NATURAL LAW IN COURT

NATURAL LAW
IN COURT

*A History of Legal Theory
in Practice*

R. H. HELMHOLZ

Harvard University Press

Cambridge, Massachusetts
London, England
2015

Library of Congress Cataloging-in-Publication Data

Helmholz, R. H., author.
  Natural law in court : a history of legal theory in practice /
R.H. Helmholz.
       pages cm
  Includes bibliographical references and index.
  ISBN 978-0-674-50458-5
  1. Natural law—History.   2. Natural law—Philosophy.
  3. Law—Study and teaching.   4. Courts.   I. Title.
  K415.H45 2015
  340'.112—dc23

                                        2014039586

Contents

Preface

This book is the result of the combination of chance, curiosity, and a challenge. These three spurs to research were later augmented by a gradual realization on my part that its subject also presented an opportunity.

The chance was this. Some years ago, an invitation came my way to attend a conference on the history of human rights and to prepare a talk on their place in the medieval *ius commune*, the amalgam of Roman and canon laws that dominated European legal education and influenced court practice from the Middle Ages through the Age of Enlightenment. I was then familiar in a general way with the concept of the law of nature, as every student of medieval law must be. I knew enough about it to think that it might help me prepare the talk. Natural rights and the place of morality in law have been strong, if contested, parts of the Western legal traditions for centuries, and the link between them and their public assertion in promoting the human rights of men and women enmeshed in Europe's legal systems appeared to be a fruitful subject for investigation in preparing the talk. So it proved to be.

The curiosity arose from a desire to see what the link between the natural law and human rights amounted to in practice—to discover the extent to which the lawyers and the parties they represented actually used the law of nature when they appeared before a judge in a court of law. In other words, did the theoretical rights founded upon the law of nature actually serve to protect the rights of men and women in the day-to-day world of legal practice? Prior work on a project on the history of the privilege against self-incrimination encouraged me to think the *ius commune* would shed some light on what might anachronistically be called "human rights advocacy" in earlier centuries. My interests as a historian have always focused more on legal practice than legal theory, and I thought that looking at the subject of natural law as it appeared in early case law might present an appropriate area for investigation. This also proved to be true. The evidence is plentiful.

The challenge came after I had considered and described the results of my initial investigations and given a talk at the conference. One of the other participants, having read and heard what I had to say, told me that I had established two things about the history of the law of nature: first, that "everyone believed in it," and second, that "it made no difference." That took me aback. True, he was thinking about American constitutional law, and he probably meant the remark as a joke. If I remember correctly, he laughed as he said it. I did not. I took it as a challenge. It prompted me to look further into the history of the law of nature, extending my survey beyond the subject of human rights. I wanted to see if my friend had been right when he said that the law of nature had no real effect on the development of substantive law. It would be less than candid on my part if I did not admit that I hoped I could show that he was wrong.

The perception of scholarly opportunity came still later. It was a result of my initial forays into modern scholarship on natural law's history. I expected to find many investigations of the place of the law of nature in the world of legal practice. Surely any thorough investigation of natural law's history would turn up accounts of its place in law courts, and concern for what it meant in the everyday world of litigation would therefore appear here and there in the large body of literature on natural law's history. So I thought. However, it soon became evident that except for a few special areas of the law, very little had been done with this aspect of the subject. The relationship between natural law and American constitutional law proved to be the only real exception to this finding, and it was a limited and controversial one. Even there, almost all of what has been written about natural law has been concerned with the great cases decided by the U.S. Supreme Court, not with ordinary litigation in state courts or even the lower federal courts. Continental and English legal historians have done slightly more with the subject, I found, but most of their work dealt with the Middle Ages, and it had not gone very far with investigations of ordinary litigation.

It seemed to me, therefore, that for all that had been written about the law of nature—and there has been a lot—almost none of it dealt with the subject of its place in law courts. I found this surprising. A few titles I came across did suggest a concern with private law and legal practice, but upon closer examination their contents proved to be unrelated to actual cases.[1] Perhaps this is because, except for the field of international relations, the law of nature today has been pushed aside by the positive law. It is theory—interesting theory perhaps—but largely irrelevant for the ordinary course of the law. Perceiving at length that there might be a scholarly opportunity for me to do something that had not been done before, something that might even prove worthwhile, I set out to discover what place the law of nature had occupied in legal practice in three different arenas: the European courts, the English courts, and the courts of the young American republic. Except for the last of these, I chose the early modern period—that is, from the sixteenth century to the mid-nineteenth century. For the last, I took the first eighty-five years after the establishment of the nation's independence in 1776. All these were periods before natural law had come under general attack from its critics. My hope was that the results would be of at least some interest to legal historians generally and in particular to anyone who has found it worthwhile to know something about the history of natural law.

All of this happened several years ago, and before coming to the subject itself and to the evidence that came gradually out of my research, I wish to mention and thank the people and the institutions that have helped me find my way. For financial support, I am grateful to the Jerome S. Weiss Faculty Research Fund of the University of Chicago. For moral support and probing questions, I am grateful to participants in workshops held in the same law school and also others held at Ohio Northern University, the University of Amsterdam, the University of Wisconsin Law School, the University of Western Ontario, and the Catholic University of America. I also benefited from having been invited to deliver plenary addresses on the history of the law of nature at the 2012 annual meeting of the American Society for Legal History and at the 2013 meeting of the Texas Medieval Association. These proved to be opportunities to test ideas and present research, and I have profited from them.

Several coworkers and friends have also been helpful and encouraging to me in my exploration of the subject. In particular, I wish to acknowledge and thank Bruce Frohnen, whose initiative got me started and whose support kept me going; Ken Pennington, whose interest in the subject and whose own scholarship have both been enormously helpful; Alison LaCroix, whose familiarity with American history and helpful suggestions gave me a leg up; and Knut Nörr, whose knowledge of the subject and friendship have meant a great deal to me over the past thirty years.

I also thank Randy Barnett, my challenger at the early conference on the history of natural rights, but for a different reason. He motivated me. He thought, probably correctly, that my early paper on the subject had not demonstrated that natural law theory made any substantial difference in fact. In the pages that follow, I hope to have shown that it did, but I cannot help wondering whether anything contained in this book will change his mind. Many of the things I discovered in the course of research did surprise and enlighten me. They convinced me that natural law did count for something. It had concrete results, even if they were not often the dramatic results many of its modern expositors assume must accompany the recognition of natural law's validity. However, I am far from sure that he will agree.

Abbreviations

Abbreviations to the ius commune

Dig. 1.1.1	*Digestum Justiniani,* Lib. 1, tit. 1, lex 1
Cod. 1.1.1	*Codex Justiniani,* Lib. 1, tit. 1, lex 1
Inst. 1.1.1	*Institutiones Justiniani,* Lib. 1, tit. 1, lex 1
D. 1 c. 1	*Decretum Gratiani,* Distinctio 1, can. 1
C. 1 q. 1 c. 1	⸻, Causa 1, quaestio 1, can. 1
X 1.1.1	*Decretales Gregorii IX,* Lib. 1, tit. 1, cap. 1
Sext 1.1.1	*Liber Sextus,* Lib. 1, tit. 1, cap. 1
Clem. 1.1.1	*Constitutiones Clementinae,* Book 1, tit. 1, cap. 1
Extrav. 1.1.1	*Extravagantes* (of Pope John XXII and *Communes*), Lib. 1, tit. 1. cap. 1
gl. ord.	*glossa ordinaria* (standard commentary on texts of the *Corpus iuris civilis* and the *Corpus iuris canonici*)
v.	verbo (reference to *glossa ordinaria* or other commentary on a legal text)

General Abbreviations

A.J.L.H.	*American Journal of Legal History*
Baker, *Introduction*	J. H. Baker, *Introduction to English Legal History,* 4th ed. (2002)
B.I.H.R.	*Bulletin of the Institute of Historical Research*
Bl. Comm.	William Blackstone, *Commentaries on the Laws of England* (1765–1769)
BL	British Library, London
Bracton, De Legibus	*Bracton on the Laws and Customs of England,* George Woodbine ed., Samuel Thorne trans. (1968–1977)

Coing, *Handbuch*	*Handbuch der Quellen und Literatur der neueren europäischen Privatrechtsgeschichte,* Helmut Coing ed. (1973–1976)
Co. Litt.	Edward Coke, *First Part of the Institutes . . . or Commentarie on Littleton* (1628)
Cortese, *La norma giuridica*	Ennio Cortese, *La norma giuridica: spunti teorici nel diritto comune classico* (1962–1964)
Councils & Synods II	*Councils & Synods with Other Documents Relating to the English Church II,* A.D. *1205–1313,* F. M. Powicke and C. R. Cheney eds. (1964)
C. P.	Common Pleas, Court of
CUL	Cambridge University Library
Ecc. L.J.	*Ecclesiastical Law Journal*
E.H.R.	*English Historical Review*
F.N.B.	Anthony Fitzherbert, *New Natura Brevium* (1704)
Holdsworth, *H.E.L.*	William Holdsworth, *A History of English Law* (1922–1966)
J.	Justice (judge of a court)
J.L.H.	*Journal of Legal History*
K.B.	King's Bench, Court of Kent, *Commentaries* James Kent, *Commentaries on American Law* (1826)
L.H.R.	*Law and History Review*
L.Q.R.	*Law Quarterly Review*
ODNB	*Oxford Dictionary of National Biography*
R.H.D.	*Revue historique de droit français et étranger*
S.R.	*Statutes of the Realm* (Record Commission) (1810–1817)
S.S.	Publications of the Selden Society
T.R.G.	*Tijdschrift voor Rechtsgeschiedenis*
Y.B.	Yearbook (Medieval English Cases)

Table of Citations to the ius commune

Canon Law

D. 1 c. 1	26, 187 n. 37	X 3.26.16, 18	54
D. 1 c. 5	187 n. 44	X 4.7.5	54
D. 1 c. 7	187 n. 43	X 5.19.4	195 n. 95–96
D. 47 c. 8	188 n. 67	X 5.39.3	48
C. 13 q. 2 c. 7	198 n. 144		
C. 14 q. 6 c. 1	68	Sext. 2.15.5	192 n. 41
C. 16 q. 1 c. 64	22	Sext. 5.2.11	56
C. 22 q. 4 c. 22	23	Sext. 5.11.48	27, 38
C. 25 q. 1 c. 16	38	Sext. 5.12.22	190 n. 5
		Sext. 5.12.48	67
X 1.2.2	190 n. 5	Sext. 5.13.4	68
X 1.2.13	230 n. 19	Sext. 5.15.5	192 n. 41
X 1.4.11	187 n. 46, 48, 50		
X 1.17.1	53		
X. 2.1.12	200 n. 171	Clem. 2.1.2	47
X 2.28.11	51	Clem. 5.11.2	190 n. 16
X 3.4.2	49		
X 3.11.2	199 n. 5	Extrav. Com. 2.3.1	190 n. 17

Table of English Cases

Table of American Cases

NATURAL LAW IN COURT

Introduction

An assessment made in the first decade of the twenty-first century concluded that "the study of natural law theories" had proved to be "one of the most fruitful areas of research in early modern intellectual history."[1] I hope this assessment is correct. It is beyond doubt that the subject has given rise to a large body of scholarship. That scholarship has been partly historical, partly theoretical. Rightly so it seems; natural law theory has been shaped by a long history, one that stretches from Aristotle to the most famous Roman jurists, then moves through the works of the commentators of the European Middle Ages and the "Natural Law School" to the era of the Enlightenment, and even into the modern era. It has played a significant part in the history of legal thought.

Although no longer the dominant opinion among lawyers it once was,[2] the law of nature has not entirely lost its adherents among them. A vocal and distinguished minority of legal philosophers has sought to begin with history in order to reclaim natural law's place in the development of Western thought and also to promote its continued recognition today.[3] Professors John Finnis of Oxford University and Robert George of Princeton University are probably the best known among its current defenders,[4] but there are others equally accomplished.[5] A simple lawyer without training in philosophy may read through their accounts with profit, if not always perfect comprehension, in an effort to uncover the main features of natural law's history. Doing so is a useful part of any preparation for research on a study like this one, an examination of the subject's usefulness as it played out in legal practice. A student needs to begin with a grasp of the basic issues at stake, and the modern works demonstrate that acquiring such a grasp all but requires a starting point in the past.

It is not a labor of Hercules in any event. The prevalent understanding of the law of nature—as presented in the texts of the *ius commune,* as taught in the European universities during the Middle Ages, and as understood in works devoted to natural law from the sixteenth century to the eighteenth—is not difficult to state or to illustrate, at least in outline. Many modern works do this quite well.[6] Ennio Cortese's masterful treatment of the place of juridical principles in the history of European law is enormously helpful for many questions.[7] Virtually every encyclopedia of law and legal theory also contains an entry devoted to the subject.[8] The accumulation of full-length works devoted to the law of nature would also fill many a library shelf, and some at least of what they show has gone into this study. These accounts differ in some ways, but they share the view that law and morality are inextricably connected. The purpose of enacted or positive law is to build upon principles of justice stated in the natural law or, in other words, to make specific the moral principles that are stated generally in legal theory. This is an obligation thought to be binding upon both lawmakers and practicing lawyers, as the following pages show in detail.

Natural law theory thus began, and still begins, with an assumption of congruence between law and basic features of man's nature as they are thought to have existed from the beginning of time. God himself was natural law's source.[9] In creating the world, He had instilled in all of his creatures a knowledge of certain principles. Most of them were known by instinct. Historically, the protection of one's person against attacks from without—a rule of self-preservation—was a common example, one much discussed by the jurists. The instinct to act in self-defense is part of human nature, the jurists said, unchanged over time. It was shared with animals. It could also be a way of righting wrongs and thus of deterring attacks in the first place. Although the right to act forcibly to defend oneself had been abridged for human beings as a consequence of their entry into society, it had not been abolished. It still made a difference. The plea of self-defense against attacks from without that is found in all systems of criminal law was itself a demonstration of its continued vitality.

Natural law also meant, in what was sometimes often called its secondary sense, congruence with natural reason, with which God had also imbued his creatures. Men and women knew right from wrong without any special training. The Golden Rule—"Do unto others as you would have them do to you" (Luke 6:31)—was a statement and example of such an instinctively known rule. Right reason had led to its recognition in every age of human history. The Bible and the great texts of Western law provided additional proof of this principle's hold on human thought and action. So stated, it did not change over time, although it might vary in the details of its application to human life, as the conditions of society themselves required. The underlying principle, it was assumed, would always matter in practice, particularly in doubtful cases. Its observance would promote the rule of justice in human life.

Although the two senses of the term *natural* might appear to stands at odds—the one a basic instinct shared by animals and humans, the other a more refined sense of justice—the primary and secondary senses of the law of nature were not then regarded as opposites. Both were necessary.[10] The two complemented each other, and both of them admitted of partial abridgement in the light of circumstances.[11] For example, the Golden Rule did not mean that criminals could not be punished. True enough, no one person would actually wish to be punished himself, but every human being could nonetheless recognize the useful function that condign punishment of criminals served. Reason taught its utility. Society would collapse if all malefactors were given free rein to harm others. Room was therefore found for a nuanced understanding of what the Golden Rule meant in practice. Like many beneficial legal rules, it admitted of exceptions and clarifications derived from a fuller understanding of the requirements of natural justice. Some of them were in fact evident in the instincts shared by man and beast. Animals acted to protect themselves from attacks made against them. They protected their "turf." So could all humans, albeit in a way that responded to the needs of communal peace. Human communities themselves had an equivalent right to protect themselves, and individuals could not assert a right to protect themselves in order to destroy the greater good.

Legal systems of positive law could take different forms consistent with the existence of laws of nature. They had done so in fact. Many varieties in their laws and institutions existed in the world as it was. However, at least in aspiration, the natural law's principles were assumed to underlay them all. Its principles remained intact despite the variety of forms taken by the positive law. They were not subject to abolition, only to modification in practice in order to meet the needs of human society. Indeed, those needs themselves formed part of the law of nature. Its purpose was to allow all men to live together in peace. The natural law's principle of "sociability" promoted that goal. It could even be regarded as "the great law of social charity."[12]

Some of the claims made for the law of nature in earlier centuries were very high, so high that one must wonder how they could actually have been applied in courts of law. From the assumption of the law's intrinsic and sublime purposes followed the famous dictum, found in St. Thomas Aquinas's *Summa theologiae* and also in many other places, that a law that contravened the law of nature was not a "true law" at all. It was rather a corruption of the law.[13] A textbook example was the decree of Herod requiring the killing of the innocent children (Matt. 2:16). It was a product of Herod's selfish fury, not a decree anyone was obliged in conscience to obey. Indeed, a greater obligation required disobedience. Herod may have been the recognized King of Judea, but it was an illegitimate perversion of his authority to issue a decree like this one and demand obedience to it. No thinking person could obey. Beyond this easy example, it was not so clear just how far that principle went or how it could be realized in fact, but the underlying sentiment illustrates the connection between law and moral reasoning that lay at the heart of the law of nature.

As this example shows, the law of nature as stated by the commentators was thought to have consequences. However, it was equally clear to them that most cases in life were not like the one potentially raised by Herod's decree. Some room for moderation—for the assumption that positive law had a moral force of its own—had to be left. Moreover, the law of nature was never a complete law. It required the creation of positive law if it was to be made fully effective in the world. So, for example, the Ten Commandments' admonition "Thou shalt not bear false witness" was regarded as an expression of one of natural law's principles.[14] Although in practice there were exceptions to this Commandment, as there were to most natural law principles, in general it was thought to be the proper task of the positive or municipal law to put this tenet of the law of nature into concrete form: making perjury a crime, ruling out the testimony of witnesses who purposefully lied, and perhaps even preventing enforcement of contracts tainted by one party's deceit.[15] These instances were regarded as expressions of the Commandment's larger intent. That intent was to provide guidance, ensuring that human law worked to secure fidelity to the aims of justice and the common good. Positive law's role was to put those aims into effect. It might do so in various ways—which is one reason that different systems of positive law existed—but the permissible ways were controlled in scope by the law of nature.[16]

This book is about that process. It deals with how natural law was employed in courts of law and translated thereby into coercive law. Focusing as it does on the practice in courts of law, the following chapters do not enter into the contentious question of what the highest and best statement of the law of nature has been. It deals with the ways in which lawyers understood it and used it in earlier centuries. Whether there has been more progress or a slow decline in the quality of thought about natural law over the centuries has today become a matter of occasional contention. To a relative outsider, the naysayers who see more decline than progress in its history appear today to stand slightly in the majority.[17] That, however, remains an open question.

Scope of the Book's Inquiry

This is a limited study of a large topic. It takes as its focus the evidence found in cases heard and decided in the courts of Europe, England, and the United States. Its coverage is limited to the early modern period for the first two—roughly from 1500 to 1800—and to the period between Independence and the Civil War for the third. Largely a product of the necessity imposed by the availability of evidence, this choice has called for several shifts of emphasis from that found in the general literature on the law of nature written by legal philosophers. Four points about the book's limited coverage require statement and brief explanation.

First, little attention is paid to the special characteristics of individual writers on natural law. The *communis opinio* that emerged from the efforts of many jurists over many centuries has been the measure used for deciding what to include. Most modern commentators regard St. Thomas Aquinas as the classic expositor of the subject, but the cases show that neither Continental nor English lawyers made much use of his treatment of the subject. Aquinas rarely appears among the many citations to authorities found in European accounts of litigation. His authority was invoked just often enough to know that practicing lawyers did regard citation to his work as of at least occasional relevance.[18] Evidently, however, the eminence of St. Thomas as an expositor of the law of nature among modern commentators was not matched by an equivalent status in the minds of jurists and lawyers in centuries before the nineteenth. I am not sure how much this matters. From the perspective of the law's application in practice, it would actually be an idle exercise to seek out the leading expositor of the law of nature. At least no one writer was so recognized at the time. As was true of the European *ius commune* itself, the law of nature was part of an ongoing tradition, one shared and augmented by generations of jurists and theologians. There were stars among them, no doubt, but like real stars, none of them dominated the sky.

Second, no attempt at formulating an exact statement of the tenets of the law of nature is attempted. It was a commonplace among the jurists that all definitions of legal terms were dangerous, and no subject illustrates the truth of their sentiment any better than the law of nature. It was hard to put into exact language and harder still to state completely. The classic authors—Aristotle, Cicero, and Aquinas, for instance—had not tried. None of them ventured to make a list of its tenets. A few authors did try—the young Hugo Grotius (d. 1645), for example.[19] He divided the law of nature into nine rules and thirteen laws, but even those he came up with were quite general statements such as "All persons may acquire and retain those things which are useful for human life" or "No persons may inflict injury upon others." Modern proponents of natural law have occasionally sought to move toward fuller and more accurate statements of its contents, but lawyers in earlier centuries shied away from such efforts at completeness. For them, it would have seemed presumptuous to pretend to state the teachings of the law of nature fully. The effort would probably have been futile in any case. This book follows the lead of the historical majority. It seeks to illustrate rather than to define what the law of nature meant in fact.

Third, little attention is paid to religious differences. Today, interest in the doctrines of natural law has become a characteristic part of Catholic thought and has been abandoned by most Protestants. Atheists usually reject natural law out of hand. This development has sometimes made it a point of sectarian contention. This modern denominational divide, however, did not exist in the centuries described in these pages—at least not on the question of the law of nature's existence and application to human life. Some of Martin Luther's more dramatic statements can be read to stand for proof of a deep religious divide in approach to moral law, but in fact almost all Catholic and Protestant jurists in earlier centuries accepted the same basic premises ascribed to the law of nature. Many of the great writers on the subject were Protestants.[20] They had not turned their backs on the traditional learning of natural law. Why should they? The Bible itself proclaimed that God had written the law of nature on our hearts (Rom. 2:15). Many of its basic teachings were inscribed in biblical texts.

There certainly were deep theological disagreements between Protestants and Catholics. Their adherents, dealing with the law of nature, sometimes traded insults, many of them quite acrimonious, even painful, to read. However, no fundamental denominational divide in approach to natural law itself marked those bitter exchanges.[21] Court practice in particular shows that the similarities swamped the differences. In the Continental accounts, it is almost always possible to discern on which side of the religious divide a sixteenth-century reporter of *decisiones* stood, but not from the approach to the law of nature found in them. It is not too much to say that the law of nature should be a shared feature of the religious heritage of Western nations.

Fourth, not much is said here about change over time. Although there have undoubtedly been developments in the ways the law of nature was described and treated during the long period covered in these pages, these developments seem not to have affected the basic features of the law of nature as it was understood by lawyers on the European Continent and in England and North America. Unlike many of the recent studies of natural law theory, therefore, this volume's theme is not about legal change. Some of the conclusions Thomas Hobbes drew from the law of nature were, of course, quite different from those of Thomas Aquinas. Cicero's treatment of it was not identical to that of the late Spanish scholastics or of Samuel Pufendorf. However, the differences between these authorities seem to have had no immediately discernible effect in legal practice. The discipline in thought imposed on lawyers by the classic texts in the Roman and canon laws also provided a source of stability throughout the period covered in this book, something that is hard to appreciate fully today. The basic assumptions upon which the law of nature was built—the division of all law into the *ius naturale*, the *ius gentium*, and the *ius civile*; the ascription of the source of the law of nature to God; and the use of its tenets to interpret and evaluate the positive law—all formed part of a long-recognized tradition. They were constants. They controlled what lawyers could do and what they could say. They limited the possibilities for change. Examination of the case law produces many differences of opinion over time. It also produces some increase in uncertainty about the exact meaning of natural law, but nothing like a "paradigm shift" seems ever to have taken place.[22] Or if it did, as some scholars strenuously contend,[23] it had little discernible effect on natural law's place in courts of law.

The book is organized into three parts of roughly equal length, each of them consisting of two chapters. The three parts deal with different geographical areas and different systems of law. Within each part, the first chapter covers legal education, reviewing the available evidence to discover as much as possible about the place of the law of nature in the training of practicing lawyers. The second chapter in each part moves to the case law, taking the seven subject matter areas in which the most frequent references to principles of natural law appeared. The cases show that considerable overlap existed between the areas of law dealt with in each of the three geographical areas covered. However, it did not amount to identity. The relations between natural law and the law of slavery, for example, figured prominently in the American cases, less so in the English, and scarcely at all in the European. The geographical overlap in usage was never complete.

The Book's Sources

Because it concerns legal practice rather than legal theory, this book's conclusions depend mainly on the author's examination of evidence drawn from cases heard in courts of law. For England and the United States, these reports have long furnished the basic building blocks for understanding law's development, and particularly for dealing with constitutional law. They have furnished one means of understanding the role played by the law of nature. For the Continent, however, the relevant sources are not well known, particularly among English-speaking students. Much less has been done with them. They are, however, quite abundant. *Decisiones* and *consilia* exist in profusion, and both of them allow the student to move from theory to practice. The first of these sources were accounts of arguments and decisions in the courts where the

European *ius commune* prevailed. The second were legal opinions written by jurists to be applied to the facts of particular legal disputes, also under the regime of the *ius commune*. They were sometimes solicited and paid for by one of the parties, sometimes solicited by the judges themselves as a way of acquiring more expert help in dealing with difficult cases. The judges were not bound by them, but the *consilia* could be influential in fact.[24] They both provided a kind of bridge between the professoriate and the judiciary.

This work draws most heavily on what is found in the *decisiones*. They usually included the arguments made by each party and the authorities relied upon to decide the case. Although there was variation in the contents found within them, normally they also stated the outcome. The earliest collections of *decisiones*, beginning in the second half of the fourteenth century, came from the papal court, the Roman Rota,[25] and in the following centuries, they multiplied beyond that court as a general class of legal literature. Literally hundreds of collections of *decisiones* are to be found in libraries in Europe and even in the United States. In recent years, they have begun to attract the attention of able scholars.[26] They deserve that attention and more. Like *consilia*, they constitute a bridge between the academic and the practical sides of the law.

Works of *praxis* have also proved useful in the preparation of this study. Normally devoted to description of the law applied in the courts of a particular city or region, many of them open a window onto the place the law of nature played in practice. Of course, general works of law are also essential to beginning any study of this subject. I have made selective use of these works, though the total numbers that exist for all three classes of juristic literature inevitably has meant that I cannot claim to have done more than to have made a sample of what is available.

In conducting that sample, I sought to be conservative in approach, not taking references and citations as relevant to my subject unless the concept of natural law was expressly introduced into argument by an advocate or into a conclusion by a judge. If the *decisio* took a position because it was "the most reasonable" reading of existing law or because the result was said to be the "most consistent with justice," I did not treat the words as a reference to the law of nature. Only express use of the terms *ius naturale, lex naturae,* or a close equivalent such as a reference to *ratio naturalis* or to *iustitia naturalis* counted.

Nor did I count situations in which the term was used purely to describe a natural phenomenon, as for example, when the fermentation and expansion of molasses during warm weather was described as a "law of nature" in one American case.[27] It is true that the term was often used to describe the inherent properties of things and even people. A good case can be made for inclusion of many natural phenomena in a complete study of the subject; it was widely accepted that the law should respect nature, and that maxim that could have real consequences.[28] I have, however, purposefully excluded such usages from consideration unless they were connected to the law of nature as it appeared in contemporary legal treatises and texts. The word *nature* has always carried a variety of meanings,[29] and the perils of enthusiasm were as obvious to me as they would be to my readers.[30]

To this self-denying ordinance, I made one exception. Invocation of a rule or maxim that every lawyer then regarded as a part of the law of nature did count as relevant to the subject. That no man should be a judge in his own cause and that an unjust law was not a true law were both principles found in the law of nature. Their connection with it would have been obvious, indeed inescapable, to any contemporary lawyer. I therefore treated them as relevant in determining the place of natural law in practice. Otherwise, however, I have treated a decision or a legal argument as being connected with the law of nature only where it was invoked in so many words.

The Book's Theme

Any theory of law or philosophical approach to law will be subjected to compromise when it comes into contact with the complexities of human life. Principles of human liberty or statements affirming the equality of all persons, no matter how praiseworthy they are and no matter how universally they are admitted, cannot be absolute. Their limitations will show up in many spheres of human life, and not least in the arena of litigation, where claims in favor of their restriction will always be made. Minds differ. Circumstances vary. So do the interests of the parties and their lawyers. It is particularly likely that variation and compromise will appear in applying abstract and general ideas such as those drawn from the law of nature to the facts of individual cases. It certainly was so in the case law that is the subject of this book. The cases heard in the courts of Europe, England, and America surveyed in the pages that follow repeatedly illustrate the practical limitations that stood in the way of full implementation of natural law's dictates. This book is descriptive in character, but insofar as this book has a unifying theme, this is it. For many and varied reasons, arguments based upon natural law did not always prevail in court. Readers of the chapters that follow will find this theme repeatedly illustrated in many different circumstances.

On this account, it may seem tempting to dismiss the significance of natural law in the history of our law. Very likely, its mixed effectiveness in practice will seem disappointing to its modern adherents. I may be mistaken on this point, but it appears to me that natural law did not achieve what they have expected it to achieve. And as for natural law's detractors, their "take away" may be that natural law did not after all really make much of a difference in the real world. They may take comfort from its very limitations in practice.

I believe this would be a mistaken conclusion. Law is not an "all or nothing" sort of discipline. It is true that the law of nature did not turn out to be a "higher law" in the sense that it swept all competing sources of effective law from its path. It is also true that the law of nature did not provide judges in earlier centuries with a roving permission to bring statutes and customs into conformity with its principles. But these limitations did not mean that the law of nature was inconsequential. Nor did not mean that one can disregard the law of nature simply as a kind of appeal to vague notions of fairness to which desperate lawyers were driven when they lost on the law.

To treat it that way, concluding that it had little effect in practice, runs into three counterarguments. First, it is the opposite of what contemporaries thought. Even while they recognized limitations of the law of nature's scope, lawyers and commentators of the medieval and early modern periods of history believed that it played an important, indeed essential, part in their legal system. They said so repeatedly. That is shown in Chapters 1, 3, and 5. To set aside their opinion makes a poor choice for anyone trying to understand the past. It comes close to asserting that lawyers of prior centuries did not themselves understand what they were saying.

Second, the negative conclusion actually stands in conflict with a considerable amount of evidence. To disregard natural law arguments because they were not sure winners is also a poor choice for historians. It looks at only one side of the evidence. One rarely knows for sure which arguments counted the most in practice, but natural law arguments seem to have made a real difference in the outcome of disputed cases at least as often as they made none. That much is shown in Chapters 2, 4, and 6. Natural law did appear to have an effect on their outcome. Some of its successes were admittedly less than earth shattering. But for the litigants and for the law itself, they did matter.

Third, dismissal of natural law arguments robs us of one source of insight into the character of law before the modern era. A great deal has been written in recent years about the "real" purposes and meanings of litigation in past centuries. Some historians have reduced it to a contest for prestige or a forum for harassing one's enemies. Starting with an examination of the premises of the law of nature offers a different and, I think, a better understanding of what litigation accomplished (and did not accomplish). To neglect the chance it offers of a special vantage point on the nature of court practice in the past may not always be objectionable in itself. Certainly other approaches are useful. It would be a loss nonetheless.

In what follows, I have sought to present the relevant evidence about natural law's place in the law courts as fairly as I could. Its real but limited success in determining the outcome of contested cases is the theme that has fastened itself most firmly upon my mind as I worked through the case law. In some ways its very malleability made it more useful in practice. This is the theme that has most surprised me and also most informed my understanding of the subject. It seems right to state it at the outset. It will be illustrated repeatedly in what follows.

1

Legal Education in Continental Europe

A N EXPLORATION OF the law of nature's impact on legal argument and court practice in European lands should begin by confronting two questions. First, what (if anything) did most lawyers know about the law of nature? Second, what role (if any) did they expect what they knew should play in their professional careers? It is just as well to start by admitting that most lawyers are not given to prolonged abstract thought, even though large ideas may enter into their working lives from time to time. If they wish to succeed in their profession, they want and need to address the immediate problems of their clients, mostly practical problems that demand practical solutions. Legal philosophy does not come into it. This is true today, and it was true yesterday. It has therefore seemed sensible to many historians of the law to pass over the learning about the law of nature found in the speculative works of theologians and jurists with no more than a momentary glance. The abstract theories spun out in academic treatises could only have been irrelevant to the professional lives of the men whose lives were spent in giving advice, drafting documents, and trying cases: individuals whose livelihood was derived from the mundane practice of law.

However sensible it appears, this is too hasty a conclusion. It may be a proper way of drawing inferences about the immediate interests of practicing lawyers, but it does not prove that these men knew nothing about natural law. Still less does it prove that they regarded what they did know as no more than abstract theory. It does not even mean that natural law was of no immediate use in dealing with the legal problems they faced every day. We must look to see. And we can see with greater clarity after having taken a slight detour to examine the place of the law of nature in the education through which European lawyers passed. English and American lawyers in earlier centuries faced a somewhat different situation; most of them did not pursue formal study of the law at a university. They learned by doing and observing—by serving as clerks, attending law courts, and reading on their own.[1] The extent of their early contact with the law of nature will be explored in Chapters 3 and 5. We begin with legal education on the European Continent. It normally took place within a university's law faculty.

The European ius commune

Although it did share some features with the training offered in modern American law schools, in important ways the legal education offered in European universities differed markedly from our own. It began with texts—the texts contained in the *Corpus iuris civilis* and the *Corpus iuris canonici*. The former, compiled at the initiative of the Emperor Justinian in the first half of the sixth century, comprised the Institutes, the Digest, the Codex, and the Novels. The latter, containing the basic law of the church, included Gratian's *Decretum* (ca. 1140), the *Liber extra*, a collection of papal decretals sponsored by Pope Gregory IX (1234) and compiled by Raymond of Peñafort, the *Liber sextus* of Pope Boniface VIII (1298), and three more minor collections added toward the close of the Middle Ages.

The curriculum centered around and continued to depend on the texts contained in these great law books.[2] Learning derived from them was supplemented by the abundant literature of the *ius commune—summae* or *consilia* or *ordines iudiciarii*, for example—and also by the many specialized works on particular areas of the law that were written by the jurists, particularly in the sixteenth century and after. Most students would also have taken some part in the argument of *Quaestiones disputatae*, in which specific statutes and practical problems would have come into play.[3] However, the texts of the two laws retained their preeminent position in the education of future lawyers. Even after partial moves toward organization of the curriculum by subject matter were made in the sixteenth and seventeenth centuries, and even when more attention began to be paid to local law during the same period, the standard texts of the *ius commune* preserved their hold on legal education. They remained the starting point.[4] They were read aloud and then read aloud a second time. They were interpreted and augmented by commentaries attached to them, but they were not shunted aside.

Texts from the two laws were virtually always accompanied by the *glossa ordinaria,* which explained and enlarged upon their meaning. Some of these glosses took on an authority of their own, establishing a *communis opinio* about the meaning and scope of particular provisions in the formal law. That opinion might be added to or subtracted from by other lawyers, even with materials from customary practice of local law or from a fuller systematic understanding of the *ius commune.* However, the texts themselves, together with academic commentaries on their meaning, remained at the center of most law students' education. Lecturers might criticize the contents of a text or gloss and puzzle over the meaning of a phrase found in one of them,[5] but their primary focus remained fixed on the texts found in the *Corpus iuris civilis* and the *Corpus iuris canonici.* One sees this dominance quite clearly from the character of the authorities that were cited before the courts; the exemplary work of Alain Wijffels on the records of the court at Malines has shown this dependence in detail. The great majority of the citations in them were taken from the basic texts of the *ius commune.*[6] What they said and what commentators made of them were what counted in practice.

The character of this approach to law did not vary greatly in substance from one university to another, and it did not change materially over the course of the later Middle Ages. In time, the very stability of this approach began to make it seem stale to critics. It gave rise to complaints—complaints that grew louder as the centuries passed. The system of legal education reacted only slowly to them. In time, some teachers did react, of course. Lecturers referred to local customs or special legal problems,[7] and eventually room was made for the formal inclusion in the curriculum for lectures on contemporary statutes and customs. These partial changes began at least from a beginning in the sixteenth century.[8] Variant approaches, such as introduction of instruction devoted directly to the law of nature that is the subject of this book or the creation of chairs for professors of national law, were also added in some places.[9] These developments augmented the scope and design of instruction.[10] However, they were "add-ons." The basic features of the traditional legal education in law remained intact at European universities. Local and customary laws were given only a subsidiary part in the ordinary curriculum; in many places they were regarded as best learned from experience in practice. European legal education was thus insulated from many of the fashions of public intellectual life. It was resistant to change in the fundamental authorities upon which it relied— hence the complaints.[11] Comic writers could lampoon its misuse of learned texts.[12] Reformers could lament that legal education had not kept up with the times. It had stagnated. Hastings Rashdall once described it as "the dreary routine of expiring scholasticism."[13]

Rashdall had a point, but the traditional features of legal education, sometimes referred to as the *mos italicus,* had great strengths, too.[14] The *usus modernus pandectarum,* beginning in the sixteenth century, if not earlier, also helped reinvigorate this approach by seeking and finding meanings in the ancient texts that earlier jurists might not themselves have seen.[15] By its application, texts from the Digest could be interpreted creatively enough to meet situations undreamt of in ancient Rome. Embracing this method was a reasonable choice to have made. Critics of traditional methods of learning—the legal humanists, for example— rarely put forward realistic doctrinal alternatives to replace them.[16] In some ways, their own attention to the texts themselves was actually greater than that of their opponents. For purposes of this survey of legal practice, however, the important point to consider is that, unlike modern legal education in the United States, the curriculum began with standard texts, some of which dealt with the basic character and purposes of law and had a close connection with the law of nature. Instructors did not plunge students immediately into the intricacies of case law. Nor did they immerse the students in complex theories of jurisprudence or social science. They began with a listing of the law's constituent elements and a statement of its high purposes. Those purposes were meant to be achieved, in some part, by applying the tenets of the law of nature.

If this approach entailed a certain separation from current court practice the students would face after the leaving the academy, it was the reality. We must take legal education as it then existed, recognizing (as we should) that in our own day a gap between legal education and the daily work of lawyers remains. We must seek first to understand the part the law of nature played in the existing curriculum so that we can better approach the role it could play in the courts. This is not a difficult task, for even a brief examination shows that European legal education during the Middle Ages and long thereafter included a significant exposure to the subject that it is the purpose of this book to explore.

The Roman Law

Progress to a law degree for students in civil law faculties at medieval universities began with the Institutes and the Digest of Justinian. The two first titles in both of these collections were *De iustitia et iure* and *De iure naturali et gentium et civili*. Lectures given each year opened with a recitation of these titles and at least a brief exploration of their contents.[17] Thus, European law students first learned what the fundamental purposes of law were. They then heard about the basic sources of law that were employed to achieve those purposes. Natural law was part of both. It was treated as a foundation for the other two basic sources of law, the *ius gentium* (the positive law common to all nations) and the *ius civile* (the positive law of particular lands).

The law of nature was referred to in numerous places in these opening titles and it appeared in the Codex as well.[18] Students thus began with texts that stated the assumption that God had implanted certain principles of conduct and justice in the hearts of men and that these principles furnished a correct foundation for all positive law. Probably it would not have been the first time students had heard this stated. The Bible repeatedly proclaimed it to be so (e.g., Ps 40:8, Jer 31:33, Heb 8:10), and most students would have known of this connection between law and justice from their own reading, if not also from repeated experience and the lives of their ancestors. The assumptions that established a law of nature were widely recognized,[19] as readily assumed to be normal parts of life as the assumption of the human appetite for material gain is today.

The law so implanted in men's hearts was meant to teach them the way to justice. The positive law, customary or statutory, was meant to build upon it, implementing the law of nature's general prescriptions with specific rules and sanctions. A basic purpose of law, students would have heard, was to do right and secure to each person what was due to him. That is what the law said. It is also what the teachers said.[20] Determining what was due in fact to each person might not have been immediately obvious to beginning law students. Indeed, it is not obvious today. However, the students would have heard that a fuller understanding of the law would come if they drew conclusions from principles of morality fashioned from the law of nature and if they looked behind the positive law for those same principles. One function of legal education was to teach students how to do this.

To judge from the contents of the *glossa ordinaria* that accompanied the texts and clarified the substance of what was being taught, students would also have heard the threefold division of the law found both in the Digest and the Institutes being discussed with examples.[21] Of these three basic kinds of law, natural law came first. Surviving notes show that lecturers gave the definitions and the attributes appropriate to it and to the two other sources of law in some detail. In reading the glosses and hearing the lectures, students would also have been directed to subsequent texts in the Digest or the Codex where they could see how the laws of nature as well as the *ius gentium* and the *ius civile* had been put into practice. They would have heard connections made between the three, and they would also have discovered where refinements in the reach of natural law principles had been made by the other two principal sources of law.

So, for example, the text of the Institutes stated that it was an obligation under the law of nature for parents to provide care and sustenance for their children (Inst. 1.2). Without nurture, all children would quickly perish. This was so natural an obligation that even wild animals followed it by instinct, an illustration of Ulpian's famous statement that the law of nature was common to both animals and human beings (Dig. 1.1.3). The medieval gloss to the Institutes then added a reference to another text in the Digest.[22] That text recognized the obligation but stated that it might not apply in practice if the child was capable of supporting himself, except in the special situation where illness prevented an otherwise prosperous child from meeting his own obligations. If such an illness intervened, it said, the parental obligation based upon the law of nature was revived, at least until the child had recovered from his illness. That text would thus have suggested to the student both that the parent's natural obligation lasted beyond infancy and that it was not necessarily absolute. Had the student looked further, examining the gloss to the text from the Digest, he would have found more references of the same sort, places where the natural obligation was expanded or contracted in light of attending circumstances. These references led to still more texts and glosses, dealing, for instance, with whether or not the obligation extended to illegitimate children and even to a discussion of whether prosperous children were themselves obliged to support needy parents.[23] This process could continue from one text with its gloss to another, always allowing students fuller access to the learning found in the *ius commune*. It could be augmented by consulting one of the many general works written for law students that gradually became available from the later Middle Ages, particularly after the invention of printing.[24] If carried out conscientiously, the search could last until all but the most enthusiastic students were exhausted.[25] However, in the process students would have more fully understood both the reach of the parental obligation toward their children and the place occupied by the law of nature in fashioning it.

Besides these basic texts, law lecturers regularly made reference to what might be described loosely as further reading.[26] A huge store of it existed. If students working through the texts paid any heed to these suggestions, they would have been led into the abundant legal commentaries the later Middle Ages produced. That task would of course have been easier to accomplish in the age of the printing press, but it was not impossible before. The commentaries of Bartolus of Saxoferrato (d. 1357) would have been a common resource for students of the civil law, although they would have had other choices, too.[27] Either way, they would have been able to learn more. In the seventeenth and eighteenth centuries they could also have chosen from a raft of treatises devoted specially to the law of nature.

Even in Bartolus's medieval commentaries, however, students would have uncovered a store of information about the law of nature and the rearing of children. His commentaries covered a lot of ground. Along with many other things, he supplied arguments in favor of regarding the natural law's obligation of parental support as a reciprocal one, applicable to children under a natural law principle and also endorsed by the Bible (Gen. 12:3)—the blessed will bless those who bless them.[28] Bartolus then discussed the concept of a public duty toward children, relating it also to the law of nature.[29] And he provided a treatment on the interpretation of statutes involving testamentary succession by children that was long and complicated enough to have tired and confused all but the most determined students, though it was also enlivened by a discussion of whether Lazarus could have recovered his property after Jesus had raised him from the dead (Jn. 11:43–44).[30] Some attention would have been paid to the important concept of legal fictions in the course of the inquiry, for they could play a role in the obligation's interpretation.[31] More than anything else, however, Bartolus showed where the Digest's texts about this most natural of obligations might lead.

Perhaps such extended excursions into works of commentary would have been unusual among law students. Legal education does not always live up to its potential. Teachers in every age have complained that their students are idle.[32] Also, some students never intend to practice law; they may have purely social reasons for enrolling in a law faculty. At a minimum, however, students intending on a career in law would have heard the basic features of natural law stated, discussed, and then expressed in the form of positive law (the texts from the Digest). If they looked, they would also have seen its dictates subjected to modification in the later texts, as well as in the works of some of the commentators on them. The parental obligation, for example, turned out to be more complex in its implications than it seemed when first encountered. The obligation might, some jurists thought, extend beyond the immediate family, and it might be reciprocal in nature. Family ties were natural ties, and they could be the source of duties the law recognized. Circumstances could also vary the applications of natural law's dictates. This meant that natural law principles were relevant in a variety of situations. However, they were not absolutes. Students might have been led quite far afield—into the law of last wills and testaments, for example, where the question of whether parents had a duty to leave some of their estate to their children was tackled, although never nailed down, by the jurists. Some of this learning would almost certainly have stuck in the mind of even the most indifferent students.

In other words, even if the texts and lectures had not led students to a full knowledge of the natural law as it applied to the law regulating the rights of parent and child, they would have learned that the parents' duty toward their children was not simply an idea. It was a practical obligation, founded upon the law of nature and put into more definite form by several of the Digest's texts. The obligation was capable of expansion, too, for the principle underlying it carried considerable weight, and it could arise in different circumstances. Under the right conditions, it might extend to grandchildren, or perhaps even to nieces and nephews. It was also possible that it could be used by analogy outside the immediate family. Some writers were willing to carry the principle into the feudal law, for example, holding that vassals might have a natural obligation to support their own lord if he became indigent.[33] Family law and feudal law might share a similar tie. The developed law could thus prove more complex than it seemed at first sight and perhaps more uncertain in its reach, but students would certainly have understood that the law of nature had definite legal consequences for the positive law that regulated family life. At least some of these consequences would have been easy for a student to fasten upon. He would probably have been able to connect several of them with the events of his own life. He would have found, for instance, that it was possible to construct an argument that, once begun, fathers were obliged under natural law to support a son's continued studies at a university.[34] The probable effect of that obligation on the son's brothers and sisters might then cause a problem that had to be considered, but that too would have taught the son at the university something useful about applications of the law of nature.[35] The same kind of extension to apparently unlikely lengths, together with incidental problems caused thereby, would also be found in many parts of the law.

The Canon Law

So it was for students of Roman law. The student whose primary studies were in the canon law half of the *ius commune* would have been led in the same direction. In many places, study of Roman law was a prerequisite for entry into study of the canon law. Even where it was not, however, the law of nature would have figured in the relevant curriculum. Its content was similar to that of the civilian.[36] Gratian's *Decretum*, the starting point for canonists, began with a statement of the sources of the law—indeed, quite a dramatic statement: "The human race is governed by two things, natural law *(ius naturale)* and usages *(mores)*."[37] It then took a more overtly religious turn than the Institutes had, adding that "natural law is what is contained in the Law and the Gospels" and giving as an example the Golden Rule. The earliest commentators on the *Decretum* endorsed and elaborated upon this understanding.[38] Throughout its history, canon law did maintain a somewhat more spiritual approach to natural law than was found in the law of the Romans— more emphasis on avoiding sin and more references to biblical precedents, for example. No surprise there. For the medieval canonist, the worship of God was a command of the natural law. Also, the "internal forum" of auricular confession, a forum where the law of nature would often have been relevant,[39] might not have mattered quite as much to the medieval civilian as it did to the canonist. However, the difference between them was not a disagreement in principle. It was only a difference in emphasis. The civilian would probably have regarded this simply as laying more stress on the secondary laws of nature. At this stage in a student's career, the common heritage of the two laws would have been more evident than the differences. The *ius divinum* was also invoked as authoritative even in Justinian's Institutes[40] so that the canonical texts relating to the law of nature pointed in the same general direction as did the civilian's.

This initial common ground that existed between the two laws turned out to be something like a historical constant. Most of the canons that followed in Gratian's first *Distinctio,* those used to clarify what the sources of law were and what they meant, were in fact taken from Isidore of Seville's *Etymologies.*[41] Isidore's work was the medium by which much of the law's classical inheritance was brought into the early Middle Ages, and Gratian's text, following his lead, took over most of the Roman law's categories, just as Isidore himself had. The sixth canon in the first *Distinctio,* for instance, used the *Etymologies,* repeating verbatim the threefold division between natural, general, and civil laws that was found in the Institutes. Because Isidore's account of the sources of law had itself made room for the *lex divinum,*[42] to have begun with him was an easy step for Gratian.

Following the texts Gratian had chosen further into the *glossa ordinaria* would have confirmed the general accuracy of the Roman law's texts for young canonists. It would have led students along a path leading to further sources, and this would itself have produced additional "cross references" to texts from the Digest as well as from the canon law itself.[43] However, it would also have shown the slightly more theological approach to law that was characteristic of the *Decretum* and the canon law generally. Thus, the established place of divine law in the world and the congruence of the law of nature and the Christian religion were stated firmly. They were insisted upon.[44] God had spoken through natural law. He had also spoken through specific commandments. In this way, the duty of the father to care for his children was supported not simply by laws found in the Digest but also by a text from the New Testament (2 Cor. 12:14), one that also appeared later in the *Decretum* (C. 16 q. 1 c. 64): "[C]hildren are not bound to lay up treasures for the parents, but the parents for the children." The Roman law's obligation was therefore consistent with Scripture.

Of course, that duty did seem to run only one way in this particular biblical text—the duty rested on the parents, not the children. Perhaps, however, the passage from Corinthians had not been meant to state the full extent of the obligation. Roman legal texts were relevant, too, and some of them appeared to point in the other direction. The gloss continued, citing another canon (C. 22 q. 4 c. 22) and also two texts from the Codex (Cod. 5.25.1–2), holding in effect that where the father stood in need and the son was capable of helping him, he must do so. The obligation might be regarded as reciprocal, it seemed. This was the same place where Bartolus had left students of civil law: in the midst of a possibility of a quite broad reading of the character of familial duty but without an unambiguous answer to the many questions it would raise in practice.

In addition to unanswered questions, students of the canon law who followed the texts of the *Decretum* and the Gregorian Decretals into the works of the late medieval commentators would have discovered things that amplified but did not seriously upset what they had first heard and read in texts that defined these institutions. It was a pattern that extended to other areas of the curriculum. Students would have found that the test for the validity of an ecclesiastical custom depended in part on its consistency with the law of nature.[45] They would have learned that even the Roman pontiff was under an obligation to comply with it.[46] They might also have encountered some discussion of natural law's treatment of the law of usury and the enforceability of men's promises.[47] All of these were touched by the natural law but not fully determined by it.

Wherever they looked in the texts, exploration of the canonistic literature would have added something new. For instance, most likely they would have come upon a fuller discussion of the consequences of the existence of *ius divinum,* or (as it was sometimes put) the *lex aeterna* than they would have found in the Institutes or Digest.[48] God stood behind both, of course. There was a large measure of coincidence between them. However, God's commands were not limited to those that had existed from the beginning of time. He had always been free to give new commandments and had done so, even in the New Testament (Jn. 13:34). By definition, the divine law securing the freedom of the church from secular control could not have been part of the early law of nature. No separation of church and state existed in the Garden of Eden. Moreover, the law of nature's reach extended to all peoples, not just Christians. So students might appreciate the reasons for keeping divine law and natural law separate even while they recognized the elements that connected them.

In works on the canon law, students would also have found a distinction drawn between the ultimate purposes of the civil law (to promote the common good of society) and the canon law (to promote the soul's health of all people).[49] This distinction was not purely academic. It could make a difference in outcome. One test of a binding statute or custom was whether it was in conformity with the dictates of reason, and the difference in purpose between the two laws meant that a slightly different analysis was required in deciding whether that test had been met in any particular situation. On the canon law side, it could more sharply be asked whether a particular statute or custom directly or indirectly encouraged sin. Some social rationality could be found in a statute, but it might fail the canonical test for this reason. Jurists thought a statute allowing usury was an example. Allowing at least a moderate rate of interest might serve a social purpose, but it might also encourage violation of God's law. On this account, the result might differ, depending on the forum in which the statute was raised in litigation. A contract might be enforced in the temporal forum but not the spiritual forum.

Admitting the differences, the aspiring canonist confronting the *ius divinum* and the slightly different test of rationality of the civilian would not have encountered an approach that varied in its basic nature from that facing his fellows on the civil law side. Assessing the strength of competing goals might be required in thinking through a legal problem. Like the law of nature itself, divine law as stated in the Scriptures could be subject to limitation or augmentation if adequate reason so dictated.[50] Many examples from the book of Leviticus were proof of that. Law could evolve in the ways in which it was applied. Polygamy might be allowed when human population was thin, for example, but rejected when it was not. Changing mores might also have intervened to require some amendment in the law. It was not always obvious what the law of nature would require in practice. In dealing with the example of usury, the student of canon law would have had to take account of the *salus animarum,* but he would also have seen the claims of commercial life stated in texts from the civil law.

Where this conjunction of parallel approaches and similar qualifications in the laws would have left beginning students of the law is hard to estimate. It is of course a situation that law students face to this day. At best, they become used to the uncertainty. Some even begin to find it interesting. They look further for clues and refinements that will serve to extricate them from the uncertainty. It is also true, of course, that in the process some students lose heart. They become discouraged and even mistrustful of the law. The risk is that they may give up or become cynical about it. The Roman law's Institutes themselves began by acknowledging the reality of this possibility and warning against it (Inst. 1.1.2). It was the reason given for students to start slowly. Experience from many centuries, including our own, teaches the utility of this ancient advice.

What knowledge of natural law the majority of law students who persevered would actually have taken away from their initial contact with the canon and Roman laws is not something we can know with certainty. Did they carefully follow the texts into the glosses and treatises written to explore their reach and meaning? Could they have taken in so much law? Almost certainly some did, and just as certainly some did not. We cannot say more than that. What we can do with greater confidence is to look at the principal features of the law of nature as they were found in the texts themselves and make a reasonable estimate of what the majority of students would have learned from hearing them stated, explained and illustrated. At a minimum, that is what all of them were exposed to, and it is this that most of them would have carried into their careers. Some of the surviving moots and *quaestiones disputatae* that occupied more advanced law students show that the law of nature was capable of being put to practical use.[51] We can summarize the main points.

The Divisions of the Law

As already noted, the Roman law divided the sources of law into three classes: *ius naturale, ius gentium,* and *ius civile.* At an early stage of their studies, law students would have heard more about each of them. They would quickly have learned, for instance, that this threefold division, although useful and true, could not be counted as complete. Some further division of the three was required, and some further expansion of the three was possible, even necessary. A degree of uncertainty about where one ended and the other began was also inevitable. The scholastic method of distinction and definition thus came quickly into play in their education. The jurists often said the task of defining legal concepts was fraught with danger (Dig. 50.17.202). Here was an example, perhaps the first most students would have confronted. A simple definition might not cover every situation.

This problem was posed immediately by Ulpian's statement that the law of nature was something that nature taught to all animals (Dig. 1.1.1). How could that be reconciled with the equally prominent premise in Gratian's *Decretum* that the contents of the law of nature were those revealed by God through reason and scripture (d.a. D. 1 c. 1)? Men and women can reason. They can understand the Bible. Wolves cannot. So what was the answer? Had Ulpian simply missed the mark and misunderstood what natural law was? That possibility would be entertained by some later writers on the law of nature,[52] although recent research on animal behavior has (surprisingly) breathed some new life into Ulpian's position.[53] Whatever the truth, medieval jurists would have found his words hard to dismiss out of hand. They took comfort from animals that apparently conformed their behavior to principles of the law of natural reason.[54] Still, the fit was admittedly not perfect. For the jurists, however, an acceptable explanation could not have been that the two texts stood at odds with each other. The Digest itself refuted that conclusion.[55] The more likely answer would have been that they were not contradictory but that a distinction was necessary to more fully understand and apply them. The law of nature should therefore be divided into its own subcategories. Usually this was put in terms of a primary and a secondary law of nature.[56] Ulpian was describing the first and Gratian's *Decretum* the second.[57] Both explanations were correct if they were understood correctly. Animals were accorded such powers of reasoning as fit their own condition. So were human beings. No real contradiction existed between them.

The process of division could and did go beyond this simple distinction, as in proceeding to sort out where various kinds of animals fit. Wolves are different from worms, for example. Worms (apparently) do not care for their young, but wolves do, meaning that a more complicated division among animals was necessary to explain fully Ulpian's statement affirming their participation in the law of nature. His apparent endorsement of the principle that by instinct or reason all parents care for their young was not without exception in the animal kingdom.[58] Most animals do, but a few do not. It depended on which subclass one was discussing. Students would here have been brought face to face with the imperfections inherent in all definitions, and they would have seen again the necessity of further distinction in order to make the system fit the world as it was.

It is easy to tire of drawing distinctions. At some point the whole enterprise can collapse, but in this case it did not. The existence of the distinctions applied to the animal kingdom did not weaken the conclusions drawn about the law of nature. They were not regarded as scholastic quibbling. Still less did they call the whole enterprise into question. The same assessment could be applied to human beings. Some men make little use their facility of reason. They act wickedly or carelessly. Lawyers describing the law of nature felt no need to account for the behavior of reprobates as anything but a human failing, a distortion of men's proper nature that was all too common in the world. Indeed, the opprobrium the failings of the wicked earned for themselves among the populace only confirmed the strength of the moral law, for it was the existence of natural law's principles that best accounted for the opprobrium. Why else would so many other men and women have felt right in criticizing wicked conduct? They could have done so only if they themselves had begun with a starting point in the moral law. Moreover, it was (and still is) true that many useful categories and salutary rules admit of exceptions. Sometimes subcategories are useful, even necessary, in the sense that they permit practical conclusions to be drawn from the material at hand. Law often moves forward by the multiplication of categories. Here was an early example—a salutary example—that was part of virtually every European law student's education.

The jurists also recognized that some of the contents of the law of nature would not have been shared by human beings with all members of the animal kingdom. These characteristics were normally put into the secondary meaning of the law of nature—meaning what was useful, necessary, and beneficial for the public welfare.[59] That no man should be unjustly enriched by doing wrong to another, one of the *regulae iuris* found both in the Digest (Dig. 50.17.206) and the *Liber sextus* (Sext. 5.11.48), was an example drawn from the secondary law of nature. It was not, however, a lesson nature had taught all animals. At least many animals did not appear to act upon it. Its truth depended on the use of man's reason. The same could be said of the Tenth Commandment, directing us not to covet our neighbor's possessions. That Commandment

would have been meaningless to a wolf. These apparent inconsistencies—
"solved" only by drawing academic distinctions and refining them further in order to fit the facts—did not bring down the enterprise. They
simply required readjustment in thought. The jurists sought to understand and apply the precepts of the law of nature, not to pick holes in
them.

A further distinction—useful for analytical purposes and for determining the legality of specific conduct—was also drawn between "permissive" and "prescriptive" natural law. The former permitted men to
exercise their liberty free from unnecessary interference from without.
The latter obliged them to do good and to avoid evil.[60] Where a right
was placed could make a difference. Religious freedom (oddly from the
modern perspective) was placed in the second category. We must be free
to worship God. We are not at liberty, however, to choose to disobey
God's commands. If we do, as of course we can, we will be punished for
our failings when we appear before God. Personal freedom, by contrast,
was placed in the "permissive" category. Men were assumed to be free
under the law of nature. This gave them the right to make what we now
call "life choices," and up to a point it also allowed them to choose to
submit themselves to the will of others if they so desired (Dig. 1.5.5).
This permission became one of several justifications given for the perpetuation of human slavery. From an academic perspective, it illustrated
one of the ways jurists found of expanding the scope of the law of
nature.

The threefold division of the law was also modified from the other
direction, rendering the boundaries open to dispute. The divisions were
not watertight. In theory, the law of nature was what all men knew from
reason. The *ius gentium* was what all nations observed by custom or agreement. The *ius civile* was the positive law adopted by individual cities and
peoples. But, it was asked, if the *ius gentium* was observed by all peoples,
what practical differences were there between it and the *ius naturae?* And,
again it was asked, if all nations followed a general law, what room was
left for rules that differed from one place to another? How were students
supposed to distinguish the one from the other? Where were they to
put specific individual laws?

The jurists were up to the challenges to the utility of the law's clas-
sifications that were raised by these objections. They conceded that there
was a strong "overlap" between the law of nature and the law of nations.

It could not have been otherwise. Both were products of characteristics shared by all human beings. However, the jurists insisted on the utility of the separate categories, adding that while the former could not be changed, the latter could be. The law of nature was not the product of agreement among human beings. The law of nations was. Standards of practice among nations could thus evolve—for example, in the rules protecting ambassadors and other foreign representatives. However, the principles that underlay the rules, as with those in the law of nature that stated the necessity for laws protecting social relations among peoples, could not.

An important point about legal practice grew out of the "overlap," one that is quite apparent in the *decisiones* and judicial opinions that are the subject of the following chapters. The jurists rarely cited only one kind of authority for any of their arguments. They rather assumed that all the three sources of law, and sometimes the divine law as well, would support their arguments. They cited all three. They did not have to make a choice between them. Why would they if they were not obliged to? Although it is true that sometimes a conflict existed between positive law and natural law, more often than not none did. They stood in harmony. This means that a question often asked in modern scholarship— is a particular author relying on natural law or positive law?—is actually a *question mal posée*. The jurists commonly assumed that all three sources of law would support their arguments. They therefore cited them alongside each other. This was a consequence both of the "overlap" between them and the assumption that positive law was founded upon the natural law, differing principally in the degree of its specificity. Few lawyers, then or now, will rest their argument on a single source of authority if they have a choice. They want as many authorities as they can cite. So it was in earlier centuries. It was in any lawyer's own interest to call upon both natural law and positive law wherever he could. That is exactly what medieval and early modern lawyers did. We shall see many examples in the chapters that follow.

The Immutability of the Law of Nature

A core assumption of the jurists held that the laws of nature were permanently fixed. They had been instilled in human consciousness from the beginning of time. Normally, their purposes were beneficent. If followed by the positive law, the law of nature, rightly understood, would ensure that law would be what it should be: "the art of the good and the equitable" (Dig. 1.1.pr). It meant "rendering to each person what that person was due" (Dig. 1.1.10). So, for instance, the Golden Rule directed that we should do unto others what we would have done to ourselves. It would not change from one era to another.[61] Neither was the coming together of men and women in physical union and the consequent perpetuation of the human race. The specific ways in which these foundational ideas were turned into positive law might of course be varied, as, for example, by creating new rules and discarding old rules in matrimonial regimes. No one supposed that the calling of the banns in one's parish church was a necessary or permanent institution required by the law of nature. Banns were not contrary to the tenets of natural law. They served a useful purpose in society. They helped to prevent bigamy and to ensure marital fidelity. However, it might happen that new or unexpected developments could come along to require a different practice. Change in circumstance was to be expected. The positive law would take account of them. The law of nature, by contrast, was a collection of ideas and policies that were thought to be immune to change in their core, yet subject to variation in the ways in which they were put into practice by the positive law.

There were, it should be said, uncertainties about exactly what the dictates of natural law required. In the law of marriage, for example, some possible unions were said to be contrary to the law of nature—a marriage between a father and daughter, for example. This obvious prohibition would last. The law of the medieval church, however, went further. It also prohibited marriages between persons related within the fourth degrees of consanguinity or affinity. At the edges, this prohibition was purely a matter of positive law. The church, it was assumed, had the power to enact such rules and had done so at the Fourth Lateran Council (1215). What was uncertain in this situation was determining exactly where the natural law stopped and where the positive law began. How close to the parent-child marriage did one have to come to violate the laws of nature? This made a real difference, since where only positive law was involved, the church could issue dispensations to permit an otherwise prohibited marriage. No such dispensations could be issued, however, to permit a union that was contrary to the law of nature. The pope himself could not make an exception to permit this. Just where the line would be drawn was the question. It was subject to doubt. The better opinion held that it was dangerous to skate too close to the edge, but there was no agreed upon way of determining exactly where the edge was.[62]

Uncertainty also marked the situation where a rule of the positive law conflicted with the law of nature or where two natural law precepts came into conflict with each other. This certainly happened. The natural lawyers were not blind to it. Slavery was the prime example, and private property was another. At the start of the world, all men had been free, in no way subject to the will of other persons, and all property had been held in common, open to appropriation by the first taker. These institutions were part of natural law, and they did not change. But how, it was asked, could one reconcile them with the realities of human life in which, it seemed, they had been so materially changed in fact? Slavery existed. So did individual ownership of lands and chattels.

Various answers were given to these difficulties, and not all precepts of the *lex naturae* were treated alike in responding to them. One possibility lay in distinction. Laws that were relaxed could be treated as aspects of "permissive natural law." It allowed for choice. It was often invoked, although this solution caused as many difficulties as it resolved. Probably the most common explanation for the current state of the world, at least among lawyers, was the answer given in the Institutes. It would have made an impact on all but the dullest of students. The law of nations, it was said there, had required variations in the law of nature according to the growth in numbers of men and women and the dictates of the usages and necessities of human life.[63] Some of the variations were unquestionably happy ones. Abridgement of the right to defend one's property and one's person, a natural right that could lead to feuds and disorder, was one. If the government provided an adequate alternative, the right to defend one's self and one's property decreased accordingly. If the right could be adequately secured in a peaceful way, so much the better.

Among other abridgements of the law of nature were the creation of private property and the institution of slavery, as just mentioned. The former, a change from the time when ownership depended on actual possession, was made necessary by the growth of human population and by the inconveniences of common ownership.[64] Gardens and farms are necessary for human survival, for instance, and no one will plant a garden if its contents remain open to appropriation by strangers. So protection of private property rights was a necessary feature of the *ius gentium*, even though it might seem to stand in conflict with primary natural law.

Slavery was slightly different, but it was still regarded as an abridgement of the law of nature that had been dictated by history and circumstance. Some said it was the result of wars. For most men in battle, being a slave was preferable to death, and captives from a losing army could be said to have freely chosen it when death had been the alternative. Other jurists supplied different reasons for slavery's existence. One argument was that the fear of being enslaved after an unsuccessful attack actually helped to keep the peace and to prevent attacks on the innocent.[65] Fewer aggressors would act on their desires if they knew that being enslaved would be the consequence of unsuccessful aggression. Some of the jurists said no more than that slavery had proved "useful" in fact.[66] It was common ground among the great majority of them, however, that slavery had entered the law through the *ius gentium* and was thus subject to change.

In neither case, the jurists held, did these developments amount to abrogation of the laws of nature. Those laws still held, and they still had consequences. In cases of extreme want, for instance, a sharing of the earth's resources and a regime of common ownership of property would return to direct men's conduct.[67] In international law, where rulers knew no sovereign, the law of nations drawn from natural law was the only present alternative. With slavery, in cases of doubt, the *favor libertatis* was to prevail over claims to own the services of another human being. This meant that where no positive law recognizing it existed, neither could slavery. And even when permitted by positive law, the statutes allowing slavery were always to be strictly construed. The jurists commonly said, therefore, that the laws of nature were not subject to abolition. They were only subject to limitation. Thomas Aquinas himself had taken note that general principles were sometimes inadequate when applied to actual cases.[68] God had intended that men and women were to live together in a society that would permit them to prosper. Sociability among men and women was the desired outcome, and that goal, as it turned out, required limitations in the reach of the general rules of the law of nature. It did not follow, however, that the rules were abolished thereby. Their consequences were merely altered.

Few features of the law of nature have caused more doubt about its worth than this one. The realities of human life and the tangled web of human history have seemed to show that the binding character and eternal validity claimed for natural law were quite contrary to what had happened in fact. If slavery had come into existence, as it had, claims for human freedom as an immutable law of nature began to seem hollow. How would students in the sixteenth century and before have reacted to this apparent gap between fact and theory? They would have heard natural law described as foundational and unchangeable, and then gone on to learn about some quite substantial changes in the consequences supposedly derived from it. Perhaps they would have taken some comfort from those precepts, like the Golden Rule, that truly did not change. Perhaps they would have simply accepted that the law of nature was meant to be a statement of abstract principles and was therefore necessarily open to exceptions. Many legal rules are, and they are not regarded as insignificant in consequence. Perhaps they would have understood this freedom as an unchanging human aspiration. It might be abridged, but it could never be entirely snuffed out. Or it may be that students would simply have waited to see what use could be made of natural law when it came to specific cases, particularly where the dictates of positive law were uncertain. The chapters that follow will return to this situation, looking more closely at the specific uses to which students put natural law after they had left the academy. They will also demonstrate how lawyers attempted to understand how natural law's precepts could have been said to remain constant over time and place despite the very real differences they led to in litigation.

The Purposes of the Law of Nature

The texts of the Roman and canon laws, as already mentioned, stated that a purpose of the law of nature was to promote the cause of morality and justice. Law students would have heard this repeated. If they had been at all thoughtful, they might well have asked how that purpose was to be realized in human life—even how it might have an impact on their own future career in the law. The law of nature was an abstract law. It stated some general principles, but most of them required refinement and specificity before they could be put into practice. That is what the positive law did. But the lessons of the law of nature were not always perfectly clear, and their "fit" with the positive law was not always perfect. Perceptive law students would soon have realized that there could often be something like a "disconnect" between human life and the tenets of the law of nature.

Would this uncertainty have made them distrustful of the law of nature? Would they have concluded that it was so much impractical speculation? It might have, but I doubt it. I doubt that disillusionment or skepticism would have set in. This is so because first, students would have seen too many cases in which the *ius civile* and the *ius gentium* put the law of nature into specific form. It was seen to have "inspired" legislation. Second, it deserved attention because students would have understood that the *ius naturale* was part of an instinct that inhered in all human beings, and they would have come across many practical examples of it. Legal commentaries, if nothing else, would have produced examples of natural law in action—examples of the exercise of a right of self-defense, for instance. And third, students were unlikely to have dismissed natural law, because they would have learned a great deal about law and lawyering from seeing how the law of nature played out in specific instances. It could have an influence even when the positive law diverged from it.

Two examples will show this. One is the promise. According to the most common understanding of the law of nature, promises were binding under the law of nature (e.g., Dig. 2.14.41). That was clear enough. The child who says, "But you promised!" to a father when he suggests postponing a long-awaited trip to the zoo is giving voice to a natural human instinct. Living together is also improved if we can count on others to do what they have promised. That was almost beyond doubt. Moreover, God himself was faithful. He made good on his promises (e.g., Heb. 10:23). Hearing this, a student might have expected that the study of human history would produce examples to illustrate the importance of promises. And in fact he would have found some if he cared to look. Examples appeared sporadically in the texts and medieval glosses of the Roman law. The art of persuasion through historical incidents was brought to a particularly sparkling form later on, most notably in the works of Hugo Grotius (d. 1645). So many examples—from Plutarch, Cicero, Plato, Seneca, Aristotle, and others—fill the pages of the treatment of the effect of promises in *De iure belli ac pacis*, they were bound to make an impression on students.[69] Although Grotius was sometimes criticized for

reasoning "from the effect to the cause,"[70] his citation of historical examples made practical sense—it did so even in theoretical terms. If natural law was an immutable part of human life, students should expect
to find that testimony to its tenets would have been expressed in many
ages, not just their own and not just in legal textbooks. Grotius sought
to show that this expectation of the force of promises had been fulfilled
in fact. There had always been something special about promising.

Ordinary academic treatments of the natural law of promises would
of course also have carried students well beyond the apparent platitude
that promises should be kept. They would have heard it tested under several circumstances. The easiest limitation to appreciate was the promise
to do an illegal act—say, a promise to kill someone. The normal answer
to that dilemma was to invalidate the promise but also to require that
the promisor repent and seek a formal release from his promise, perhaps even subjecting him to some form of punishment for breaking it.
Killing an innocent person was a greater wrong than breaking a promise,
but breaking a promise was still a wrong. This way of thinking could
have consequences in practice. Students would have learned this lesson
as a matter of course.

They would also have learned some of the other limitations fastened
upon the rule that promises were to be kept. The best known of these,
at least today, is the requirement of consideration, or *causa,* as the civilians called their own analogous institution. Not all promises are made
with the same seriousness or the same intent. Not all involve the same
reliance by the promisee. Our lives—not to speak of our courts—would
be in a pickle if we were legally obliged to perform every promise we
ever made or else made to pay damages for every promise we have broken.
For the sake of convenience and peace, some limit has to be put to the
rule that promises are to be observed, and the requirement of *causa* or
(in England) consideration was one result. Broadly speaking, in the civil
law *causa* meant a legitimate reason for the promise. To be enforceable
in a court of law, such a reason had to exist. In the course of time this
requirement took on a life of its own, one that involved many limitations and amplifications. Common lawyers of today who have worked
through the doctrine of consideration in their study of contract law will
recognize the difficulties that lurk within what is at bottom a simple idea.
But starting with the natural law of promises would have been a sensible way of approaching it.[71] Otherwise (as sometimes happens today),

the complications seem almost to swamp the promissory obligation. They come to occupy center stage, the place where the original promise ought to be.

A second example of the utility of the law of nature for a law student—and perhaps a better one—is the law of usucaption and prescription, usually called adverse possession in common law countries. It meant acquisition of title to a thing belonging to someone else by possessing that thing for a period fixed by law (Inst. 2.6; Dig. 41.3). In essence, long-time possession had (and has) the effect of transferring ownership from one person to another after the passage of a sufficient length of time. A thoughtful student, first coming upon this institution, might well have asked, "How can that be? It seems to contradict what I learned from natural law—that the law should not take A's property and give it to B." So it did. It might therefore have been a stark reminder for him of the limited power of the law of nature when confronted with purposive civil law. But he would also have learned that there were arguments in favor of the doctrine's utility. If the true owner neglected to claim his property, if indeed he lost track of it, how was ownership to be established? Someone must have title, or there would be an endless *res nullius.* No purpose was served by allowing ownership of chattels (or anything else) to remain forever uncertain.[72] The neglectful owner could also be said to have "slept on his rights." Usucaption was the law's solution and prescriptive title the result.

In exploring the subject, the attentive student would have noticed that the role of the law of nature in prescription or usucaption was an active one. It was not simply an obstacle to be overcome to solve a problem. It affected the developed law in several positive ways. One was in ensuring that the period of prescription was long enough. The Emperor Justinian himself lengthened the period for movables from one to three years.[73] This was to legislate as the law of nature suggested; it minimized the extent to which one person could claim title to another's property. A second was to require good faith on the part of the possessor. Here the canon law came into play.[74] If it was a wrong for one man to take another's property, but circumstances nonetheless dictated that the practice be allowed, at least it should be restricted to a blameless possessor, usually someone who believed (wrongly but honestly) that he was entitled to the property. The man who sets out with a design to take another man's chattels for himself is a thief, not a possessor the law should protect (Inst. 2.6.3). Rewarding him would not be consistent with the law's goal of doing justice. A third was to provide a way of dealing with new situations. The natural law of prescription might also apply in part in situations not found in the Roman law texts. Of this possibility, the discovery of the New World presented the greatest challenge. Did the native peoples have title to the lands on which they hunted, or could these lands be taken by the Europeans as *terra nullius?* There was little within the positive law directly applicable to the situation. Jurists were thrown back on what was found in the sources: the law of nations and the law of nature.[75] It would not be sensible to enter into this contentious subject here, except to say that a lawyer's early study of the law of nature would not have been irrelevant to it. It provided him with a starting point for thinking about the strength of the claims of each side.

The Potential Uses of the Law of Nature

During their years in a medieval law school, students would have seen something of the diverse uses to which the law of nature had been put. They would also have confronted some of the limitations fastened upon its application in practice. What most law students would probably not have seen quite so clearly is the (mostly untapped) potential that existed behind the law of nature laid before them. Wider possibilities were there to be uncovered all the same, and natural law's potential might have become more apparent to some lawyers as they entered more fully into the world. So far, this survey has looked mainly at what the texts and glosses compiled during the twelfth and thirteenth centuries had to say about the law of nature. But we might look up from them just a bit. Interpretation of the law of nature did not stand completely still. It gave rise to a School of Natural Law in the sixteenth and seventeenth centuries. Three examples of expansive use of the law of nature—all possible developments in the positive law that were later derived from these texts—will show what it could mean.

The first lay in the possibilities opened up by the concept of equity. It was a commonplace of the *ius commune* that *aequitas* should sometimes prevail over *rigor iuris*. Equity provided motivation for fresh enactments in the law (e.g., Dig. 6.2.17), and in appropriate situations it was to be preferred to the harshness of written law (Cod. 3.1.8). So said the Roman law's texts, and their teaching was carried over into the canon law.

Equity was the "mother of justice" (d. p. C. 25 q. 1 c. 16 § 4). Its connection with the law of nature was firmly asserted, if indeed it was not self-evident.[76] Exactly where these teachings led might not have been obvious to law students, except in the specific instances laid out in the texts, but they would have been taught that the texts cited contained examples of the possible reach of ideas underlying them. The texts themselves were not necessarily limited to the specific situations in which they happened to arise. This knowledge allowed for their expansion by analogy. In practice lawyers might properly use them in situations that were similar to, but not identical with, those found in the texts. We look at some examples of what this meant in Chapter 2 when we examine law practice on the Continent. In England the importance of equitable principles gave rise to separate courts of equity, preeminently the Court of Chancery, which had (some said) the power to correct the strictness of the common law through the application of equitable principles. The chancellor could invoke underlying principles to avoid obviously unjust results. Their invocation was also operative in the law courts themselves, to be applied as needed by the common law judges in reaching their decisions.

A second example of the potential inherent in the law of nature was the law of unjust enrichment. No person should be enriched by injuring another. That principle was stated clearly in both the Digest (Dig. 50.17.206) and the canon law (Sext. 5.12.48). It was and is an easy sentiment to agree with in the abstract, but its reach in law has always been more uncertain. The classical Roman law had not treated it as an independent source of obligation. Law students might therefore have passed it quickly by. There were, however, examples in the Digest where the idea was used as a way of securing redress for an injury, and in the course of time, lawyers seized the opportunity to expand the scope and function of the maxim.[77] The potential latent in them to create an independent source of legal remedies was realized in time, although never perfectly. To this day the extent of the impact of this European development on the law of England is a matter of doubt, even of dispute.[78] There is little doubt, however, that an English law of unjust enrichment exists today.[79] The potential inherent in this simple idea, one derived from dictates of natural justice that were found in the Digest,[80] is well illustrated by what happened on both sides of the English Channel.

Third and finally, there was the large idea. Lawyers have involved themselves in government from time immemorial. That they have played significant roles in political controversies that shaped our history is not a matter of disagreement.[81] Who can assess the impact on men of ideas first encountered in a classroom? That "all men are created equal; [and] that they are endowed by their Creator with certain unalienable rights" is a sentiment derived ultimately from the law of nature—one that lawyers would have first heard as students. Little in the way of practical results might have come from the idea during lectures in the law faculties. It was a principle limited by countless examples from life as well as by other authoritative texts in the law. These limitations would have been presented to the students.[82] But there it was all the same: a statement of what once had been and what might possibly be again. Who knew where it might lead? In the minds of a few it might even have inspired something like the powerful lament: "Man is born free; and everywhere he is in chains."[83] This book is about natural law in courts, and large ideas like this one played a limited role in that arena. Their existence is worth remembering all the same.[84] In time, some of them would come to matter a great deal.

Conclusion

Students who set their sights on a university degree in law during the Middle Ages and after looked down a long road. Six to ten years of study were the average times they could expect, depending on the degree they sought and their choice of canon law, Roman law, or both.[85] We cannot be confident in stating exactly which aspects of the law of nature those years would have brought home to average students as they progressed along that road; we know little enough about what teachers taught and less about what students learned in the law faculties of European universities.[86] However, we can be confident that those years would have brought students into contact with the law of nature. In their first lessons, it would have been a direct contact. The basic books of both Roman and canon law opened with texts recognizing its existence and stressing its centrality in shaping the law's purposes. As their education proceeded, a student's contact with the law of nature would have been more sporadic. It would probably not have been at the center of his study, even after the rise of the Natural Law School. From time to time, however, ordinary students would have come upon specific texts and commentaries where the law of nature had been put to practical use. The commentaries would also have taught them something about the complexity involved in drawing concrete conclusions about the positive law's foundations in the law of nature. Rarely was this a simple matter of nullifying a statute or custom because it did not conform to the dictates of fundamental laws. More often, the law of nature was treated as a tool for understanding and interpreting the law. It furnished a start for legal analysis. It was not the last word. Even the reach of the *ius divinum* was sometimes subject to limitation through analysis and argument, and all but the most indifferent students would have been exposed to the limitations characteristic of its reach.

It will be the object of the following chapters to explore the results of this approach to fundamental law, an approach quite characteristic of the *ius commune* and one that also had an impact on the development of the common law both in England and the United States. The chapters will explore the many uses to which the law of nature was put in litigation. In that exploration, however, it should not be forgotten how different on this score medieval and early modern legal education was from that which prevails in most of today's law faculties. For lawyers educated in those earlier centuries, the dictates of the law of nature were not platitudes. They were not theory. They were living law.

2

The Law of Nature in European Courts

THE RELATIONSHIP BETWEEN what law students learn in classrooms and what they require in practice is a legitimate subject of inquiry. The form of the question relevant to a study of the history of the European *ius commune* is whether the introduction to the law of nature students received served their needs as practicing lawyers. It was meant to. The nature of the university education in law described in Chapter 1 is proof of that intent. But did it serve that purpose in fact? That is not the same question. Today, one source of occasional complaint among lawyers and law students is that little of what they are taught in law school has any relevance to their work in "in the real world." That complaint is not new. It was leveled against the legal education that prevailed in past centuries, and some of the discussions of the nature of fundamental law found in medieval and early modern treatises do appear to support it. What they contain can seem more like abstract theory than usable law. But, again, to find out, we must look at the evidence.

To do so, this chapter surveys what is shown in collections of *decisiones* made between the late fifteenth century and the eighteenth century.[1] Used together with the other available sources—treatises, works describing regional jurisdiction, and scholarly *consilia*—the *decisiones* provide a way of testing whether what students had learned about the law of nature in university law faculties had any connection with what they did in practice. More than that, they suggest answers to help in determining whether the law of nature made any real difference in deciding cases that affected the governance of society. In conducting this survey, I was able to work through significant parts of some ninety-five early collections of *decisiones* and also to consult something like a quarter of that number of *consilia*. I used about the same number of contemporary works of *praxis,* the guides to procedure and legal substance applied in individual European courts.

The Sources and Problems of Method

These sources, even if examined selectively, produce a quite considerable body of relevant evidence. The law of nature, taken up and used as a source of legal argument and decision, appeared within virtually every collection of *decisiones* and *consilia* consulted. This is not to say all of them, of course. In my survey, in perhaps five or six, nothing at all related to the law of nature emerged. Very likely, this absence was the result of fatigue on my part; some days it was difficult to keep going. Still, what did come to the surface was positive enough, and the pattern was repeated often enough to support my supposition that natural law was then regarded as relevant to legal practice. I cannot give statistics. I kept none because it was impossible to see how any could meaningfully be compiled. References to the law of nature were, however, clear and repeated in the reports—enough to show that it was not simply abstract jurisprudential theory.

Finding some use being made of the law of nature in the *decisiones* did not come as a surprise. It was only to be expected. As shown in Chapter 1, Continental jurists became familiar with it in university law faculties. Its application to legal issues was routinely mentioned in the treatises and commentaries on the law they turned to for help in dealing with specific cases.[2] Its place in the formal law was not controversial, and its possible relevance to some specific legal issues would have been clear to any competent lawyer. A right to defend oneself against attacks from without, for example, was regarded as a right founded upon natural law. Lawyers might have referred to it without self-consciousness in speaking or writing on behalf of a client being tried for murder or assault. The argument would have carried some weight with the judges. Just how much weight is hard to say, but definitely *some* weight. It would actually have been surprising if the law of nature had not sometimes appeared in a conscientious lawyer's argument. And where it was relevant, many *decisiones* show that it did.

For all the regularity in the collections consulted, however, express reference to the law of nature was not a particularly frequent feature of the *decisiones*. It was necessary to look for it. Its invocation did not jump out from the pages. Only occasionally is it possible to conduct an online word search of the old titles, and it is even rarer to find a separate entry for the law of nature in the indices provided in the early modern editions of these works. True, finding aids were almost always added to Continental treatises in earlier centuries. They made (and make) use of sources like the *decisiones* easier, but it was rare for a note or an index entry to flag the importance of natural law in their texts. I took advantage of the exceptions whenever I could. But the opportunity rarely occurred.

Moreover, there were also quite a few cases where the law of nature could easily have been cited but was not. Some jurists chose to cite only contemporary statutes and the opinions of other jurists in cases where the law of nature would have been relevant. So, for example, even though the necessity for an adequate citation of a defendant was derived from a natural law principle, sometimes the reporter of a *decisio* who was faced with a case involving possible application of the principle cited only legal authorities drawn from the positive law.[3] Natural law and divine law may have been in that reporter's mind, but seemingly only in the back of his mind. He chose not to invoke the authority of the natural law, relying instead on existing precedents or on treatises dealing with the positive law of civil or criminal procedure.

This absence of direct citation is probably what one should expect from the contemporary understanding of the relationship between natural law and positive law. The latter was built upon the former, making concrete what was abstract. The two were thought to be mutually supportive, both in theory and reality, rather than competitors or alternatives. In other words, positive law was one means by which the law of nature was designed to be made effective in practice. That was a working assumption of the jurists, and they believed that it had happened in fact. They sometimes noted that specific laws and statutes had given the force of positive law to the law of nature—what the Germans call *Positivierung von Naturrechts*.[4]

Under contemporary understanding, therefore, a connection between positive and natural law was something that could be assumed in most circumstances. Where this was so, it was possible and even proper for lawyers to cite specific laws and statutes when they had the choice, making little or no reference to an underlying principle derived from natural law. Lawyers usually prefer the specific to the general; an argument involving a legal right is stronger for having a statute or recognized jurist to cite as authority instead of a general and contestable principle drawn from the law of nature. This choice appears to have been made quite often in the cases. For instance, a Portuguese case involving the fundamental principle that no one should be deprived of his property or personal freedom without fault was invoked in one *decisio*, but it was supported only by one text from the Digest, one from the Codex, two from the Gregorian Decretals, and one from the *Liber Sextus*.[5] The lawyer did not mention the law of nature. He could have, but he did not. This was an oft-repeated pattern.

However, whether by taste or necessity, lawyers and judges did also cite the law of nature expressly in many *decisiones* in which they also cited positive law. Indeed, combining them was not at all unusual. To take only the simplest and most frequently found examples, in one *decisio* the proposition that unowned property belonged to the first possessor was supported by citation to the law of nature as well as a text from the Digest.[6] In another, a statute fixing the positive law by setting a monetary penalty for adulterers was defended both by legislative authority and by principles of natural law that were "consistent with justice and reason."[7] In a third, the right of all men to fish in public rivers was asserted as guaranteed by "the law of nature itself," as well as being recognized by specific texts from the positive law.[8]

An only slightly more unusual example comes from a case heard in the city of Florence in the mid-seventeenth century. It involved the issue of a criminal defendant's right to procedural due process. The court used natural law to distinguish an earlier decision of the same court where the facts were roughly equivalent. The judge in that case had given a sentence against a man accused of a crime in circumstances similar to the case at hand, and it had been affirmed on appeal. The second case went the other way, disregarding the earlier case, and the reason given for doing so was that the prior sentence had been contrary to the law of nature.[9] Prior decisions did sometimes serve as precedents in the European courts; if identical issues were involved, there was good reason to do so.[10] Why reinvent the wheel? However, in this Florentine case a prior precedent's apparent violation of the law of nature was given as the reason for *not* following it. The situation called for invocation of principles of justice to avoid following an unfortunate result in the prior case, and it was the law of nature that supplied the means of answering that call.

The more common situation, in which no specific reference to the law of nature was made in a *decisio* even though it could have been, should not come as a surprise to modern lawyers. Something very like that has happened in American constitutional law and seemingly also in similar situations within other legal systems.[11] Over the years a line of cases based on the text of the Constitution takes on a life of its own, sometimes putting the words of the document itself into the shade. Doctrine once applied directly from the First Amendment and the Contracts Clause of the American Constitution has developed that way. Gradually the case law has lost close touch with the exact words of the Constitution itself, and lawyers commonly and sensibly pay more attention to the line of cases than to the original text. There are always exceptions—cases in which the original meaning of a constitutional term becomes important. But the normal case depends more often on gradually evolving precedents than it does on the wording of the Constitution's text. Some lawyers lament this, but it is the fact. They are obliged to respect it if they wish to prevail in litigation.

Following the law of nature into the mature *ius commune* produces a similar, although not quite identical, result. Academic commentaries on the positive law were cited in profusion in the *decisiones*, sometimes to the exclusion of relevant natural law principles. The parallel to modern law is this. No one would say that a provision in the American Constitution was irrelevant to modern law simply because a line of cases interpreting it is cited in a recent opinion, seemingly to the exclusion of the original text. Neither should one conclude that natural law was irrelevant in cases where it was not mentioned directly. I have opted for a more cautious approach, but this has been for reasons of prudence. Even so, that choice has not proved unrewarding. Patient fishing for explicit references to the law of nature produces a sizable catch.

Applications of the Law of Nature

Working through the Continental *decisiones* and other titles devoted to court practice produces more than general conclusions. The survey produced several specific areas of the law where the law of nature appeared regularly, more so than in others. In some aspects of the legal practice—for example, the law regulating the use of public buildings or the repair of parish churches—it rarely came into play. Only positive law or (for the latter) divine and canon law did. It should therefore be said that although the law of nature was virtually always mentioned in general descriptions of law's purposes—and normally mentioned with fulsome praise for its worth and importance—it was not necessarily relevant to cases in all fields of law. It was assumed that the law should be consistent with reason and also that statutes and customs should be interpreted and tested for congruence with natural law. These were commonplaces of the *ius commune.* They stated principles that could matter in the outcome of specific cases, and they did seem to matter in some *decisiones.* However, there were also specific areas where the law of nature was scarcely mentioned at all. The practical uses that appear in the first group well illustrate the contemporary understanding of what the law of nature could and should accomplish in individual cases, but it should also be said that what they show is not duplicated in every area of the law.

Procedural Law

One of the areas where natural law mattered most was in the law of civil and criminal procedure. That procedure must be consistent with the law of nature was an operative principle of the European *ius commune.*[12] It was an accepted starting point, but also something more. It sometimes led the jurists into complex and minute conclusions about the details of court practice.[13] One basic principle ascribed to natural law—that what was determined in one proceeding should not prejudice the rights of third parties not then present in court (Cod. 7.11.1)—was, for example, the source of many testing cases.[14] In them, lawyers often chose to cite both positive and natural law. It is not hard to see why. Citation of both sources of law made a stronger case. The positive laws would illustrate how the natural law had been understood, but citation of natural law would also show clearly that justice stood behind them. It also helped to interpret and guide the positive law's meaning in practice.

The law of nature also came to the fore after the introduction and elaboration of summary procedure in European courts. Many cities and kingdoms in the late Middle Ages passed statutes authorizing legal process to be conducted summarily: *simpliciter et de plano ac sine strepitu iudicii et figura*—that is, simply and plainly without the noise and form of full legal process.[15] The church endorsed this abbreviated procedure, enacting a rule that its courts could lawfully act "so that only discovery of the truth" mattered. This meant that full compliance with the formalities of legal process outlined in the existing *ordines iudiciarii* (Clem. 2.1.2) was not required. This express adoption of abbreviated procedure may seem antithetical to principles of justice, but it happened, and it is not hard to see why. Full compliance with the *ordo iuris* could be a millstone around the neck of a conscientious officer of justice. It could extend the length of hearings, increase costs, facilitate evasion of court orders, and in the end allow malefactors to escape their just deserts. The complexities of a process designed to prevent unfairness could themselves be used to do just the opposite: to pervert justice. It appeared they were being used that way. No procedural system should encourage that result, and adoption of summary procedure was intended to provide a way of preventing the injustices made possible by manipulation of procedural technicalities. Therefore, the real question in practice was not whether these statutes were permissible. It was assumed that they were. The real question was rather how they were to be interpreted. They were vague, seemingly purposefully so. What exactly did it mean to proceed "simply"? How should a judge actually proceed by discarding everything except what mattered for discovery of the truth? Here the law of nature helped to supply an answer.[16] It furnished a means of deciding exactly how much abbreviation of process these statutes permitted. Repeatedly in the *decisiones*, the question was, does a particular reading of the statute accord with the law of nature? That was a test used to determine the statute's meaning and to settle its practical effects.

A persistent example of the test's application arose in the question of whether the statutes authorized judicial proceedings if there had not been an actual, personal citation of a person adversely affected. The possibility was tempting. Contumacy was a frequent problem. If only truth was to be respected, the statute might be read literally, allowing a court to proceed whenever the truth was manifest and clear. The proof against a person might be so clear that a conscientious judge needed no further evidence of its veracity despite the absence of a citation of that person. But, it was answered, proceeding without hearing both sides would violate a principle based on natural law. Justice required that every person affected by litigation be cited and heard by an impartial judge.

The ability to speak in defense of one's own person and property was a right that could not be denied to any person consistently with the law of nature.[17]

The latter position was rooted in the right to self-preservation, a right established by the natural law (X 5.39.3). It was assumed that in the start of human society, every person had the right to defend himself and his property against predation.[18] Originally, all men had held the right to take such action themselves. It is a rule preserved today for nations in international law.[19] However, for most of the population, that primitive right had long since been abridged. When men agreed to live together in peaceable society, they had ceded a part of the right to protect themselves and their property to their governors, who, in turn, undertook to provide a system of justice that would provide them with adequate remedies against dispossession and injury. Imaginary or not, this agreement was regarded as something like a trade in the common interest of all concerned. One right was surrendered in exchange for another. Fair enough, but it was always assumed that in this trade men had not completely surrendered their right to protect their lives or their possessions. Because there were bound to be limits to what a government could do, they had merely parted with a portion of their natural rights. What they had preserved meant that life and property could not be taken from them without lawful justification. All men had preserved for themselves the right to prevent this injury from happening to them, at least in circumstances where they had no other choice.

This line of reasoning had consequences for procedural law. It was read to mean that all men were entitled to adequate notice in litigation so that they might defend themselves against unjust deprivation of their property. They might have surrendered some rights to self-defense, but not *all* rights. In practice, they had a right to be summoned and then given a chance to defend themselves. The textbook expression of this principle was God's call to Adam in the Garden of Eden (Gen 3:9). Adam richly deserved the fate that would be meted out to him, and God surely knew Adam's guilt in advance. God had nonetheless cited Adam by calling out, "Where art thou?" He had then given Adam the chance to present what justification he could muster before pronouncing a final sentence. The lesson seemed clear to early lawyers. As inapt as this biblical story may now appear, it was oft repeated by the early modern jurists—too often in fact to have been simply a counterweight. They did bolster it further with an argument from their understanding of its history. In the organization of human society, they thought, rational men would never have surrendered a right to defend themselves without some guarantee that they would not be treated arbitrarily by the law. This required that an adequate means of defending themselves be made available to them. From this supposition emerged the adoption of a rule based upon both divine and natural law—one that could be applied in courts. Adequate citation and a day in court were guaranteed by the law of nature, as well as being stated by divine law and specific texts from Roman and canon law.[20] It was "the first and most important part of a judgment; without it a right derived from the law of nature would be taken away."[21] It may even have included allowing witnesses for a person being prosecuted in a criminal matter the chance to testify in the person's behalf.[22]

Cases involving this principle came before European courts with surprising frequency. They also turned out to involve unanticipated complexities. In a 1587 case heard by the Roman Rota, for example, it was held that a bishop could not remove a cleric for nonresidency from the canonry he occupied in the cathedral church unless he had first been properly cited to appear before the bishop's court.[23] The law made clear that habitual absence was sufficient cause for deprivation (X 3.4.2), and there was little doubt that this man had been absent for long enough to invoke this law. The theoretical difficulty was that he had not been cited. He had not been given the opportunity to explain himself. The practical difficulty was that the very fault for which he was being deprived had also prevented him from being cited. He was not around. Of course, contumacy was a problem the courts of the church faced repeatedly, and various expedients were devised to deal with it, none of them entirely successful. In this instance the Rota seems to have hesitated. Because adequate citation was a right guaranteed both by the positive law and the law of nature, in the end the auditors held that the existing sentence of deprivation was invalid. However, the *decisio* went on to state that if the canon had been long absent, he could in fact be removed, but he must first be given a threefold citation (presumably at his cathedral stall or residence) rather than the single peremptory citation that had become the norm in court practice, and also that a final sentence could only be handed down following a six-month interval from the time of the third act of citation.

This was probably not a bad compromise. Natural law rules were not meant to become the source of judicial paralysis, but neither were they to be lightly disregarded, and the Rota's decision in this case seems to have respected both aspects of the requirement. In ordinary court practice, it had also become the rule that a written citation left at a person's residence would suffice if he was not at home and could not be cited personally; it was called citation *viis et modis* in the usage of English ecclesiastical courts.[24] However, removal from an ecclesiastical dignity must have been regarded as a more serious matter than a run-of-the-mill consistory court proceeding. Equally different were the chances that the canon would return to his cathedral stall to find any citation left for him. The Rota's approach took account of those differences. It thus recognized the force of the law of nature without being paralyzed by it.

Many of the cases involving the principle resembled the Rota's decision. In them, the natural law's requirement of citation was weighed against the circumstances of the case, the needs of society, and the exigencies of court practice. The natural law's principle requiring personal citation was regularly affirmed in the *decisiones,* but it turned out to have been eaten away by many exceptions. If the defendant was a vagabond and could not readily be cited in person; if he had announced in advance that he would not come to court under any circumstances; if he had hidden himself so that his whereabouts could not be discovered; or if it would have been dangerous to cite him in person, then the citation could be made *per edictum.* That could amount to no more than formal adherence to the rule.[25] It was a dangerous experiment. It invited disregard for a rule of principle. The author of one work that discussed the existing exceptions at great length was of the opinion that no further exceptions should be made.[26] But in time others were.[27]

Many difficult and disputed questions on this subject arose in the *decisiones.* For instance, were all the creditors of a deceased man entitled to personal citation in a judicial proceeding to approve his last will and testament? It was held that they were not.[28] Did a bankrupt debtor keeping to his house to avoid his creditors require a citation before he could be imprisoned if it happened that he deliberately left the house, thereby rendering himself subject to bodily seizure and imprisonment? It was held that he did.[29] Could a person cited to appear for one cause be required to respond to a different or additional cause without a fresh citation? It was held that he could not.[30]

If anything, most of the *decisiones* suggest that often more weight was placed on needs of practice than on strict compliance with requirements imposed by the law of nature. It is true that the compilers of the *decisiones* were probably attracted by hard cases. What one finds in them probably underestimates the strength of the requirement of citation in ordinary litigation. There is some evidence to support this opinion: the attention the jurists paid to setting out the contents necessarily given in citations,[31] their endorsement of providing fresh citation before formal sentence was pronounced,[32] and the care they took to secure the most nearly adequate substitute where personal citation was impossible.[33] These additions were expressly tied to the law of nature. All the same, for understanding the citation's role in procedural litigation, the exceptions to the requirement multiplied the number of holes that could be drilled in the surface of a salutary rule of natural justice. That is a theme running throughout the procedural cases.

Within the field of criminal procedure, the law of appeals makes a meaningful comparison with the law of citations. Like the citation, the ability to lodge an appeal was considered to be part of the natural law's right of self-defense, and the principle reached into the details of the law. Julius Clarus, the Italian proceduralist, noted that "an appeal was a form of self-defence granted by the law of nature, and consequently should not in any event be taken away by law or statute."[34] Cardinal Tuschus, the encyclopedist of the *ius commune,* shared this view: "A statute abridging the appeal is odious because it takes away [a person's] defence."[35] The example of St. Paul's appeal to Caesar (Acts 25:11–12) served as biblical confirmation of the institution's availability and importance. Paul's appeal had been allowed as a matter of right. Texts from the Roman and canon laws lent support to this principle. One from Ulpian placed in the Digest (D. 49.1.6) held that appeals in criminal cases were not to be impeded; they were allowed *ratione humanitatis.* Technical objections should not stand in their way.[36] The canon law seemed to endorse the same conclusion. "Even in minor matters appeals are permitted," stated a text in the Decretals (X 2.28.11). Establishment of the right to appeal to the papal court had been an important step in the reform of the church in the eleventh and twelfth centuries and also in the creation of effective papal rule over the Western church.[37] From the perspective of natural and divine law, appeals appeared to stand on all fours with citations.

The reality, however, turned out to be rather different, particularly in criminal cases. By statute and custom, allowance of an appeal against a criminal sentence became the exception rather than the rule. A seventeenth-century Catalan jurist, for example, stated (surely with some exaggeration) that until 1599 no appeal of a criminal conviction had ever been allowed in his native land.[38] He himself was critical of the exclusion, noting specifically that an appeal was a form of defense accorded by the law of nature. He praised the change that had taken place in 1599 as one in which the courts had "newly opened their eyes" to reality.[39] Yet, he recognized that the earlier pattern of denial had a long history. In fact, it remained the more normal practice in many European courts.[40]

Several justifications were given for these apparent inconsistencies with the law of nature—none of them wholly convincing. First, appeals had not been invented so that they might become a defense of iniquity. Yet, they were all too often used in that way. Better to choke off the evil at its source.[41] Second, proof in criminal cases was required to be "clearer than the midday sun" in the *ius commune,* and if this was so, there could be no good reason for allowing an appeal. The reason for having appeals was to prevent unjust sentences, and by definition no sentence based on proof that met the "midday sun" test could have been unjust.[42] Third, virtually all penal sentences were "arbitrary" in law. This was meant in the sense that setting the most appropriate penalty always involved the exercise of judicial discretion. As a result, there could be no meaningful standard of review and no legitimate purpose for allowing an appeal.[43]

This was not the end of the matter, of course. These three reasons were matched on the other side by substantive disagreement, and also by a counterargument based on interpretation of the statutes barring appeals. It was that the statutory law itself did not in fact bar *all* appeals but only *some* appeals. The statutes and customs prohibiting appeals, it was said, were meant to apply only to "frivolous" appeals.[44] Meritorious appeals, by contrast, were not ruled out. This was an argument *a contrario sensu,* made to distinguish the texts that, on their face, forbade appeals. Statutes should always be interpreted to accord with the law of nature, and distinguishing "frivolous" from "meritorious" appeals might do the trick. By rejecting the former, the statutes were actually allowing the latter. That was the argument. If so, natural law's contribution was actually vindicated by distinguishing one kind of appeal from another.

This was not necessarily a winning argument, however. It required considerable stretching of the apparently clear meaning of the relevant enactments, and it invited endless dispute over whether or not a particular appeal was frivolous or meritorious. So disagreement there was, and the results in practice varied from place to place. No resolution of the basic argument, except occasional recognition of the force of customary practice, seems ever to have been reached.[45] Other means of redress against unjust sentences had to be found. It stands to the credit of the jurists that they were.[46]

Law of the Family and Succession

Chapter 1 contains several examples in which the law of nature's requirement that parents provide nurture for their children was used to reach legal conclusions that lasted beyond the child's infancy. It also mentioned the possibility of extending the requirement so that a child might be obliged to support a parent in situations where there was special need. The obligation, as it seemed to some jurists, might actually be reciprocal in character.[47] Those examples do not, however, fully reveal the complex set of familial obligations that would eventually be built upon this apparently elementary requirement of the law of nature. It could be stretched quite far, sometimes even to the breaking point. The law of nature was cited to reach conclusions so far removed from the parental duty to nurture a young child that nature itself all but disappeared from view. When this point was reached, the connection with some texts from the Roman civil law was closer than that with the law of nature. They were more often cited.[48] But this was not the normal case. Normally, even where these extensions did not depend entirely on natural law, in litigation they were routinely supported by its authority, and the statutes embodying the obligations were routinely tested against natural law's tenets. Few areas of the law were determined more fully by local custom than the law of succession during these centuries,[49] but even within this regime, natural law could matter.

One example where no stretching was required and natural law prevailed was the extension of the obligation of support to illegitimate children. Children born out of wedlock were no favorites of either the civil or the canon law. They were, for example, barred from entry into Holy Orders (X 1.17.1). In most places they took no share of the estate of parents who had died intestate leaving legitimate children. Some jurists considered that a father's attempt to legitimize his bastard children would violate the rule of divine law that no one should allege his own turpitude.[50] All medieval lawyers of course recognized that no fault could be attributed to the illegitimate children themselves from the circumstance of their birth. The fault lay with the parents. Yet, they reasoned—if that is the right word—that "in detestation of the crime itself" (adultery or fornication), it was proper to exclude children born out of wedlock from most of the privileges of legitimate children. Family stability and discouragement of sin were also said to justify the second-class status of illegitimate children in the world.

This hard conclusion, however, did not apply to a child's right to nurture and support, and the more lenient result was ascribed to the law of nature. Nature drew no distinction between different classes of children.[51] No such distinction existed at the beginning of the world. It was a creature of the positive law. Ulpian's famous parallel with the animal kingdom was also relevant. Animals, wild or domestic, drew no distinction between spurious and lawful offspring.[52] Neither, it seemed, should human law, at least unless there were good reasons for it. A plausible reason for it did exist for some purposes, but that did not mean that one existed for all purposes. Indeed, equitable principles backed up the support obligation's extension to all children, illegitimate or not. Without it, none of them would survive to adulthood. Here the canon law avowedly followed the original law of nature (X 4.7.5). The law of the church expressly imposed an obligation to nurture illegitimate children on the parents, thus "correcting" any deficiency found in the Roman law's texts.[53] It was an obligation enforceable in the courts of the church, and the *ius commune* gradually incorporated it into the general law.

A second consequence was the *legitima pars liberorum*—roughly speaking, the child's right to take a part of a parent's estate. It was not ordinarily allowed in favor of illegitimate children, but it did apply to legitimate offspring. Generally called *legitim* in English practice, the notion was an established part of the positive law in most European lands. An obligation, resting on the parents, was recognized in the Roman civil law (Inst. 2.22; Cod. 3.28.36; Nov. 18.1), and it was endorsed by the medieval canon law (X 3.26.16, 18). Although it was a disputed point,[54] the consensus view among the jurists was that some obligation to care for a child, derived *ex iure naturae,* could be understood to endure to the time of the parent's death. The principle was the same. Children in need should be left something where the parent's assets sufficed. However, the extent of the obligation differed, because in matters of inheritance, the needs of illegitimate children were outmatched by concerns for family stability—again illustrating the pliability with which principles drawn from the law of nature could be interpreted and applied in fact.

The questions related to the *legitim* raised most often in litigation were two: the conditions under which other circumstances could excuse parents from the obligation and the extent to which a custom or statute could regulate and reduce it.[55] The textbook example of the situation where the obligation was excused was the case of the ungrateful child. Exclusion for ingratitude was part of Roman law, but it raised additional problems of its own. For example, allowing children to marry against the wishes of their parents, as the medieval church did, presented a hard problem for excusing payment of the *legitim*. It was clearly an example of ingratitude, but children had the ability to marry whomever they chose under the canon law.[56] Jurists were loath to admit that following religious law could be a source of legal wrong or a cause of familial disorder. The more common view therefore separated the two questions, allowing exclusion from inheritance of a disobedient child but preserving a child's right to marry without parental interference. In other words, it appears that the *communis opinio* of the jurists stepped back from facing the problem head on. The law of nature was open enough to allow that disposition.

Statutes or customs that enforced a regime of primogeniture so strictly that only one child took most or all of the parental estate raised similar difficulties. On the one hand, they might require virtual extinction of an obligation toward the other children, one that was itself based upon the law of nature.[57] On the other hand, splintering estates caused social instability and led to shared poverty. The opinions of the learned therefore differed. The law of nature itself sometimes seemed equivocal. Eventually the legal problems associated with the *legitim* would fill a treatise of 730 folios divided into two hundred separate *quaestiones*.[58] In some of them the law of nature was relevant enough to be cited directly as controlling the outcome, as occasionally happened in the *decisiones* themselves.[59] Probably it would be accurate to say the *communis opinio* among the jurists was, first, that a statute could diminish but not entirely take away the right to *legitim* and, second, that the regime of primogeniture was not unlawful but that within it some financial provision should always be made, either inter vivos or at death, for all the children born lawfully within the marriage.[60]

A third consequence of recognizing the law of nature as a source of positive law might be described as a procedural disqualification. In contemporary understanding, parents and children were so tied together by a bond of nature that it would be more than awkward for a child to bring suit against his father. It would be contrary to the dictates of nature. Equally so would be allowing a child to testify against his father in court. "For sons to reprove their fathers would cause the law itself to blush in shame."[61] It would be contrary to the teachings of nature. Modern law still recognizes a doctrine of parental immunity very like that found within the *ius commune*, although it is usually justified by ascribing it to a societal consensus that courts are likely to get things wrong if they intrude too far into the circle of family life. In earlier centuries an almost identical rule was explained by the law of nature.

As is also true in modern law, the rule of the *ius commune* forbidding hostile legal action between parent and child also made room for exceptions. The immunity did not extend to bar complaints about a parent's excessively cruel treatment of a child. Nor did it offer protection where the father's crimes were particularly heinous. A child might bring an accusation against his own father, for example, where the father had killed his wife, the accuser's mother,[62] or where, for example, a son knew his father to have committed an act of treason, he was admitted to testify against him, this despite the natural bonds of kinship. The law of nature was not meant to contribute to the subversion of a legitimate government, and the enormity of particular crimes called out for exceptions. The needs of justice could outweigh the tenets of the law of nature.

Under the medieval canon law, the same hard rule held true for heresy. The son who knew his father to be a heretic was not only entitled to give evidence against him, he was said to be obliged to come forward and denounce his father (Sext. 5.2.11). In support of this admittedly unnatural requirement, canonists cited the words of Jesus: his followers must be willing to forsake their own mothers and fathers if they are to inherit eternal life (Matt. 19:29). Exceptions like these were entirely normal parts of the *ius commune*. They were noted both in inquisitorial handbooks and occasionally in the *decisiones* themselves.[63] The commands of the law of nature always had their limits, and here was a particularly easy one for medieval canonists to endorse.

These areas are samples—probably the most frequently mentioned in the cases—of how the law of nature was used in litigation involving family life. They show something of the consequences of invoking the natural law. The *decisiones* demonstrate that arguments founded upon the law of nature were not assured of success. Particular statutes and arguments based upon the needs of society could blunt their force, at least where they could be supported by citations to the *Corpus iuris civilis* and the opinions of other jurists, as almost all of them could. Sometimes the arguments advanced in litigation had the effect of putting the natural law into the shade. Sometimes they brought it into the light. It is a mixed picture, one quite characteristic of the *ius commune*.[64]

These three most common examples do not exhaust the subject. The law of nature also turned up in some (now) quite unexpected settings involving the law of families and inheritance. One such case involved a challenge to the local custom of inheritance that limited intestate succession to persons descended from anyone who died intestate, thus excluding any person on a family tree reached by ascending upward through the parents. The argument against allowing this custom was that it was irrational. It could allow persons more distantly related to a person to take his estate, to the exclusion of those more closely related. An uncle might be closer kin than a great-nephew. The argument in its favor depended on the law of nature. As rivers in nature flow only downward, so, it was said, should the law of inheritance.[65] The custom was therefore defensible. It was rational in the sense that it followed a path identical to one found in nature itself.

A second and perhaps a better example is a *decisio* from a dispute involving a married man who left his family to fight in a war, leaving a son behind him.[66] While he was gone, the child was brought up by his father-in-law, and when the soldier returned some years later, the father-in-law greeted his arrival by bringing suit against him to recover the cost of the child's upbringing. The natural law was relevant to the case. It furnished an answer to the soldier's argument that the father-in-law had acted simply out of piety and kindness. In the law of nature, the duty to provide *alimenta* belonged first to the father himself; that was enough, the argument went, to overcome any presumption that what the father-in-law had furnished to the child had been meant as a gift.

It saved any necessity of inquiring what the actual motives of the father-in-law had been.

A third, and perhaps even better, example involved an Italian city's statute restricting the right of a married woman to alienate her property without the consent of both her husband and her closest relatives.[67] It was held not to apply to a woman's provision of a dowry for her daughter. The provision of the daughter's dowry was regarded as a product of "maternal piety." It formed one part of a mother's natural duty toward the children to whom she had given birth and then had reared. It was thus an exception based on a natural tie. The *decisio* unfortunately does not contain the text of the statute, but it mentions nothing in the statute's wording that would justify the exception—nothing, that is, except one found in the law of nature.

A fourth example, illustrating the length to which natural law could be taken, was raised by the attempt by one brother to have another brother committed to prison for failure to pay a debt the brother owed to him.[68] On one side, it was said to be an act of unnatural cruelty for a brother to hate his own flesh and blood. The controversy should be settled amicably. Charity should begin at home, argued the debtor's lawyer. For the other side, it was said that the claim of fraternal affection was not really a fact of life. Brothers were often rivals. So it had always been, as the example of Cain and Abel showed. The law was bound to recognize this characteristic, particularly where a duty to pay a legitimate debt was involved and where one party was seeking a special privilege to block it. The judge decided to allow the imprisonment; the reasons based on natural ties that were advanced by the debtor were, as he saw it, "too general" to carry the day.

Criminal Law

A substantial number of Continental *decisiones* dealt with crimes, and in them the law of nature did occasionally come into play. One area already mentioned was the right of self-defense. It was a staple feature of the *ius commune* and was commonly ascribed to the law of nature, in theory because it had been exercised by all men prior to the organization of societies and the partial abridgement of the right that had followed it. In practice, the right had assumed a variety of forms. Guides to lawyers provided practice tips on how to assert them.[69] Most basically, it justified killing in defense of one's person, at least if it was the only reasonable alternative to being killed by the assailant. This was a right "derived from nature and available to everyone, even to brute animals."[70] It also extended to repelling attacks on one's children, and probably also to attacks made on one's kinsmen as well.[71] Just how far it could be taken was a matter of controversy; that it also applied to the case of an attack being made against a companion and friend was a harder, but not an impossible, argument to make.

More difficult still was its use as a means of preventing theft of one's property. That might be extending the natural law's principle beyond the point where it made sense. Should a life be taken to defend a purse? A piece of timber? Would it allow a creditor to kill a fleeing debtor if the creditor knew for certain that the fugitive would never return to satisfy the debt?[72] Obviously, the underlying principle was capable of expansion in cases like these. Equally obviously, it could be taken too far. Sometimes the balance weighed against the exercise of a right supported by the natural law, but sometimes the balance of reason went the other way: in favor of its extension. The law of nature provided a starting point and a solution to clear cases, but not more than that.

The principle itself was cited with approval in a wide variety of situations in the *decisiones;* it was said to extend, for example, to justifying a defamatory statement made in answer to a personal attack on one's character. No liability ensued if the speaker was merely defending himself, even if he used otherwise defamatory language.[73] To answer in kind was a natural impulse. The same might be said where the initial slander had been an attack on one's personal honor.[74] It would be unnatural for anyone to suffer such an insult in silence. It bears saying again that these were arguments, arguments made by lawyers in favor of defendants in litigation. They did not always carry the day. The principle has always been clearer than the practical conclusions to be drawn from it. It was an easy principle to invoke, but it was harder for a judge to be sure about its extent.

As a practical matter, the law of nature's most frequent mention in the *decisiones* involving criminal law probably came in determining whether a defendant found guilty of a crime had been accorded due process. The right to fair treatment in court was regarded as part of the same right to defend oneself from harm found in the law of nature, and the principle could come up in any case where that right had not been adequately afforded to a defendant. The possibility is well illustrated by a case from the high court of Naples from the sixteenth century. A statute had been enacted punishing by immediate death any man taken at night in the act of climbing a ladder he had set up under the window of a house in which maidens dwelt, presumably to make an assault on their chastity.[75] The climbers could be executed by the magistrate with the barest of legal process. Exact adherence to the *ordo iuris* was not required, and no appeals were to be allowed. This draconian decree—reminiscent of some in Shakespeare's *Measure for Measure*—was put into effect, and in one such instance it was challenged as contrary both to the law of nature and to provisions in the established *ius commune* that built upon it. The argument was that the right guaranteed by the law of nature had to be a meaningful one. It included a right not to be condemned without a fair trial. It could not be taken away. By so drastically abridging it, the defendant's lawyers contended, this Neapolitan decree had offended against the natural law. The statute should not be applied against their client.

That was their argument. In the event, however, it failed. The *decisio* held that the enormity of the crime, the alarming increase in the frequency with which it was being committed in Naples, and this defendant's undoubted aim in first setting up his ladder and then climbing it—taken all together—were sufficient to uphold the statute's application in the case. The defendant, who had been caught in the act of climbing, was rightly condemned. A hard result for the libidinous young men of Naples, no doubt, but any among them who were also law students might not have been caught entirely off guard by the decision. The maxim that "crime should not go unpunished" was often forceful enough to overcome arguments based on the law of nature, particularly when coupled with a panicky reaction to social disorder.

Sometimes, of course, the results were happier (for the accused) than in this Neapolitan example. In a seventeenth-century case involving application of a statutory penalty of death for simple theft, for example, natural law was invoked to justify a lesser sentence. In the beginning, all property had been held in common, the argument went, and it would require special reasons for the law to visit so terrible a penalty upon a man who had taken back what, in a state of nature, he could conceivably have held by right.[76] The statute should thus be read to apply only to cases of heinous theft. To be sure, this was not the only argument made in the case; in fact, its use may even then have seemed a bit of a stretch. The lawyer also invoked the Bible (Prov. 6:30–31) and Roman law (Inst. 4.1.1–2), as well as the opinions of other jurists, to secure a lesser sentence for his client. He acknowledged that death might be the appropriate penalty in more serious cases. He did not attempt to invalidate the statute. He was not disputing its validity but rather its applicability to one case: his case. This crime, he said, seemed more like a simple case of conversion than of heinous theft, and the law of nature was only one of several laws that pointed in the direction of leniency. What finally happened in the case, unfortunately, we do not know.

A similar example is found among the *decisiones* of the Avignonese Rota in the sixteenth century.[77] A defendant in the case invoked the law of nature after having been convicted, he claimed, without the fair trial it guaranteed to him. The judges agreed, but they merely reduced his sentence from death to perpetual service in the galleys. There had been a clear failure of due process. What had been done was contrary to a right founded upon natural law. That failure was admitted, but the man's crimes were many, and his guilt of the one for which he was being tried seemed at least highly probable to the auditors of the Rota, even if the trial had not been conducted in full accord with the standards of procedural due process. The circumstantial evidence was strongly against him. His accomplice had implicated him on the gallows. The consequence was that he was treated more leniently because of the admitted failure of legal process, but he was not exonerated. In this situation, as in most, the law of nature was not a trump card.

A third common use of the law of nature in the criminal law related more directly to the punishment of criminals than it did to their procedural rights. It emerged from the distinction drawn between crimes that violated the laws of nature and those that did not. The former deserved, and in fact received, more serious punishment than the latter. Therefore, it was necessary to know which was which.[78] Roughly speaking, this was quite like the distinction modern criminal law still draws between a crime that is *malum in se* and one that is merely *malum prohibitum*. It sometimes differed, however, in where the line was drawn. Premeditated murder, rape, and treason were then treated as violations of the natural and correct order of human society, and over the centuries these crimes have largely retained their status as particularly serious offenses. The laws covering their gravity have remained pretty much the same, though we have ceased to speak about the law of nature in giving reasons for the severity with which they are punished.

However, some things have also changed in substance between then and now. Then, blasphemy and sodomy, far from being protected by a constitutional right of privacy or freedom of speech, were regarded as particularly heinous violations of the law of nature. They called for the harshest repression and the most serious forms of punishment.[79] Now they do not. In today's climate of opinion, this conclusion may seem hard to understand. Even where they are still prohibited by the positive law, they are widely regarded as "victimless crimes." However, in the understanding of earlier centuries, the harsher treatment made sense. The author of the law of nature was God himself. To blaspheme was to curse God. To set oneself against one's creator in a particularly pestilent way—not by neglect but by express denial of his power and goodness— was a real crime.[80] To commit it would likely call forth God's wrath. Sodomy was equally a crime against nature, as its description in the English common law long asserted.[81] God's own action in visiting and punishing Sodom taught all men that lesson (Gen. 19:5, 24–25). From sodomy no good could come, only ill; indeed, it was a "crimen detestabilissimum." The jurists seemed almost to compete in the extravagance of the language they found suitable for its condemnation. Sodomy and blasphemy were not crimes against men but crimes against God himself,[82] and God's vengeance would very likely be forthcoming. Proper punishment might help to forestall that day, and citation to the law of nature in the cases provided some of the justification for it.

Apart from these three common functions, other instances where the law of nature was raised and put into practice appear here and there among the criminal *decisiones*. For instance, one case drew a distinction between a crime against natural law and one that was purely statutory in dealing with criminal acts committed by foreigners who were ignorant of the laws of a particular city. Strangers without knowledge of the statute should be punished only if their crimes violated the law of nature.[83] If they did, they would have had the necessary *mens rea* because the natural law in their hearts would have told them so. Another case allowed the passage of time to mitigate the punishment to be meted out to perpetrators of crimes, but only as to those crimes that were not in violation of divine or natural law.[84] A third allowed mitigation in the punishment of the crime of incest, limiting the concession, however, to incest that fell outside the degrees of consanguinity defined as incestuous by the law of nature.[85]

Criminal cases involving mistreatment of animals that cited the law of nature also appeared in the *decisiones,* although not with any frequency. One of them allowed an exception to established local practice of not punishing simple attempts to commit crimes. The case dealt with a man who had intended to sodomize an animal.[86] He was caught before he could bring his intent to fruition, but the character of his crime, one clearly against natural law, was used to justify his punishment despite the established exception's existence.[87] Natural law, in other words, was used to augment his guilt.

Cases involving the trial and punishment of animals themselves also occasionally raised questions in which natural law was cited.[88] That their actions—sodomy for example—could be said to violate the law of nature seemed sufficient in the eyes of some jurists to justify this strange practice. This was the argument, even where the animals were themselves victims of men over whom they could exercise no control. If, as Ulpian held, animals knew the rudiments of the law of nature by instinct, they should know enough to flee the sodomite's touch.[89] If they had not done so, they were justly punished. The answer was given, however, that their lack of the full use of reason might excuse them in crimes that required the existence of *mens rea.*[90] They were victims, not perpetrators. The merits were thus open to doubt. The results varied. Such crimes were thought to involve violation of the laws of nature. That made them worse in theory than crimes that did not, but even admitting this, the crimes of animals might be subject to excuse or mitigation. Here, as elsewhere, natural law did not require a fixed result.

Economic Regulation

The law of nature reached into the field of economic regulation and social life. It dealt with the regulation of many forms of trade. The *Mare liberum* of Hugo Grotius is the most famous example of its reach. It provided a means of proclaiming and protecting the freedom of the seas.[91] The economic thought of the "Second Scholastics" in Spain provides another example. Only recently have the contributions to economic thought of men like Leonard Lessius and Luis de Molina been recognized. Economics was not then a separate academic discipline but rather a special aspect within the field of moral thought. It is only to be expected, therefore, that natural law should have appeared in court cases involving commerce.

So it did. The contents of the Continental *decisiones* demonstrate natural law's perceived relevance to economic questions. A rule in favor of freedom of navigation on rivers and seas, for instance, was attributed to the law of nature and used to prevent the imposition of new and onerous tolls on navigation in the river Scheldt near Antwerp.[92] It was also used to prevent the Duke of Savoy from imposing prohibitions against fishing in public rivers by his vassals and their men.[93] *Decisiones* like these augment and support the findings of Wim Decock's impressive recent study of the moral dimensions of the commercial law developed during the sixteenth and seventeenth centuries.[94]

Of the many individual subjects involving commerce regularly touched upon in the *decisiones*, one of the most frequent and intriguing is usury—particularly so in the context of the study of the law of nature because it provides an example of doctrinal development within the supposedly immutable tenets of the law of nature. Today, it is hard to take seriously the invective commentators once leveled at what is now considered to be a necessary and largely beneficial part of economic life, lending money in return for the payment of interest. The common understanding of usury was, however, very different in the Middle Ages. Defined in the simplest case as taking back more than had been lent, the practice stood condemned in the Old and New Testaments. It was also condemned in the clearest of terms within the canonical half of the *ius commune*.[95] Thought to be destructive of the sinews of a just society, among its several vices the practice of usury was said to be contrary to the law of nature. An ostensible reason given for the latter was that in nature, money, unlike humans and animals, cannot generate more money.[96] Coins are sterile. Aristotle himself had so stated, and many medieval jurists applied his analogy to contemporary commercial practice.[97]

Whatever one thinks of this reasoning, strains between the strength of the old prohibition and the needs of a more commercial society surfaced in the later Middle Ages, and scholarly efforts were made to reach some accommodation between them. Several sophisticated modern studies of those efforts have been made.[98] Most of the accommodation took the form of refinements in what was meant by the term *usury*. Shared risk in a contract, for example, might take the contract out of the category of usurious transactions. This survey of the *decisiones* and works of practice does not lead to a challenge of the conclusions found in recent scholarly work; in fact, it does quite the reverse. One's admiration increases. It may be said with some measure of truth that the subject did lead many of the Schoolmen into "a quagmire of contradictions."[99] But it probably should have. Usury was never an easy subject. The Schoolmen were working toward a sensible goal within the restraints of a tradition they had neither the wish nor the ability to discard.[100] Within that constraint, they did not do badly.

The survey of evidence from the law courts does show that the assertion that usury was contrary to the law of nature continued to be made there. Lawyers regularly invoked traditional assumptions about it.[101] *Decisiones* recorded invocations of the law of nature in efforts to prevent enforcement of allegedly usurious transactions.[102] It was sometimes contended in argument, for example, that usury could not be permitted under natural law, even when it served the cause of public utility.[103] Formidable authorities in support of that hard line could be amassed.

However, the tide of scholarly opinion was running in the opposite direction, and this change had consequences in the courts. Most revealing of the movement were *decisiones* in which a statute that allowed a moderate rate of interest to be taken was challenged as contrary to both the law of nature and the *ius commune*, but was nonetheless validated and upheld.[104] These statutes were enacted in many parts of Europe, and the *decisiones* seem mostly to have decided in favor of enforcing them.[105] A German constitution setting only a moderate penalty for usury—loss of a quarter of the profits—survived a challenge that it was contrary to natural law's prohibition of usury.[106] So did a papal grant allowing Jewish bankers to take a reasonable rate of interest from Christians, despite the doctrine that the popes were bound by the law of nature.[107] An Italian statute allowing the taking of moderate interest on a loan, when challenged as contrary to natural law's strictures against usury, was also defended successfully as both moderate in rate and useful in contemporary commercial life. That made it consistent with the common good.[108] In another case, an Italian merchant was excused from the criminal penalties exacted against usurers because of the existence of such a statute.[109] Whether or not his conduct had violated the law of nature as understood in the juristic literature seems most often to have been a moot point. At any rate, this particular prosecution of a lender based upon his violation of the law of nature did not succeed.

Cases like these appear to demonstrate the falsity of the claim that the law of nature could not change. They seem contrary to the assumption that it was immutable, and in a sense they do refute the claim. However, some jurists had an answer. They claimed this was too mechanical an objection to be accepted uncritically. The natural law's true purpose in condemning usury was, and had always been, to prevent wrongful conduct. Usury provided a way of taking advantage of the poor and the needy. This was the immoral purpose being condemned by usury's prohibition, and this purpose did not change from one age to another. Experience and reason had shown, however, that allowing a moderate rate of interest (but no more) achieved that goal and also fit the needs of the community better than a widely evaded absolute prohibition against taking any rate of interest no matter how small. Such an approach served the law's true purpose.

Thus, some modern apologists claim, no fundamental change in the church's stance occurred at all. Rationalization? Perhaps. Accepting it does (and did) require both some redefinition of what was objectionable about usury and some tinkering with the meaning of the concept of change.[110] The object seems to have been to save the reputation of the law of nature and the Catholic Church. However, the argument is not without plausibility. The results in practice were not greatly different from the treatment given some statutes that had nothing to do with usury. Provisions in them might come into conflict with the law of nature, but when they served a useful purpose, normally they were given effect. Across the board, there was room for development in the understanding of what was useful and what violated the law of nature. The existence of private property, for instance, was itself contrary to the law of nature, but it served a larger goal of civilized society. Circumstances changed, but not the basic purpose of the natural law.

The *decisiones* also show repeatedly that the law of nature was supple enough to admit the validity of rules that seemed to bring it into line with society's needs.[111] On this account it does not seem unreasonable either simply to take the claim that the law of nature forbidding usury was immutable *cum grano salis* or else to accept the claim that, properly speaking, natural law itself was not subject to change but that its application within the law of usury allowed for variation and fuller development over the course of time. Any treatment of the law of nature that dismisses that possibility out of hand is incomplete. Whatever one thinks about usury, rejection of the law of nature because it permitted some change over time is inconsistent with the evidence of what it had always been meant to do in practice.

The same spirit of accommodation to time and situation animated the tests of restrictions on commercial freedom that are found in the *decisiones.* For example, a statute adopted by the governors of one of the papal states forbade the export of grain from the territory where it had been grown. This was challenged as an onerous restriction on the liberty of those who had grown the grain, one contrary to human liberty and therefore beyond the power of the governors to impose. Like many similar commercial restrictions, the statute was nonetheless held to be enforceable. Looked at impartially, the restriction served the public interest in times of hardship, even if it might infringe to some extent upon the growers' freedoms. It was even said in its support that "natural reason" supported the retention of what was grown in one territory for consumption in the same territory.[112] Crops were most naturally consumed where they had been harvested.

Most such local commercial enactments seem to have passed muster when challenged as contrary to the natural liberty of potential traders.[113] The grant of an exclusive right to print a book was challenged in one *decisio* as a "monopoly adverse to the liberty of trade that nature provides" and "condemned as harmful by the common jurisprudence of all peoples."[114] The answer given by the grant's defenders was that similar restrictions were in force throughout the world and that they in fact served a useful purpose. They rewarded effort. The judge in the case allowed the restriction to stand, reserving the question of whether this was a harmful monopoly for future determination. Some restraints on commercial freedoms were permissible when challenged as violations of the law of nature, and some were not.[115]

Also promising for the future was the example of the *ius commune's* part in the creation of something akin to a law of restitution. The Digest and the *Liber sextus* both contained this *regula iuris:* "By the law of nature, it is unjust that any person should be enriched by an injury done to another person" (Dig. 50.17.206[207]; Sext 5.12.48). The principle was implemented in the Roman law by allowing a *condictio* under appropriate conditions (Dig. 12.6.14) and in the canon law by the rule that no one should be absolved from sin unless he had first restored the fruits of that sin (C. 14 q. 6 c. 1; Sext 5.13.4).[116] These were what a European jurist would have called "pregnant texts." They were capable of application and expansion in a wide variety of circumstances, certainly including commercial ones. To allow unjust enrichment in commercial dealings was challenged as "repugnant to divine law, natural law, human law, and equity itself."[117]

Of course, the term *unjust* did not define itself. The very elasticity of the terms used in the texts meant that they could be invoked in legal argument in a variety of circumstances. In fact, they were so invoked in the *decisiones,* mostly in a context where the result of its application seems consistent with what any decent legal system would hold. Thus, the son and heir of a manifest usurer was not allowed to inherit his father's property without first meeting the father's outstanding obligations of repayment.[118] Similarly, papal absolution from an unlawful oath might excuse a man from fulfilling a rash promise, but it did not excuse him from having to repay the money he had received as an inducement for making it.[119] Neither situation fit very well within the ordinary laws of contracts or delict. It was the invocation of the law of nature that helped make room for a just result. The concept underlying these cases invited more development than is found in these simple cases, and an admirable study by Professor Jan Hallebeek has shown where it did lead in an academic environment.[120] By comparison, the cases coming from a survey of the Continental *decisiones* seem more like simple applications of a rule of justice, one that was found within the law of nature. Where applying that rule caused more problems than it solved, the secondary meaning of natural law developed from practical reason usually prevailed. It did allow enforcement of most commercial regulations.

Interpretation of Statutes

One obvious starting point for any examination of the relationship between the law of nature and statutory interpretation is the oft-repeated maxim that an "odious" statute, even if valid, should always be strictly construed. It should be accorded enough deference to give it some actual effect, but it should not be extended beyond that scope. The law of nature offered an appropriate way of determining whether any particular statute was in fact "odious," and it was regularly so invoked in the case law. An ordinance of the church of Toledo, for example, forbade the grant of any benefice to a person descended from a Jew, a Moor, or a heretic. In a decision of the *Rota Romana,* this requirement was said to be contrary to principles of natural justice. No actual fault could be ascribed to the descendant caught by the ordinance. It was also contrary to the accepted canonical rule that every person was presumed competent to hold an office until the contrary had been shown. In the event, however, the auditors of the Rota did not invalidate the ordinance. Because of its "odious" character, they simply concluded that the path of descent had to be proved beyond doubt for it to be applied.[121] Hearsay testimony and opinion testimony did not count as proof. The auditors could not undo the ordinance, but they could interpret it strictly. It did not dictate the result in a case where they had a reasonable choice.

Another starting point is the famous statement that to be a true law, every statute must stand in conformity with the natural law. Hugo Grotius, for example, wrote that "the municipal law can neither command what the law of nature forbids nor forbid what the law of nature commands."[122] In so saying, he was building upon a medieval tradition. St. Thomas Aquinas stated that "the first command of the law is that good is to be sought and done, evil to be avoided."[123] For him, it followed that unjust laws did not deserve the name of law at all; they were "corruptions of the law."[124] Even the powers of emperors and popes were constrained by the law of nature.[125] The similarity between this approach to natural law and modern judicial review of legislation does seem apparent.[126]

Good reasons nonetheless exist for caution in seeing modern judicial review in natural law's past. Stefan Vogenauer's excellent survey of the history of statutory interpretation elucidates many of the continuities and the differences.[127] In the context of the study of natural law's role in the process, it is also particularly important to keep in mind that some long-established human institutions were contrary to the law of nature—slavery and private property, for instance. No one then believed these institutions could be treated as nonexistent simply because of their lack of congruence with the law of nature. They existed. Courts enforced them. They served a purpose.[128] We have looked already at examples of the result. More than a few of the *decisiones* surveyed also show that courts regularly weighed arguments based upon the law of nature against the pressing needs of the community. In that balance, the law of nature did not always prevail. Evidently, a regime that recognized the validity and even the primacy of natural law left room for exceptions based on society's interests. Some of the statutes in which those interests outweighed the law of nature were not treated as "odious" at all. When supported by strong reasons, they were actually treated with deference.

In thinking through the meaning of these cases, we will do well to remember that statutes did not have quite the same force under the medieval and early modern *ius commune* as they have under most modern regimes. Under the right circumstances, valid statutes could be displaced by contrary local customs. They were subject to extinction through desuetude; they were open to the power of dispensation held by a competent authority; and they could even fail if they had not been "received" by the community for which they were intended. A study of natural law's relevance in the courts is not the right place to explore these limitations on legislation's force in practice, except to take note that they were limitations occasionally mentioned and applied in the *decisiones*.[129] They still should be kept in mind while examining this study's subject. They affected how statutes were understood.

The *decisiones* and other works of practice contain many challenges to the enforcement of statutes, and some of them depended on the law of nature. The challenges rarely resulted, however, in what is known in American law as "striking down" an unconstitutional statute. Judicial review in this modern sense did not fit within the juridical assumptions of European lawyers.[130] Instead, their assumptions led them to a search for an understanding of a statute that was consistent with natural justice and, where no such understanding could be uncovered, to a reluctance to apply the terms of the statute in the matters that came before them. The formal law (Cod. 1.22(25).2) and their oaths bound them to do justice. That is what they tried to do in the cases brought before their courts.[131] For this, the law of nature was a useful tool. It did not, however, grant them the power to overturn laws simply because they contained a violation of nature's laws.

Probably this pattern, found throughout the *decisiones,* can best be appreciated by specific examples. The textbook example—one known to every civilian—involved a Bolognese statute punishing any person who shed the blood of another person in the public streets. The statute was intended to restrain public quarrels and to prevent bloodshed, but if its terms were read literally, it covered a doctor who opened the veins of a man on the streets as part of an effort to restore him to health. Must the doctor be punished? This example was long used to show that judges should not read statutory language in a wooden way. They must consider the statute's larger purpose. Legislators could not have foreseen every circumstance where the words of their statute might apply, and judges were invited to compensate for an inability the legislators could scarcely have avoided. Judges might legitimately ask: What would the legislators have done had they actually had this case before them? This query provided the entry point for the laws of nature.

The Bolognese example was not a purely academic exercise. Similar cases arose in fact. One comes from a sixteenth-century *decisio* involving a statute of the Italian city of Genoa that denied the losing party in litigation the right to rely upon a particular point on appeal unless he had presented it within twenty days of its violation. This statute was raised against a party who had interposed a technical objection during the twenty-day period, making it impossible for the appellant to meet the deadline in objecting to a different fault. The twenty days had passed in arguing about the first objection. The words of the statute, however, forbade any exceptions to this strict time limit. In the *decisio*, the party caught in this trap objected that the statute should not be read "to open the way to the malice and trickery of litigants." This would be contrary to natural justice, he said, and no good reason for permitting this to happen had been offered, none except the words of the statute read literally. And so the litigant prevailed against the statute. Today, we might reach the same result through invocation of the doctrine of estoppel. Then, the court reached it through invocation of the law of nature.

Another *decisio*, one with a quite different outcome, challenged a sixteenth-century ducal decree from Piedmont that purported to impute responsibility for injuries inflicted upon an abbey church and its monks to the city in which the abbey lay. Under the decree, the whole community was required to compensate the monks for their losses. After one such injury, the municipality challenged the decree as "contrary to divine and human law and [also] against natural reason," adding that "where there is no guilt, neither should there be punishment."[132] This was a settled principle of natural law.[133] It was against natural justice to do the contrary. The city's inhabitants should not be made to pay, the argument ran, unless they had actually been at fault, and no proof whatsoever had been offered that they had. However, a counterargument was also made. Numerous outrages had been inflicted upon the abbey, the abbey's lawyer said, and the duke was duty bound to prevent them. Similar statutes that punished men without fault had passed muster elsewhere. They had been challenged, but they had been approved and enforced in other *decisiones*. God himself sometimes visits punishment on men who had committed no provable crime (Gen. 19:24–25; Exod. 11:5–6). And as for the principle that unjust statutes are not true statutes, that principle applied only to statutes enacted without a good reason.[134] This decree was not one of those. A good reason for its enactment was self-evident. The statute might not be applied where it was known who the actual malefactor was, the lawyer conceded, but where no one could be identified, it was right that the decree should be enforced as written. If it were not, "crimes would remain unpunished."[135] This second lawyer's argument proved to be the winner. The inhabitants had to pay.

In some ways these two *decisiones* appear very like many modern disputes that animate constitutional litigation in the United States. Disagreements about the meaning of constitutional provisions and their application in different circumstances fuel disputes. Each party to the dispute conceives it has right on its side. The parallel between the current situation and that of earlier centuries appears to be a quite close one. Perhaps it is even an inevitable feature of any developed legal system. Nonetheless, differences existed between then and now. Two should be stated.

First, the consequence of the initial case, the Genoese *decisio* dealing with the right to appeal, was not to invalidate the statute being challenged.[136] The judges did not "strike it down." They simply did not enforce it in the case before them. Their reasoning was something like this: A statute cannot have been meant to work injustice. The purpose of a statute, as indeed of all positive law, is to do justice. If enforced exactly as written, the statute's enforcement would frustrate that purpose, its own purpose. No overriding justification for such a mechanical reading had been suggested to the judges. They therefore concluded that the statute did not apply to the case before them, but they did not invalidate the statute itself. It could apply in other cases.

Second, the decisive question in the other *decisio*, the Piedmont case involving damages to the abbey, was not whether the natural law had been violated. It was conceded that it had been. Punishment without fault was contrary to the tenets of the law of nature. What permitted the court to apply the ducal decree nonetheless was that the arguments advanced on its behalf were strong enough to justify its application in the case before the court. Statutes like it were founded on the need for justice in the community, there was no obvious alternative to them, and they were supported by the authority of other *decisiones* and other jurists. The community itself held both rights and duties under the law of nature, and protection of a monastic house was one of the latter.[137] These two Italian cases do seem to have reached different results in interpreting a legislative act. What unites them, however, is that, in both, the law of nature furnished only a start for the legal arguments. It was not the end.

When they felt called upon to generalize about their approach to natural law and statutory interpretation, the early jurists said some apparently contradictory things. Karl Llewellyn could have taken notice of them as examples of law's habitual incoherence.[138] Sometimes jurists said that statutes should be construed strictly according to the words they contained. It would not be right to inquire into the reasons behind a statute, they argued, because lawmakers were presumed to have had a good reason for enacting what they had. Nor is it possible to give a reason for every legislative act. They should, therefore, be applied as written.[139] Sometimes, however, jurists said pretty nearly the reverse. The words of a statute were merely its shell. Reason was the soul and the spirit of the law.[140] The "mind" of the law was what mattered, and that "mind" was presumed to stand in accord with principles found in the law of nature.[141] The words of an enactment should therefore be brought to an understanding that was "sane, good, civil, and alien to evil."[142]

These spacious and seemingly inconsistent approaches were stated with particular clarity by Andreas Gaill (d. 1587): "As a rule *(regulariter)*," he wrote, "statutes are to be taken as they are written. Their words are to be followed, and the opinion of the legislators is to be accepted as reason." In the very next sentence, however, he added, "This rule does not apply *(fallit)* if the words are general and would lead to a result that is absurd, iniquitous, or injurious to the rights of others."[143] In such cases, he thought, a judge must look beyond the bare words in order to do justice. He was not tied to a literal reading of the statute's commands. Were Gaill's two statements internally contradictory? Perhaps they were, but they were not dishonest. They describe what the cases show.

Examples of each approach appear throughout the *decisiones*. A statute had the effect of taking away a man's right to leave his property by last will and testament. Academic opinion was cited to show that this was

contrary to the tenets of the law of nature,[144] but there was also learned
opinion that justified restrictions that amounted almost to abolition of
the right.[145] Judges had to think through this problem. A local statute
restricted entry of outsiders into a company of merchants to those who
married the widows or daughters of existing members. It was attacked
as contrary to the right to marry and the freedom to conduct commerce
said to be part of the law of nature.[146] But it was also defended as a restriction useful in trade, one that was "neither iniquitous, impious, nor
dishonest."[147] Judges had to weigh the two arguments. A third statute
allowed lords to forbid hunting in their lands by their vassals. It was objected to as contrary to the "liberty of hunting granted by the laws of
nature and the law of nations."[148] It was also defended, however, as
founded upon a "just and reasonable cause." Hunting could have unhappy consequences. The argument ended by asserting that "many things
permitted by natural law may be forbidden by positive law when justified by the needs of public utility and equitable government."[149] Judges
had to make a reasoned choice. The *decisiones* show that in weighing the
law of nature against the needs of public utility, they did not always make
the same choice.

    One additional point to be made about these cases—indeed stressed—
is that most of the statements cited formed part of arguments being made
by lawyers in the course of litigation. We should not concede more weight
to the arguments than they bore at the time they were made. That much
is made clear by a curious feature of the *decisiones* themselves. Which
side in the end had the better of the arguments was not always stated.
The accounts did not invariably include the judge's decision—to us a
strange finding for a class of legal literature supposed to describe decisions. However, *decisiones* were meant for lawyers—men who sometimes
needed a plausible argument more than they needed to know how an
earlier case had come out.[150] Knowing the outcome might be useful, of
course, but in a legal system not strictly based on judicial precedent, it
was not always essential.

    What one can see most clearly in the evidence is that the law of na-
ture was regularly used in arguments made in the European courts. It
was a tool of statutory interpretation, one employed to put into practice
the assumption that a statute could not have been intended to reach a
result that contained either absurdity or iniquity.[151] The law of nature
was used less often to challenge the validity of statutes than to interpret

them. When it was invoked, the assumption that statutes should not be accorded respect if they were out of step with the law of nature was a strong one, but it was also one that could be answered and even overcome. Some answer to arguments based on the law of nature there had to be, but there usually was. The *decisiones* show both sides.

Restraints on the Exercise of Power

At least in English language scholarship, few subjects involving the *ius commune* have attracted more attention and more diversity of viewpoint than determining the extent to which it served to protect ordinary men and women against abusive exercises of power by society's governors. On the one hand, the Roman and canon laws are said to have legitimated absolutism, endorsing the unchecked powers of emperors and popes.[152] The legal regime developed from their texts was also characterized by the systematic persecution of honest men and women.[153] On the other hand, the same laws are said to have been the source of human rights.[154] Whatever abuses of power did exist (and that some did exist few historians doubt), this happened in defiance of the learned laws, not in furtherance of their principles. Law is a malleable discipline. On this subject, it provides evidence for both sides. Kenneth Pennington's examination of the evidence found in texts and treatises provides a praiseworthy introduction to understanding this subject.[155] So do the works of his teacher, Brian Tierney.[156] The *decisiones* and works of *praxis* upon which the present study is based also yield additional information. They give examples that show that the law of nature did play a role in defining what counted as an abuse of power and in determining what could be done in response for its victims. Though far from a cure-all, its invocation served to prevent some excesses.

Many of the *decisiones* and *consilia* simply replicate the conclusions drawn from the examination of statutory interpretation. Statutes could be instruments of tyranny. Construing them according to purposes found within the law of nature provided a way of avoiding that result. However, a little more can be added to this on the basis of evidence found within the *decisiones*. Some of the things princes and legislatures did were no different from things done by ordinary men and women. When princes promised to do something or when they acted wrongfully, orthodox thought of the time sometimes invoked the law of nature to keep them to the paths of justice. Even the mighty must, for example, keep their promises when they entered into an ordinary contract with one of their subjects.[157] Living up to one's word was part of the natural law. Princes were bound by it. They were not above the law of nature; the law of nature was above them, and this principle required them to do what they had promised to do.[158]

It is true that there were exceptions to this general rule that promises should be kept. For instance, the existence of "very great prejudice to the Crown and to the public good" might be sufficient to excuse performance of a promise made by the prince.[159] Courts started with a presumption of legality in judging the actions of a sovereign, a presumption not always available to others. The existence of such exceptions, it may be said, gave rise to the possibility of cynical manipulation of the law by the ruler. No doubt that is true, but too much should not be claimed for it. Subjects will not enter into contracts for long with a ruler who regularly breaks his promises. Moreover, courts can deal with the contracts of princes on the basis of the ordinary rules of law.[160] Normally, they did just that. European courts might ordinarily invoke a presumption that rulers were acting for a good reason, but they were not bound to follow the presumption blindly. The possibilities were sketched in the legal literature of the time. In them, it is noteworthy that most jurists did endorse a presumption of legality for the actions of a ruler, but they also held that it would not necessarily apply in cases where those actions contradicted the law of nature.[161]

In the European cases where the law of nature was invoked, it was half-command, half-interpretive guide. A fair example from the highest court of Naples in the seventeenth century involved the meaning of a lord's restoration of a vassal to his fief after the vassal had rebelled against the lord, thereby committing the *crimen laesae maiestatis*.[162] Did the restoration also restore a special privilege granted as part of the original feudal contract between them, or was a new grant required? The court held the former. The privilege remained intact, and the reason given in the *decisio* was that the lord's contractual promise was binding under natural law. Commission of the *crimen laesae maiestatis* had given the lord the right to deprive the vassal of his fief under positive law, but the crime did not of itself necessarily invalidate the lord's promise. *Pacta sunt servanda*. The lord could have made renunciation of the vassal's privilege a condition of the restoration of his fief. The force of a promise could be overcome by subsequent events or destruction of the thing upon which the promise was based. But if the lord had not chosen to take advantage of the possibility, the promise remained binding.

Decisiones like these illustrate what might be called the "internalist" role played by the law of nature. It was used to discover the meaning of existing laws, to help supply the answer to a legal question where the import of positive law was uncertain, and to discover the meaning of actions taken by the parties to litigation. In cases like the one just mentioned from the Neapolitan court, the law of nature served as a supplementary role to the positive law. Its force could have been evaded by better planning on the part of the lord. Where he had not acted, however, the law of nature's dictates remained binding upon him.

A more aggressive reading of the cases, however, illustrates a stronger, though not absolute, role sometimes played by natural law. If a conflict between the ruler's command and principles of justice founded upon the law of nature existed, there had to be a good reason for the command if it was to pass muster. A lawyer's ordinary assumption was that no conflict between the two existed, and that assumption might be carried quite far. It would allow a judge to suppose a tacit condition in the lord's command that its effect was meant to stop short of iniquity.[163] It might even allow the judge to suppose that a ruler's concession to one of his subjects had only been the result of repeated importuning and was therefore invalid. The judge might assume, in other words, that what the grant seemed to contain had not been in accord with the ruler's true intent.[164]

European judges also seem to have been willing to take this "maximalist" approach more often to invalidate governmental actions taken by subordinate officers than when they had to deal with the decisions of a sovereign. The dean and chapter of the cathedral church of Toledo, for example, were appropriately kept under a relatively tight rein, while the Spanish monarch was given more leeway.[165] One also sees something like this in a *decisio* recorded by Matthew de Afflictis. A royal ordinance allowed a cleric despoiled of his benefice by another cleric to have recourse to a secular court.[166] The objection to the ordinance was that it encroached upon the church's jurisdiction, but the *decisio* nevertheless found no serious objection to its enforcement. The king had a special duty to defend the weak and the oppressed. This statute was a reasonable way in which that obligation could be realized. In fact, this particular sort of royal intervention was itself a duty "founded upon natural and divine law." So it stood. If the intervener in the church's affairs had been a guild or a mayor rather than the monarch, it would have been a harder case.

The point is also particularly well illustrated by a *decisio* involving an action taken by a Renaissance pope. Canon law held that popes were bound by natural and divine law but that they stood somewhere above the positive law.[167] For this reason, ordinary courts could not cite or judge the Roman pontiff. But what would happen if a pope did something contrary to natural law or the law of God? That would seem to be unlawful. It might be challenged, albeit indirectly. Just such a possibility arose with regard to a grant made by Pope Julius III (d. 1556) to his sister.[168] Out of the Roman church's patrimony, Julius had made a grant to her of property worth 1,200 *scudi.* After his death, the validity of this grant was contested. The contestants were ready to show that the *causa* expressed in the grant was nonexistent or false; it was stated only in general terms as having been in repayment of an obligation and (they said) there was no proof that any such prior obligation had actually existed. They claimed the grant was simply an illegal gift. On that account they argued that it could not stand. The property must be returned to the church.

The contestants' argument was taken seriously, but it failed to convince the judges before whom the complaint was made. Their *decisio* dismissed their objection without requiring a showing of positive evidence of the reason for the grant. It was strongly to be presumed that the pope had a good reason for making it. Indeed, it would be most absurd to suppose that the vicar of Christ would voluntarily subject his soul to the fires of eternal damnation for a simple human advantage.[169] In fact, the *decisio* actually invoked natural law in favor of the grant's validity. Charity begins at home.[170] It is a natural impulse to do good to one's own flesh and blood. The *decisio* thus held out the possibility of invalidating *some* papal actions under *some* circumstances. This could happen where either of two situations existed: where the *causa* stated in the grant was false on its face or where the injury to the church caused by the grant was a matter of great moment.[171] But this was not such a case. The contestants had failed to overcome the ordinary presumption of legality. The gift (or repayment) stood.

Whether or not one finds these arguments convincing, this particular *decisio* does bring to the fore one of the most salient features of the law of nature as it was understood and put into practice in earlier centuries. It provided a starting point for thought and argument, but it was not the end of the matter. This was particularly true where the acts and orders of the sovereign came into play. To a degree, although a lesser degree, it was also true of actions taken by guilds and officials somewhere down the ladder of authority. Throughout, however, something like a presumption of validity in favor of legislative acts existed. It was respected in fact. In most cases, the search for a rational explanation of the sovereign's command produced a reason for upholding and enforcing it. The presumption of validity became slightly weaker as one moved down the pecking order of society's institutions, but the possibility of justifying an objectionable exercise of power by lesser authorities never vanished entirely. A good reason for the exercise had to be found—a slightly harder task perhaps, but rarely an impossible one.

Conclusion

At the very least, the evidence found in the early European *decisiones* and works of *praxis* shows the relevance of the law of nature to what happened in courts. Lawyers put into practice what they had first learned as students. In giving advice and in arguing cases, they drew upon the experience with natural law they had acquired. It served various ends: to create presumptions, to interpret statutes, to evaluate commercial transactions, to solve disputes within a family, and to restrain arbitrary exercises of power. In all these functions, the law of nature usually played a subsidiary role. Rarely was it the final word. Virtually always, it was cited together with precedents from the positive law or the *ius gentium*— that is, statutes, texts from the Roman and canon laws, and opinions of the commentators, great and obscure. Natural law was called upon for help when it was helpful. It underlay the positive law and was used to undergird the assumption that the positive law was a force for justice. Under the common assumption of the times, overlap between positive and natural law was actually a sign of the influence of the latter, not an indication of its lack of consequence.

Perhaps that understanding of the law of nature provides a partial explanation for the one function it was designed to serve for which my survey found virtually no evidence in the Continental *decisiones*. In theory, an important function of the natural law was to fill gaps in the positive law. Where no positive law to govern a particular subject could be found, recourse was to be had to the law of nature. That was orthodox learning. Judges were to look to its precepts to discover the correct outcome when they found no guidance in existing texts and precedents. Of this function of the law of nature, my survey of the *decisiones* scarcely produced an example. At least I found none in which a judge or lawyer conceded that no relevant legal authority save that of the law of nature could be found.

It is difficult to offer a satisfying explanation for this absence from the *decisiones*. It may simply call attention to the richness of the resources found within the *ius commune* and to the skill of advocates in reasoning by analogy. Proceeding *de similibus ad similia* was their watchword (Dig. 1.3.12), and the range of possible similarities to be found in the texts of the *ius commune* was great. In a world in which the "mind" behind a statute or a legal text might count for more than its words, it was a rare case where no authority at all in the positive law could be found for an argument. Reasoning by analogy opened up some (to us) quite unexpected possibilities. A law defining the qualifications necessary in a Roman praetor might be used as a statement of principle that defined the requirements of officeholders long after Roman praetors had disappeared from the scene. The law might serve to confirm or to invalidate the decrees of an officer of a medieval kingdom that knew nothing of praetors. Recourse to first principles was therefore unnecessary. A text from the Digest might suffice.

It is important to remember too that the three formal sources of law were assumed to stand in harmony with one another. Existing sources in both positive law and natural law were meant to work together toward the attainment of justice. For the most part, that had happened, and it may help to explain why the law of nature alone was not often used to fill gaps in the positive law. The coincidence between the sources of law was not complete, however. This was admitted on all sides. Few lawyers supposed that natural law and positive law had been blended perfectly in the world as it was. In reality, the regime that existed, one in which the law of nature was recognized as a basic source of law by all lawyers, turned out to be no paradise of due process.[172] The lawyers who worked within the system admitted this. From time to time they lamented it. One example among many comes from a Neapolitan lawyer in the seventeenth century. Discussing the principle that no man could lawfully act as judge in his own cause, he observed how often it happened in practice that men in authority violated this clear rule of good sense and natural law. Yet, he observed, the men who paid it no heed rarely suffered any harm in consequence. The courts did not prevent it. As he brooded on the situation, this reprehensible practice seemed to him to be an almost daily occurrence. Searching for an explanation, he could only ascribe it to the inveterate vices of human nature.[173] Those vices were all too prevalent in his day. Too often they had proved more powerful than the dictates of the law of reason. One noteworthy thing about his discussion, however, is that this lawyer did not rail against natural law's weakness. He did not even argue that courts were obligated to give it a greater place than it had received. He did wish for something better, something more in tune with a rule of natural justice. But he did not expect it. Perfect justice was something God would provide. As things stood, it was unlikely to be achieved in the courts of men.

3

Legal Education in England

C ROSSING THE CHANNEL to assess the place of the law of nature in English courts raises the same preliminary question about legal education and the relevance of theory to practice that surveying the subject on the Continent did. The difference is that its answer is more difficult to discern. The exact question is: What did English barristers, the men whose professional lives were spent in the courts of the common law, know about the subject? How would they, as students, have learned anything at all about the law of nature, and how could they have absorbed sufficient knowledge of its tenets and techniques to apply them in practice? Continental lawyers, as was shown in Chapter 1, learned about natural law's place within their own legal systems while they were students at a university. The subject was put before them directly at the very start of their studies, and it recurred from time to time as they advanced further into familiarity with the resources in the Roman law's Digest and with the texts and glosses of the *Corpus iuris canonici.* This was not so in England.[1] Aspiring common lawyers did not start with Justinian's Institutes or the Digest. They were not required to progress into the commentaries of Bartolus or Panormitanus. Civil law faculties did exist at Oxford and Cambridge, but only rarely were they sought out by lawyers destined for practice in the central courts of the common law. The formal education of most common lawyers took place at England's "Third University," the Inns of Court in London, and it did not begin there with the texts that described the law of nature.

The Inns of Court

What, then, did aspiring English lawyers actually learn during their years at the Inns of Court? What were they taught? There is doubt about this, and it appears to have varied from one period to another. Some things can be said, however, and most of them do not point to any obvious source from which fledgling lawyers acquired a working knowledge of the law of nature.[2] It is true that points of entry into the subject did exist, some of them outside the training offered in the Inns of Court in London and some of them within. For instance, it was not unusual for future English lawyers to spend a year or two at Oxford or Cambridge.[3] They need not have studied the civil or canon law there. We know that some did,[4] but most as it seems did not. Whichever direction they turned during their stay at a university, however, they might at least have come into contact with the subject, perhaps in their own reading of classical literature, perhaps in meeting with students in the civil or canon law faculties, or perhaps even in perusing a contemporary treatise on law taken from the ample storehouses of the *ius commune*. Reading Cicero would have made a start. We know from various sources that these openings to the subject existed and were sometimes exploited.[5] It may be, however, that our awareness of these contacts actually signals the reverse of what they seem to show. Acquisition of learning drawn from European *fontes* may have been unusual enough among English common lawyers to have made it the subject of remark. Its very rarity made it worthy of note. It is hard to be certain what conclusion to draw.

Something of the same uncertainty recurs as one follows a student's course of training in the common law. A medieval English lawyer's normal first direct step into his profession was entry into one of the inns of Chancery in London. There students became familiar with the writs available at common law, learning in the process what situations the writs covered, what remedies they offered, and what had to be included in their wording. Students would also have learned something about the nature and structure of actions on the case. In the end they would have gained a familiarity that would later enable them to advise clients and even to draft an appropriate writ or bill. This was an important and a useful expertise. But it would be a stretch to think of it as the equivalent of a civilian's introduction to the aims and nature of law.[6] We look in vain in Registers of Writs for any general affirmation that the attainment of justice was the highest goal of the law or for a discussion of the laws of nature and nations as the foundation of all positive law. Such statements were indeed found in Justinian's Institutes, the starting point for Continental lawyers. They were conspicuous by their absence from the basic learning tools of a common lawyer.

The common law writs did of course contain material capable of raising questions related to the law of nature—the use and necessity of summoning parties to court, for instance, or the extent of every person's right to defend himself and his property. These subjects might appropriately have been discussed in examining the possible uses of the writs available in Chancery, because their contents sometimes called forth matter to which the law of nature was pertinent. If one wanted to know more about the place of writs in securing justice in the common law, turning to a treatise on the law of nature would not have been a wasted effort. There was a general congruence between them, at least an indirect connection, and an alert student of the common law might have seen it.

Examples show this possible congruence pretty well. Fitzherbert's *Novel natura brevium,* for instance, stated that men and women who were labeled as villeins by men claiming rights over them as masters enjoyed a procedural advantage when disputing the claim in order to secure their own freedom. They were entitled to a presumption that they were free until they were affirmatively proved to be villeins. Until that presumption was overcome, that is, they were to be treated as holding the rights of a free person. This privilege was granted, the text stated, not simply by reason of the normal allocation of the burden of proof but "in favour of liberty." An English student might easily be curious about exactly what that statement meant and where it came from. He might wish to know how far the presumption extended. That would be no more than natural curiosity. At most, however, hearing such a statement in the *Natura brevium* offered up the opportunity to discuss an underlying principle found in the law of nature.[7] It does not prove, of course, that the opportunity was seized. Fitzherbert's text did not mention any source, and what it does say could have been treated simply as one more feature of the common law in England. Other examples are similarly ambiguous. So it is certainly possible that students would have left an inn of chancery without having had anything but the most incidental contact with the law of nature. It would have been relevant to some of what he had learned, but that he would have been brought to see the relevance is only a possibility. We cannot know more than that.

The next step on the path of entry into the ranks of the profession was entry into one of the Inns of Court. The nature and worth of the education offered there have long been matters of uncertainty and debate among historians. Some historians have found little to praise; they have presented a bleak picture of what it meant to study the common law. Its study left little room for anything but drudgery and certainly none for large questions of jurisprudence or discussion of moral principles drawn from the law of nature. To its critics, the law of England presented at the Inns seemed to be "a formless, confused jumble of undigested particulars, successfully resisting all efforts at simplification or systematic statement."[8] That is one modern student's assessment of the education offered, and there is evidence to support it, particularly as time passed and the Inns declined into social organizations, attractive for well-born gentlemen, to be sure, but lacking the requirements necessary to foster real learning in the law.[9] Even while they flourished, however, the eyes of students were seldom lifted above the confused technical rules of the common law. Students of the law either continued with the effort required to learn them or simply abandoned their studies. Law's high purposes, not to mention the law of nature, figured little or not at all in what they learned.

This stark picture is supported by many bits of evidence, but it cannot be the whole truth. Other scholars, no less versed in the subject, have reached an almost directly opposed conclusion. For them the evidence actually shows that "[t]he inns of court were centrally involved in making English law into a coherent science."[10] There was room within them for men with ambitious horizons of thought.[11] From the perspective of this book's inquiry, one cannot expect to see their training in grand jurisprudential terms, but each of the three main components to legal study at the Inns of Court could easily have helped participants to gain some familiarity with the law of nature.[12] First, there were the formal exercises: the readings and moots, the expositions of the statutes and formal arguments in which students participated. Second, there was attendance at the courts—that is, listening and learning from what experienced lawyers did in Westminster Hall. Third, there was independent reading in books of the law, guided by experienced lawyers and fellow students.[13] We need not assume that every aspiring lawyer applied himself assiduously to each of these tasks, but it would be overly cynical to suppose that they learned nothing at all from them. They spent something like seven or eight years as "inner barristers" at one of the Inns. They could not have understood, let alone taken part in, the complex arguments raised in so many of the moots had they been either altogether idle or discouraged to the point of apathy with study of the law.[14] In fact, a closer examination of what happened in the Inns makes it appear likely that they would have come into contact with the law of nature in the course of those years.

Readings and Moots

Not many of the "case-putting exercises" that occupied students of the common law at the Inns have found their way into print,[15] but what has now become available demonstrates the possibility that lecturers included references to the law of nature in their instruction. The privilege of self-defense and the limits to the rights of a lord over his villeins—both staples of discussions of the practical effect of natural law principles—were cause for invocation of the "ley de raison" in one compilation of such exercises.[16] As Christopher St. German explained, English lawyers commonly employed the vocabulary of reason when invoking principles drawn from the law of nature.[17] Both terms were also used, seemingly also interchangeably, on the Continent.[18] Here was an example of that English usage. An attentive student might have taken note of the source of law that lay behind it.

This particular example should of course be set alongside the moots that made no mention whatsoever of natural law principles.[19] Most probably did not, and none of those so far uncovered made it a focus of discussion. The land law seems in fact to have been a much more frequent subject of interest in them than anything else, and under English law as it then stood, the intricacies of the law of real property rarely called for application of any facet of the law of nature. Its complexities, of which there were many, did not lend themselves to discussion of law's moral dimensions, although the initial acquisition and subsequent protection of property rights were subjects that came within the scope of natural law.[20] At best, therefore, reference to the law of nature in the moots seems to have been an occasional thing.

Conclusions drawn from the formal Readings at the Inns devoted to statutes appear similarly ambiguous. Sir John Baker's fundamental research has shown how many of them were given from the mid-fifteenth century to the reign of Charles II.[21] Most have remained in manuscript, so conclusions can only be tentative. Some of those that have attracted a printer do make at least passing reference to the law of nature.[22] Some do not.[23] Some leave the reference uncertain.[24] A few are simply puzzling. The printed version of the Reading by Thomas Williams (d. 1566) on the Henrician statute regulating the appearance of jurors at Nisi Prius (35 Hen. VIII, c. 6), for example, begins with a preface containing an elaborate encomium to the law of nature, but the actual Reading as it has come down to us contains only a recitation of the words in the statute and an exploration of some of the effects of the statute under varying circumstances.[25] The Reader cited no authorities whatsoever, and he discussed no opinions at variance with his own. Still less did he deal explicitly with the law of nature's impact on practical questions.

More puzzling still is the 1503 Reading of Thomas Marowe on Justices of the Peace as set out in the Statute of Westminster I (1275).[26] The Reading contained no reference to the law of nature; indeed, its only citations were to other statutes and a few Yearbook cases. However, its treatment of killing in self-defense contained a discussion of the degrees of consanguinity required between the person being attacked and the person who killed the attacker very like those that appeared in the Continental literature and quite unlike most treatments found in English law.[27] Likewise, he described royal commissions of justices of the peace in terms that would have better fit a natural lawyer's analysis of the effect of papal or episcopal grants of ecclesiastical benefices than an English monarch's. If made to an unqualified person, Marowe held, they were void.[28] But whether any of this came from a source that dealt with the law of nature, as it well might have, we cannot tell. Only the congruence with the subject is clear.

Observation of Trials

The second means of learning open to law students was attendance at the royal courts in Westminster Hall. They went there and observed what was done and said. The question here is whether the experience of seeing the courts in action would have taught them anything about the law of nature and its place in practice. Happily, this question has been the subject of several excellent studies, most notably that covering the medieval period by Norman Doe.[29] His conclusion, based upon a careful reading of the Yearbook cases and contemporary treatise literature, was that the law of nature per se was infrequently cited in the Yearbooks and commentaries but that references to conscience and to the law of reason as components of the common law occurred with regularity.[30] Judges rejected legal conclusions that were "against reason," and lawyers invoked the "the law of reason" as a means of dealing with ordinary problems in litigation. These invocations had concrete results, as we shall see in more detail in Chapter 4. Later on, the concept of "natural justice" or "natural equity" became a normal conduit for appealing to the law of nature, although variants of all three terms also continued to be used.[31] They embraced what Continental jurists classed as the secondary meaning of the law of nature.

Had Professor Doe come to his subject from an examination of Continental *decisiones* in mind, he would have found further confirmation of his conclusions. Cases appeared in the English Yearbooks evaluating procedures by whether it had been sufficient to secure the citation of defendants.[32] So did cases asserting the existence of family ties based upon the law of nature.[33] Cases drawing distinctions between the treatment of crimes that were regarded as against the law of nature and those that were not were heard in English courts.[34] References to divine law as a source of English law were also sometimes made in the course of argument.[35]

Attendance at the Court of Chancery would have brought students into contact with similar arguments based upon the claims of conscience and the force of equity. Arguments made there were sometimes drawn from the stores of the law of nature.[36] Attentive students would have heard them. Perhaps they would not have recognized the similarity of these interventions to the references to the law of nature found in the European *decisiones,* but they would have identified the same underlying sources of authority that were being cited in them. The general similarity with what was found in Continental works is clear enough today, and it would have been even clearer then. Of course, there were some differences, too. We shall follow their trail more closely in examining the later English cases.

Private Reading

The third part of the education for students of English law came from reading legal works, either on their own or under the direction of a more

learned and experienced guide.[37] In the course of time, independent
study in fact came to be the chief method of broader education available to common lawyers. By the eighteenth century, if not earlier, reading
in the chambers of an established barrister had become the course taken
by most aspiring common lawyers.[38] It was coupled with the performance
of severely practical tasks: drafting documents and becoming conversant
with the work of the courts. As one would expect, it produced diver-
gent results. Some saw it as unceasing drudgery, but others were luckier
in the choice of mentors and learned a great deal.

The books on the law that students would have read as part of this
"system" may conveniently be divided into two categories: general works
on English law and more specialized works on specific legal topics. In a
study of the place of the law of nature in legal education, it makes sense
to limit coverage to the former. They were the more likely to have been
consulted by young men just beginning the study of the law, and they
were surprisingly abundant. Many such general introductory works were
written in the sixteenth and seventeenth centuries—all the more surprising because most of them have disappeared from the view of historians.[39] This disappearance has probably been inevitable. None of them
attained the level of sophistication or enjoyed the success of the treatise
known as *Bracton* (ca. 1360) or the *Commentaries* of Sir William Blackstone (1765–1769), both of which took repeated and respectful notice of
the law of nature. *Bracton* began with definitions of justice drawn from
the same Roman law texts by which civilians became familiar with its
tenets.[40] Blackstone mentioned the law of nature at many points and
always with respect; for him it was part of the law of England.[41]

Even putting aside these two great works, however, the lesser and
shorter works had their uses, and almost all of them paid at least some
attention to the law of nature.[42] John Brydall's *Enchiridion Legum* (1673)
opened by reciting the same threefold division of the law found in the
Digest and Institutes; it thus began with the law of nature.[43] Sir John
Dodderidge's *The English Lawyer* (1631) described the law of nature as
one source of the rules and maxims of the common law.[44] The opening
chapter of Sir Henry Finch's *Law or a Discourse Thereof* (1613) was entitled "Of the Law of Nature." William Fulbecke's *Direction or Preparative
to the Study of Lawe* (1600) began with a mixture of civilian and common
law learning, repeating many of the maxims drawn from the law of
nature.[45] *Studii legalis ratio* by William Philipps (1662) opened with a

general discussion of what an aspiring lawyer must know; that knowledge required included the law of nature.[46] William Sheppard's *Faithful Councellor* (1651) began with definitions of law that were apparently lifted from the opening sections of the Roman law's Institutes, although without acknowledgment of their source.[47]

At the opposite end of the spectrum in amplitude of coverage were treatises devoted specifically to the law of nature. They were available to students, and some had been translated from Latin into English. Hugo Grotius's *De iure belli ac pacis* (1624) is only the most famous of such works; it was translated into English in 1654 and reprinted several times thereafter. Samuel Pufendorf's *De legibus naturae* appeared in an English translation in 1672. To them, one should add the English authors on the law of nature: John Selden, Sir Francis Bacon, Richard Cumberland, and Thomas Rutherforth. And, of course, Christopher St. German's *Doctor and Student*—many times reprinted in the sixteenth and seventeenth centuries—should also be counted among their number.[48] Repeatedly, it made connections between the law of nature and the common law. It is true that we do not know how many law students consulted these works and absorbed the learning in them. We know only that they could have. We do have one further clue; these works are sometimes found cited in the English Reports, so they cannot have been wholly without utility for common lawyers.

English Legal Treatises

The accumulation of evidence makes it likely that the education of most active English barristers would have brought them into at least minimal contact with the law of nature. It would not have been a primary focus of their study, and much of what they were required to master—the extent and meaning of existing writs, the requirements of pleading, and the intricacies of the English land law—would have been quite far removed from large questions involving the moral purposes of the law. What they heard about the law of nature might also have flown quickly from their minds or been swamped by other learning. However, under various circumstances they would have heard invocations of the principle that law should not be "against reason." They would also have heard (or read) recognitions of the existence of the law of nature, and probably they would have understood some of the results that followed from its principles. That may be all. At least it is all that can be demonstrated without invoking the uncertain claims of possibility. But it was surely enough to have made students cognizant of the law of nature's existence.

When one turns to the treatise literature, even that dealing with some quite specialized legal topics, the picture becomes clearer. A search through the legal literature of the time produces a very long list of English common lawyers who accepted and wrote positively about the law of nature. The authors recognized it as forming part of the law of England. They used it in describing the principles that underlay and influenced the common law. The list includes Roger Acherley (d. 1740),[49] Thomas Ashe (fl. 1600–1618),[50] Sir Francis Ashley (d. 1635),[51] Sir Francis Bacon (d. 1626),[52] Matthew Bacon (d. ca. 1757),[53] Henry Ballow (d. 1782),[54] Daines Barrington (d. 1800),[55] Anthony Booth (fl. seventeenth century),[56] Timothy Brecknock (d. 1786),[57] William Bohun (fl. 1732),[58] Britton (fl. 1300),[59] John Brydall (d. ca. 1705),[60] William Burge (1787–1849),[61] Charles Butler (d. 1832),[62] Robert Callis (d. 1642),[63] Sir Charles Calthrope (d. 1616),[64] William Cawley (fl. 1680),[65] Sir Edward Coke (d. 1634),[66] Henry Colebrooke (d. 1837),[67] Richard Crompton (fl. 1573–1599),[68] Henry Dagge (fl. 1760),[69] Michael Dalton (d. 1644),[70] Sir John Davies (d. 1626),[71] Sir John Dodderidge (d. 1628),[72] Sir William Dugdale (d. 1686),[73] William Eden, Baron Auckland (d. 1814),[74] Thomas Egerton, Lord Ellesmere (d. 1617),[75] Sir Robert Filmer (d. 1653),[76] Heneage Finch, Lord Nottingham (d. 1682),[77] Sir Henry Finch (d. 1625),[78] *Fleta* (fl. 1290),[79] Sir John Fortescue (d. 1479),[80] Sir Michael Foster (d. 1763),[81] Abraham Fraunce (d. 1592/1593),[82] Sir Geoffrey Gilbert (d. 1726),[83] Edward Hake (d. ca. 1604),[84] Sir Matthew Hale (d. 1676),[85] Sir Christopher Hatton (d. 1591),[86] Michael Hawke (seventeenth century),[87] William Hawkins (d. 1750),[88] Sir John Holt (d. 1710),[89] Giles Jacob (d. 1744),[90] David Jenkins (d. 1663),[91] Sir William Jones (d. 1794),[92] William Lambarde (d. 1601),[93] Sir Thomas Littleton (d. 1481),[94] Gerard Malynes (fl. 1586–1641),[95] Walter Mantell (seventeenth century),[96] Samuel Marshall (d. 1823),[97] Thomas More (d. 1535),[98] William Murray, Lord Mansfield (d. 1793),[99] Michael Nolan (d. 1827),[100] Roger North (d. 1734),[101] William Noy (d. 1634),[102] Mark Ord (d. 1805),[103] Sir Roger Owen (d. 1617),[104] Henry Parker (d. 1652),[105] John Perkins (d. 1545),[106] William Philipps (fl. 1660),[107] Edmund Plowden (d. 1585),[108] Francis Plowden (d. 1832),[109] John Joseph Powell (d. 1801),[110] Robert Powell (fl. 1609–1642),[111] Charles Pratt, Earl Camden (d. 1794),[112]

William Prynne (d. 1669),[113] Ferdinando Pulton (d. 1618),[114] Francis Rodes (d. 1589),[115] Christopher St. German (d. 1540),[116] John Selden (d. 1654),[117] Granville Sharp (d. 1813),[118] William Sheppard (d. 1674),[119] John Somers (d. 1716),[120] Sir Henry Spelman (d. 1641),[121] Sir William Staunford (d. 1558),[122] William Style (d. 1679),[123] Simon Thelwall (1659),[124] Sir John Vaughan (d. 1674),[125] William West (d. 1598),[126] Bulstrode Whitelocke (d. 1675),[127] Thomas Williams (d. 1566),[128] Edmund Wingate (d. 1656),[129] Richard Wooddeson (d. 1822),[130] Edward Wynne (d. 1784),[131] Charles Yorke (d. 1770),[132] and, last (although out of alphabetical order), Anonymous.[133]

Not only did a search for common lawyers who recognized the existence of the law of nature as a source of law produce a considerable harvest, it was also not matched by lawyers who took the other side. Among English lawyers whose works reached print, it was possible to find common lawyers who took no apparent notice of natural law's existence.[134] Seemingly their subjects did not call for it. But, with the notable exception of Jeremy Bentham (1784–1832) and David Hume (1711–1776), neither did the search come upon writers about the law who actually denied the existence of the law of nature. Bentham's views require a mention. He regarded the law of nature as "a hodgepodge of confusion and absurdity."[135] He railed against its recognition by the Bar. His example at least shows the possibility of skepticism about its value, but of course neither Bentham nor Hume was a lawyer. Bentham in particular was an enemy and harsh critic of many of the assumptions embedded in the common law. And apart from these two writers, this search through the pre-1800 literature of the common law turned up no other authors who stated, as a matter of fact or opinion, that natural law was "an exploded superstition." Perhaps they existed, but if they did, this search did not uncover them.

Conclusion

Even against this background of widespread acceptance of the law of nature's legitimate place as a source of law, modern historians of English law have sometimes taken the view that the law of nature had no real following among common lawyers. Writing about the fifteenth-century work devoted expressly to the subject by Sir John Fortescue (d. 1477/1479), for example, Sir Frederick Pollock concluded that it was "at best the artificial performance of a champion wielding unfamiliar arms in a strange field."[136] "Express invocation of the Law of Nature," he continued, "seems rather to have been purposely avoided" by common lawyers.[137] Maitland himself regarded the ultimate victory of the common law in the seventeenth century over Roman law and prerogative courts as a defeat for the law of nature.[138]

On the available evidence, that conclusion is difficult to sustain. David Ibbetson and Michael Lobban, two able English historians currently active in this field, agree in rejecting it, or at least in qualifying it quite substantially. Both have concluded that in some measure natural law jurisprudence worked its way into parts of the common law during the seventeenth and eighteenth centuries.[139] As they themselves acknowledge, an exact measure of the extent of that influence is impossible to attain. No reliable statistics are possible. Only examples are. Chapter 4 explores some of them. They show many substantive similarities to the arguments that were being made in courts of law on the Continent.

4

The Law of Nature in English Courts

B EGINNING A STUDY OF natural law's place in the practice of the English courts inevitably calls to mind two larger questions. Both have been long discussed and long debated. The first is whether the English common law was influenced in any meaningful way by Roman law.[1] Because the law of nature was an established part of the civilian tradition, English lawyers' acceptance of natural law might be one example of such influence coming from without.[2] The second is whether the English common law ever recognized a "higher law" that limited the powers of king and Parliament.[3] The law of nature is the obvious candidate to have been that "higher law." Common learning proclaimed that it stood above all other laws, except perhaps the divine law, and this learning was known in England. The limitations on legislative power that natural law could encourage may even have been akin to "judicial review" of legislation as applied in the modern constitutional law of the United States. Investigation of natural law's place in the law reports would also be significant in tracing the road taken by English law itself, a road that led gradually away from reliance on natural law toward full recognition of parliamentary sovereignty. This has meant, at least until the most recent years, rejection of the possibility of anything like judicial review of acts of Parliament.

These two questions are not simply variants of the same inquiry. A new idea may be hit upon without having been lifted from an alien source, and "higher law," no matter how well settled, may be insufficient to give judges the authority to annul the acts of their sovereign. Continental law is proof of that. Explanations for the shape of English common law that recognize similarities without admitting the existence of influence may account for what the case law shows. If these explanations are correct, the history of English law may require only the slightest consideration of the law of nature as it was drawn from European sources.

Nonetheless, these two questions are often connected, and not without reason. By the end of the eighteenth century, natural law was the subject of an enormous legal literature on the Continent. Some of it was well enough known on the English side of the Channel to have captured the imagination and interest of common lawyers. Works by Burlamaqui, Grotius, Pufendorf, Vattel, and others were translated into English and printed, though most lawyers could certainly have read them in Latin. The influence they exerted might have carried other parts of the common law of Europe with them, including the law of nature. Equally, the possibility of judicial "control" over legislation might have been among the ideas imported from Continental sources. Statements that customs and statutes that contravened natural law were "void" were found in many Continental treatises. They may also have found a home in England. Present-day historians who believe the Roman and canon laws influenced English common law in a significant way will therefore more readily accord a place to the fundamental law derived from the *ius naturae* and the *ius gentium*. Those who reject that view will be more skeptical about the possibility that natural law could ever have been seriously invoked to influence the course of the common law or to limit the powers of the king and Parliament.

This chapter does not enter into either of these contentious questions directly, although it may shed a bit of indirect light on them. It has a more immediate and limited goal: to discover whether the law of nature was used in English court practice and, if it was, to describe the purposes it served. This is much the same approach taken in investigating the Continental *decisiones* and works of *praxis* in Chapter 2. However, the two large questions just discussed lurk in the background of any evaluation of the English case law in a way they do not for European law. The chapter returns to them briefly at its end.

Applications of the Law of Nature

Tracing the appearance and usage of the law of nature in the English law reports—the immediate object of the research upon which this study is based—is not free from difficulties. The English cases contain many fewer citations to precedent and learned commentaries than do the Continental *decisiones*. They can leave their readers guessing. No indices or guides to their contents exist, except what little help can be found in the early abridgements. The headnotes attached to many reports are also rarely of use, at least for this topic. The task of finding treatment of a particular subject has nonetheless become considerably easier today than it was twenty-five years ago. Certainly it is easier than working one's way through folio after folio of *decisiones*. The reports are now available online. Word searches are feasible and fruitful, even though for this topic they proved to be insufficient by themselves. Reading some of the case reports from start to finish and gaining some familiarity with contemporary treatises on individual areas of the law turned out to be productive. In fact, they proved to be necessary. Without them, too much pertinent material would have been missed. I tried to cast as wide a net as possible, and what follows seeks to categorize and summarize what came of the search.

General References

As was true in its treatise literature noted in Chapter 3, the English case reports contain praise in both general and specific terms for the law of nature. It both coincided with and undergirded the common law. "The law of nature is part of the common law" was the oft-repeated refrain.[4] A few English lawyers did express reservations about its actual utility in establishing firm legal conclusions, but many more took the position that it had played a positive role in determining the shape of the common law. Michael Dalton, author of the much-used manual *Countrey Justice* (1618), was typical in regarding the positive laws of his country as "receiving principally their grounds from the laws of God and Nature."[5]

A clear, if today unpalatable, example was English law's refusal to give legal force to the practice of adoption of children. The maxim that "only God can create an heir" was one of several ways reliance on the law of nature was then expressed. Adoption was contrary to the natural order of things, and that opposition provided a reason for rejecting it as nothing more than a matter of convenience and charity.[6] The law should imitate nature, it was said, and in this instance the English common law did so.[7] Adoption, though a significant part of Roman law, was not taken into English practice. Heirship and succession to estates should not be determined by mere human whim. They should rather be fixed by the natural order of things. Of course, exactly this once unacceptable result did eventually occur. But that was not until 1926.[8] Until a basic change in sentiment had occurred, more objective criteria had prevailed. Rejection of adoption was regarded as a consequence of nature's law.

As was true of medieval arguments against adoption—in most instances where English advocates and judges expressed this close connection between law and nature—they did so with a concrete object in view: to support a legal claim. It was part of an argument. That object is readily and repeatedly apparent in the reports, and it should not be overlooked in assessing natural law's role in litigation. In one seventeenth-century case involving the order of payment of a testator's legacies and debts, for example, a lawyer argued that if the judges moved away from what he described as the existing rule, the change would require "the breaking of the law of God, the law of nature, and of the land."[9] In another, the argument was made that the English law of inheritance, at least as interpreted by the lawyer involved, had itself been fashioned "by nature and God's law."[10] It was no arbitrary system, this lawyer contended. It followed the lines of descent established in nature itself, and it told in favor of his client.

Arguments like these were made too often and too readily to have been simple matters of convenience or necessity. The lawyers who made them could not have hoped for success unless they had struck a chord that rang true. Lord Mansfield was particularly fond of expressing this way of looking at the common law, holding in one case (involving the qualification of witnesses) that the common law "works itself pure by rules drawn from the fountain of justice."[11] He meant the law of nature.[12] In making such a positive assertion about natural law's place in England, he cited the works of Hugo Grotius and Johannes Voet (among others). He referred to specific precedents from what these two learned jurists would have called the municipal law—that is, the English common law— to make its connection with natural law certain. Municipal law and natural law were, Lord Mansfield thought, in harmony with each other. That is how they were meant to be. And that is how they were. This was not a new sentiment. The established rule of the positive law that an agreement between two persons could not prejudice the rights of a third was cited as dispositive in an earlier case, precisely because it was based on a principle of "the law of nature and reason."[13] It had itself become part of the positive law. Lord Mansfield also applied the same reasoning to disputes involving religion. To him, persecution of free men and women for religious reasons violated a natural human freedom. Persecution seemed just as "inconsistent with the rights of human nature" as it was "iniquitous and unjust." It was something that could be applied only with the clearest warrant in positive law. Happily, he thought, English law left only the narrowest openings for it.[14]

Some of the general assertions running along these lines that are found in the reports now seem quite extravagant, reminiscent of the boastful claims about the merits of English law made in Sir John Fortescue's *De laudibus legum Angliae*. An example is the claim made in an Elizabethan case involving the law of feoffments to uses; the lawyer claimed extravagantly that "there is nothing ordained in our law contrary to nature or reason, or the law of God, but our law is agreeable to them all."[15] He did not argue that the Statute of Uses was dictated by the law of nature, but only that it was not opposed to any fundamental part of it. The law of nature provided an independent measure by which the statute's provisions could be measured, and he thought they passed the test with flying colors. Other speakers took much the same position in forensic argument.[16] Still others, confronted by a situation where no statute or precedent provided an adequate answer, acknowledged the customary harmony between common law and natural law in order to apply the default rule that where no local law could be uncovered, recourse should be had to the law of nature. It might fill the gap.[17] All these were commonly found in works devoted to the law of nature, and whatever their immediate sources may have been, they were regularly invoked by English common lawyers to show that their own municipal law fit neatly within its pattern.

Although harmony between natural and positive law was the normal rule, it was never all there was. Lawyers knew that. Not every English legal rule stood in accord with this pattern of congruence, and in occasional cases lawyers spoke frankly about divergences between their own law and the law of nature. A particularly clear example was the law of wardship. In England, at the death of a tenant who held land by knight's service, the common law had long granted control of a minor heir's person and lands to the tenant's lord. This practice stood in conflict with the laws of nature. They favored the claims of the family over the artificial ties of feudalism.[18] English lawyers' usual response to these situations was to seek a plausible harmonization of the two, but on occasion they admitted the contradiction, as a lawyer did in one late-seventeenth-century case. English law, he said candidly, "takes more notice of the relation between master and servant than it doth between father and son."[19] There was something to what he said. It was a clear example of disharmony between natural law and positive law.

Statements like these were not necessarily meant as criticism of existing English law. Mostly they appear to have been descriptions of it. Everywhere, aspects of the law of nature had been subjected to variation and amendment by the positive law. If they had been challenged, defenders of the common law could have answered by pointing to many similar contradictions that existed in the law of every European land. Custom—the tacit choice of the people subject to the law—was a valid source of law. It was everywhere given a wide scope in determining what was actually required in judicial decisions, even though it might have seemed to stand at odds with a principle derived from the law of nature.

A few English common lawyers went a little further, though not to the point of rejecting the existence of natural law. Closer to overt criticism were the instances in which the English common lawyers objected to intervention by the Court of Chancery in legal situations where they claimed exclusive competence. Some of their barbs were directed at what they regarded as overly aggressive application of the laws of nature. Granting relief against penal bonds subject to conditional defeasance was a particular bone of contention. These written obligations required a debtor to pay twice the amount owed if he failed to pay the principal debt on time, seemingly an occasion for usury as well as a hard bargain. Relief against their enforcement was available in Chancery in cases where there had been special hardship or oppression,[20] and it was sometimes justified by principles of natural justice.[21] On occasion, the common law judges objected. They thought the bonds should be enforced as written. Their position in this long-running quarrel, however, was not an overt rejection of the law of nature. They simply argued that they themselves were its proper interpreters. They had ample authority to assess the rationality of the common law's rule without interference from Chancery. The strict enforcement of these bonds made both commercial and moral sense. Promises should be honored. That was itself a principle of natural law. The penalty for nonpayment too made practical sense. It provided an effective sanction against defaulters.

In this same fashion, when John Selden famously criticized the scope of the law of equity as being determined by the measure of the current lord chancellor's foot,[22] he was disparaging some of the arbitrary uses that had been made of the law of nature. He was not questioning its existence. Selden elsewhere wrote about natural law with the approbation characteristic of most English lawyers. He did so with greater learning than most common lawyers possessed. What he regarded with disfavor was the way it was sometimes used. All in all, therefore, the attitude of common lawyers toward the law of nature was one of respect, coupled with occasional objections to how it was applied. That was not far removed from the sentiments that appeared in the Continental *decisiones,* where arguments based on natural law were often challenged and overcome by positive laws and sound reasoning.

Procedural Law

The English common lawyers were not faced with quite the same problems that were caused by the adoption of summary procedure on the Continent. There, as described in the Chapter 2, natural law was commonly used to clarify what "shortcuts" in procedure could be put into place without objection. Natural law helped to draw the line between the permissible and the unlawful. In England, although exceptions were made to allow summary treatment of some crimes in some courts,[23] no general adoption of summary procedure took place. The shape of common law procedure in the royal courts, including the use of royal writs and reliance on lay juries, had been established at an early date. It would not change in ways that raised the same issues that adoption of summary procedure on the Continent did, and its principal features seem not to have come under serious question until much later.

From today's perspective, however, this apparent stability did not mean that the procedures men and women accused of crimes faced once they came before a judge were immune from criticism. They were sometimes criticized, and the law of nature provided a ready source of complaint. Thomas More, for example, objected strongly to some of them when he was tried for treason in the reign of Henry VIII, and his complaints were based, at least in part, on principles drawn from the law of nature.[24] It is remarkable, given More's status, how little agreement the substance of arguments like his evoked at the time—not simply in his own case but across the board. English lawyers considered their system of criminal procedure, flawed as it seems today, to stand in accord with the basic principles of justice. This may have been blindness on their part, of a piece with the common law's long continued refusal to allow professional lawyers to defend accused criminals, but it was an attitude widely shared among them.

In this opinion they were not without company. Their opinions about criminal law found considerable support in contemporary legal thought. Denying criminal defendants the right to representation by a lawyer and prohibiting appeals against sentences, for example, were then regarded as necessary and even useful aspects of European criminal procedure. When taxed for lack of fairness in their own procedural system, English lawyers extolled the virtues of leaving decisions in the hands of juries of laymen. It allowed the truth to emerge. They also threw the example of torture in the face of critics from the Continent. English courts did not permit torture as an ordinary part of criminal procedure; on the Continent, by contrast, it had found a home.[25] True, its application there was hedged about with safeguards against abuse, but reading through sixteenth-century treatments of criminal procedure produces little or no indication that torture's use in judicial proceedings was regarded as a violation of the laws of nature by European lawyers.[26] It was regarded instead as a legitimate part of legal process, to be called upon when necessary, though never recklessly or inadvisably. Everywhere, it seems, criminal procedure admitted such compromises. Invocation of natural law did not exclude them.

One situation where the law of nature did appear purposefully in the English procedural law is found in the same place as Continental literature: the requirement of a citation. One must be called and heard before being punished or deprived of one's property. A lawful summons was a sine qua non of English law, just as the citation, its equivalent on the Continent, had proved to be. This was clearly asserted by a royal justice in 1721: "It is certain that natural justice requires that no man shall be condemned without notice."[27] William Fulbecke used it as one of his "Parallels" between the common law and the *ius commune*, ascribing it to the law of nature.[28]

The requirement was raised many times before the English courts.[29] In one such challenge, the testing case arose of the defendant who had proclaimed in advance that he would not obey the court's decree under any circumstances. Continental lawyers had made an exception to the requirement where a defendant had made such a statement, reasoning that there was no sense in requiring something known in advance to be pointless. In the equivalent English case, however, an ingenious lawyer answered that this exception was itself "founded upon a most abominable doctrine" that such a man "could not repent."[30] At a minimum, he said, the law of reason required that he should be given a fair chance at amendment of life. The law therefore required that he be summoned no matter what he had said. So he was in the case. In another case involving the same basic issue, one involving at attempt to deprive a man of his degree at Cambridge University, the judge added that he had heard "a learned civilian" make the point by invoking God's citation of Adam in the Garden of Eden (Gen. 3:9), the standard "proof text" in the *ius commune*.[31] On this point the English positive law and natural law stood in harmony, and both were noted in the reports.

A forum for dispute about how far the principle extended arose in administration of the Poor Law. It must have been tempting for the men entrusted with the task of putting its difficult rules into effect to act without listening at length (if at all) to the men and women affected by their proceedings. To society's governors, the facts would often have seemed too plain to require demonstration. The poor were also hard to summon and harder to listen to with respect. But exactly that requirement was founded in natural law. It had not been eaten away by exceptions, and if the Poor Law's administrators did fail to summon them and were later challenged for the failure, in most cases their excuses were set aside.[32] Their proceedings and their orders were nullities. An adequate summons was taken to be one of any legal system's most basic requirements. That was a rule based upon the law of nature, and it applied even in dealing with the most unfortunate members of society.[33]

The principle applied more widely, too. The common law judges enforced this principle against the judges of England's ecclesiastical courts, issuing writs of prohibition to prevent the civilians who controlled those courts from taking action against men and women who had not been adequately informed in advance of the nature of the offenses of which they were suspected. Unless persons summoned before the spiritual courts were given adequate warning of the cause for requiring their appearance, the spiritual prosecutions could not lawfully proceed.[34] The judges in the royal courts took that view and enforced it by issuing writs of prohibition upon application by the parties affected.[35] This was not simply a means of restricting the scope of ecclesiastical jurisdiction, although it certainly was that. It was also a requirement of the law of nature. The common law judges acted accordingly in their own courts. Certainly it would have been awkward if they had themselves ignored this principle within their own bailiwick. On this score, all judges were bound to observe rules of natural justice. Not mindlessly of course. Exceptions existed. As was true elsewhere, the law of nature could be opened up to admit them. But it required a good reason before judges did so.

Law of the Family and Succession

Principles regulating relations between members of the same families were fundamental parts of the law of nature as it was then understood. Blood counted. Marriage, too, built upon the laws of nature, even though most of its incidents were matters of positive law only. Chapter 2 showed something of the role natural law played in questions involving family life in Continental *decisiones*. In the English common law, that role turned out to be more restricted than it was in the European courts. Fewer cases referred to it. A possible explanation for its relative absence may be ignorance or lesser interest on the part of most common lawyers. The system of primogeniture they accepted as basic law also sat uncomfortably with principles drawn from the law of nature.[36] It appeared to ignore the duty a father owed to all his children. Although that regime was open to contrary local custom,[37] the common lawyers began thinking about their own law of inheritance with an institution in which natural law seemed to have been shunted aside by customary law.

An additional reason for paying lesser heed to natural law than was appropriate on the Continent was jurisdictional. In England, matters like the provision of support orders for illegitimate children were long left to the courts of the church. So were most matters involving succession to movable property. This was not so on most of the Continent. One result of that jurisdictional divide was that questions involving a child's right to inherit some part of the father's property, the so-called *legitim* that claimed so much attention in the Continental *decisiones*, did not come up as frequently in the royal courts as it did across the Channel.[38] Primogeniture excluded it in most English cases dealing with succession to rights in freehold land, and a jurisdictional divide between church and state meant that its real home in England was the ecclesiastical forum.[39]

This limitation did not mean, however, that the law of nature was altogether irrelevant to the common law related to familial and inheritance questions. It only narrowed the scope and changed the ways in which it was used. A parental duty to children was in fact put into statutory form as part of the Elizabethan Poor Law enacted in 1601.[40] Thereafter, at least in some circumstances, the duty was brought within the jurisdiction of the royal courts.[41] Echoes of natural law doctrine on the subject also sometimes appeared in the reports. For instance, the Court of King's Bench held in 1719 that a son-in-law was under no duty to support his wife's parents, even if they were poor. The reason given was that "the law of nature does not reach to this case."[42] The law of nature also served to support the famous rule that to take land by descent, one had to be of the blood of the first purchaser.[43] And it also helped to uphold the validity of conveyances within a family that might not have passed muster if made between strangers. Natural family ties supplied sufficient consideration necessary to execute a use raised by a covenant to stand seised made in favor of a member of the same family.[44] No less a figure than Sir Edward Coke held the opinion that "every man by the law of God, of nature, and of nations was bound to provide a competent living for his wife, his children, and for the payment of his debts."[45] One consequence of that sentiment was to validate grants made to family members that would otherwise have been legally questionable for lack of a bargained for consideration.

Natural law principles seem to have figured to a greater degree in establishing inheritance rights in litigation in Chancery than in the common law courts.[46] Concepts of equity opened the door for natural law to come in, and once inside it could easily be called upon as an interpretive tool. It did sometimes serve that purpose. An example of natural law's potential comes from a case in which it supplied an absent term to a marriage settlement. The words of the grant of the property involved were "to [the grantor's daughter], but if she died before her husband," then to her brothers and sisters.[47] The Chancellor read these words as meaning "but if she died without issue before her husband," thus supplying the additional term "without issue" to the settlement. That addition would enable any children to be born to the couple eventually to take the property granted. The reason he gave for adding these words, which were admittedly absent from the document, was that "parents were, by the law of nature, bound to take care of their issue." Being so motivated, the Chancellor reasoned, the father must have meant to benefit any children born to his daughter and her husband. As the document had been drafted, this goal might have been frustrated. Children born to the marriage would have been excluded from taking the property if the daughter died before the husband. That is what the settlement said. But that would have been an "unnatural result." As reinterpreted, if any children were born to the couple, the children would take the property no matter which parent died first. In other words, the Chancellor assumed that the additional term "without issue" had been left out of the settlement by carelessness or mistake. He supplied it, doing so based upon an assumption derived from the law of nature.

Of course, the case could have come out differently. Had there been no ambiguity at all in the settlement's terms, it probably would have. The ability to dispose of property according to one's own desires was a part of English law. How far it extended was the question, a question that had been disputed and answered in different ways, but the law of nature was a factor in answering it. Whether freedom of testation formed any part of the law of nature was itself a matter of doubt. Godolphin seems to have thought it was at least derived from natural law.[48] Blackstone described it as "a kind of secondary law of nature."[49] If it did qualify, it was certainly an equivocal kind of freedom, one that admitted of more than one exception.[50] The medieval English rule of primogeniture for land held by knight service was only the best-known example in which testamentary freedom had been curtailed.

This was an important but difficult part of the law in England, as it was on the Continent. Customary and positive law had everywhere made inroads into its "family-first" principles. By 1550, the common law had left a wider room for individual choice than the law of nature seemed to require. Testators were free to ignore ties of kinship, except, some thought, in cases "bordering upon necessity."[51] Although common lawyers acknowledged that "by nature and God's law, every man is bound to love, prefer, and advance his own blood before any stranger,"[52] this did not mean that the courts would necessarily intervene to prevent a man from disregarding what the law of nature required. The Court of Chancery might do so for reasons said to be connected with natural law's dictates,[53] but only under quite special circumstances. The Chancellors did not normally seek to impose the dictates of the law of nature on the common law courts,[54] and natural law itself recognized many reasons a conscientious man might wish his property to end up outside the circle of his own family. The claims of charity and the vagaries of family circumstance were among them. In matters of succession, the law of nature was not a straitjacket. When lawyers said that all men were "bound" to do something by the law of nature, they did not necessarily mean the word *bound* to be understood in a literal sense. It was an obligation founded upon natural law's tenets, but in most matters of testamentary law, judges would not compel its performance.

Despite such apparent inconsistencies, as a general matter English lawyers seem to have regarded their own law of inheritance as consistent with the law of nature's tenets.[55] They "proved" this in various ways. One was to pick out those rules that fit. As noted earlier, one reason given for the rule that the real property of a man dying intestate should descend (but not ascend) to his kin was found in nature itself, as well as in the laws of Moses (Num: 8:12).[56] The natural ties of blood could also furnish a rule of decision where an ambiguous devise of land required interpretation.[57] A testamentary trust perpetuating the settlor's name was said by one lawyer to be enforceable, indeed beyond reproach, because it was based upon "a passion implanted in the mind as a laudable incentive to industry."[58] In other words, English lawyers dealing with rules of inheritance sometimes found in the law of nature resources they needed to explain and justify specific rules of law.

However, harmony was not an invariable feature of the English law of succession. As another lawyer assessed the situation, the law of nature actually played a limited role in this corner of the common law. A large part of the law of inheritance, he thought, was "grounded only on our particular laws." It had neither needed nor received guidance from without.[59] In support of this proposition, this advocate actually cited a passage from Hugo Grotius's *De iure belli ac pacis*. Grotius had pointed to natural law as a uniting principle for European laws of succession, but as this English lawyer pointed out, Grotius himself left room for some large variations in the relevant positive law.[60] For this English lawyer, that permissible variation showed that his own description of English law could actually have been applied to the law of succession in virtually every part of Europe. As he saw things, testamentary law's connection to the law of nature may have existed, but everywhere it was a loose tie at best, too loose to have coercive force. Certainly this was so, he thought, in his native land.

Even under this view, there some special situations within the law of familial relations where the ties were closer. One in which the law of nature played a more overt role in English law occurred in defining the degrees of consanguinity and affinity that prevented a valid marriage from being contracted. When the English church struck out on its own during the Protestant Reformation, one of the institutions it rejected was the system of prohibited degrees that had been enacted by the Fourth Lateran Council in 1215. The canon law on the subject had led to a system of papal dispensations that allowed couples to marry despite the existence of kinship between them. Dispensations were issued under a system that Englishmen had come to regard as "exorbitant and unwarrantable." Without warrant in reason or holy scripture, they served principally as a means of filling the papal coffers, and they were swept away at the Reformation.[61] Once this step had been taken, however, the inevitable question was to determine what would replace the prior law. Recreating the papal system by allowing the king or archbishop to issue equivalent dispensations was not acceptable. A regime of unlimited free choice was also not a live possibility, although the English church's answer came close. The solution was to reject all matrimonial dispensations based on kinship and to permit all marriages, with the exception of those that were actually forbidden by the laws of God and the laws of nature. An attractive answer, no doubt; however, it was not altogether easy to know exactly what the laws of God and nature required in this corner of the law. Uncertainty reigned for a time, but a reasonable approximation was at length forthcoming. In 1563, Archbishop Parker published a table of prohibitions that included some sixty specific kinds of kinship.[62] In taking this step, the leaders of the Church of England believed they were doing more than eliminating an abuse. They were correcting existing law to make it better conform to the lessons of reason and religion. This was one of the roles the law of nature was meant to play in shaping human life. One of its broad functions was to help determine the shape of the positive law, and in this instance it did exactly that. It provided a way of thinking about a difficult problem—and even of solving it after a fashion.

The Law of Slavery

The study of the English common law's treatment of slavery has long been dominated by the opinion of Lord Mansfield in *Somerset's Case*.[63] The dispute involved a Negro slave brought temporarily into England from Virginia, the master's ultimate destination being Jamaica. A writ of habeas corpus was brought on the slave's behalf in order to try the legality of his detention, and the Court of King's Bench held that he could not be confined or held as a slave in England. Nor could he be forced to leave the realm and thus returned to servitude. In the course of decision, Lord Mansfield used the law of nature to define slavery's status in English law.[64] By natural law, all men were free. It was the positive law or the *ius gentium* that had introduced slavery into human society. That result had been reached by various means, the most frequently cited in the juristic literature being warfare.[65] Defeated soldiers, forced to choose between death and enslavement, invariably chose the latter. They thus became slaves by an act of their own free will. Why that event should also have bound the voluntary slave's descendants in perpetual servitude was never satisfactorily explained, but the customary law of many nations had long since reached that result. It is what had taken place in the world, and the law recognized that it had. The natural law had been at odds with this aspect of the positive law almost from the start. Slavery's existence thus depended only on positive law, and Lord Mansfield accordingly held that slavery was "so odious that nothing can be suffered to support it but positive law."[66] England had no such positive law. Hence the Negro could not lawfully be treated as enslaved within its borders, whatever his status in Jamaica or Virginia would have been. Nor could he be forcibly transported back to a slave country. From the perspective of the law of nature, this was not a particularly startling decision. It did not "free the slaves." It held only that the master's right could not be enforced in England. It did accomplish one thing the law of nature was meant to do: it applied principles of natural justice to the facts where no positive law could be found.

The concept of an "odious" law—of which a positive law permitting slavery was an example—was a quite familiar one to the Continental jurists.[67] It meant a law at odds with principles founded upon the law of nature. On that account it was a law not to be extended beyond its own terms and its own jurisdictional boundaries. Continental jurists often contrasted an "odious" statute with one that stood in accord with natural and divine laws.[68] The latter received an expansive interpretation. The former did not. Even an "odious" statute would not necessarily be wiped from the books, but it would not be applied when a choice existed. That was essentially what happened in *Somerset's Case.* Positive law permitting slavery existed, but it came from outside England. The question in the case was to be decided by the law of England, and the absence of a positive law permitting slavery required an outcome in favor of freedom.

For all its renown, *Somerset's Case* was not the first English decision to deal with the institution of slavery in this fashion. A 1696 action for trespass for taking and withholding a man the plaintiff claimed as his slave was defeated in the King's Bench. Counsel for the defendant argued to good effect that it was "against the law of nature for one man to be a slave to another," so "if the plaintiff had any right to the servitude of this negro, that right is now divested by his coming into England."[69] Similarly an action of trover brought to recover a Negro claimed as a slave in 1706 was also defeated. The reason given was that "[b]y the common law no man can have a property in another. . . . There is no such thing as a slave by the law of England."[70] The subject was admittedly complicated by the long history of villeinage in England and also by the availability at common law of an action for enticing a servant to leave a master's service.[71] Both seemed to recognize the possibility of holding a property right in another human being. These precedents were successfully distinguished from slavery, however, and by the eighteenth century, the rationale of *Somerset's Case* had come to represent the generally accepted view in England. Why a determined search for similar cases in the Continental *decisiones* did not produce any result has remained a puzzle to me.

Economic and Commercial Regulation

The variety of roles played by the law of nature in regulation of economic life in England make its place harder to define than it proves to be in describing the law of slavery, but that natural law was sometimes called upon as an authority in commercial litigation is not open to doubt. One example is a famous one for law students. The common law's development of the requirement of bargained for consideration to establish the enforceability of contracts can be regarded, with only slight exaggeration, as a life-and-death struggle between the natural law principle that oral promises were binding where seriously intended and the sensible reluctance to treat a person's words, without more, as creating an obligation enforceable in a court of law.[72] The struggle took many twists and turns, ending in a body of law that remains perplexing to the present day.[73] Its subtleties are part of every modern law student's life, and in their historical development, natural law as found in the works of Grotius and Pufendorf played a part.[74]

If one leaves aside that old and contentious subject, as it seems prudent to do, several other and less contentious invocations of the law of nature in commercial law quickly appear in the English reports. The law of unjust enrichment is probably the most evident example,[75] but it is far from the only one. For one party to a contract to have concealed relevant material circumstances from the other party, for instance, was said to be sufficient "to vitiate all contracts upon the principles of natural law" in one reported case.[76] Equal treatment of creditors in the law of bankruptcy, it was claimed, was required by principles of "natural justice" in another.[77] Similarly, the argument in favor of the existence of a common law of copyright was supposed to have been "founded on natural justice" in several eighteenth-century cases.[78] Without it, a copyist "would be converting to one's own emolument the fruits of another's labour." In a different setting, it was held that a local custom could not restrict the use of land any further than the high-water mark of the sea. "[B]eing against reason" and restrictive of the rights of navigation under the law of nations, the custom could not hold.[79]

The argument for the defendant in the famous case of *Paradine v. Jane* (1647) also depended in part on "the law of nature as well as of nations."[80] In it, suit was brought to recover rent due for lands leased to the defendant, who sought relief from the payment when the land under lease was invaded by Prince Rupert, an alien enemy of the Crown. The Prince's troops had expelled the defendant from the land under lease. The defendant argued that he should not have to pay rent because he had been deprived of any use of the land wholly without fault on his part. His lawyer's contention was that "by the law of reason it seems that [the defendant] ought not to be charged with the rent, because he could not enjoy what was let to him . . . and the civil law, the canon law, and the moral authors do confirm this."[81] In the event, his argument failed, effectively overruling a similar case heard fewer than twenty-five years previously—

Williams v. Hide—in which the virtually identical argument had prevailed.[82] In *Paradine v. Jane,* the law of nature thus played a part in legal argument, but it did not control the outcome.

The treatment of the law of usury in the common law courts was also touched, if not finally determined, by the law of nature. Taking interest on a loan was sometimes described as "against natural justice" in argument before the courts.[83] This was a traditional theme among civilians, and a surprisingly large body of English legal literature elaborating it came into being during the sixteenth and seventeenth centuries.[84] Usury was said to be tolerated in law only for reasons of the strictest necessity. Where the exact boundaries of legality were located had long been a question open to discussion,[85] but just as had also happened in many parts of the Continent, statutes had interrupted the ensuing speculation. Laws enacted by the English Parliament allowed moderate rates of interest to be taken.[86] These statutes were not treated as invalid simply because they appeared to violate tenets of the law of nature. They were treated as valid, even if perhaps "odious" in character. They served a legitimate purpose. They were also a concession to the realities of commercial life. Normally only their extension and their interpretation were affected and resisted on the theory that "all usury is damned and prohibited, as being against the law of God, the laws of the realm, and the law of nature."[87] Whatever the lawyers thought of the intrinsic merits involved, however, most of their discussion of usury in the English cases centered around the proper interpretation of parliamentary statutes, not around usury's impermissibility under the laws of nature. Just as had occurred in European courts, usury's oft asserted impermissibility under the law of nature was not enough to invalidate statutes allowing it in moderation.

Probably the most famous of the English cases dealing with commercial law that used the law of nature had nothing to do with usury. It was the great contest involving the legality of monopolies, summed up by *Darcy v. Allen.* The case itself was argued at length in the Court of King's Bench in 1602.[88] By patent, the king had granted the plaintiff an exclusive right to import and make or sell playing cards within the realm. The defendant had infringed this patent. Suit was brought against him on that account, but the judges found in his favor, holding the royal patent invalid as an unlawful restraint of trade.

The complexities of that famous case have been clarified by a patient and praiseworthy exploration of the records by Jacob Corré.[89] As a result of his labors, the case can no longer stand unequivocally for the heroic limitation of the powers of the Crown that it may appear to be in Sir Edward Coke's report of the case. The evidence relating to the case, however, does show that it was thought possible to challenge the monarch's creation of an "odious monopoly" on the basis of a subject's right to carry on a lawful trade.[90] They were so treated in some Continental *decisiones*.[91] In England, monopolies were similarly subject to attack as being "without authority of law or reason."[92]

Legal authority to the same effect could certainly be found in England's positive law at the time that *Darcy v. Allen* was decided. Coke cited what he could from both sources in his report of the case. The arguments they afforded him converged to stand in favor of commercial freedom, an aspect of permissive natural law. As the lawyers themselves recognized, there were as many exceptions to this principle as there were complexities to the issues raised in the case's argument in King's Bench. When the difficulties had been fully recognized, however, Coke's understanding of the case's meaning must have struck a chord among England's governors. The principle he espoused in the case was put into statutory form a few years later.[93] In a sense, this example shows the law of nature in the service of purposes for which it was designed; it had prevented abusive use of royal powers in more than one situation, and then it had helped to shape the positive law.

Interpretation of Statutes

The place accorded to principles taken from the law of nature in the construction of statutes was so evident to English lawyers that they often applied them without taking any notice of their source. As was true on the Continent, the common lawyers had long been "prepared to take liberties" in dealing with the texts of "odious" statutes.[94] These liberties were often shaped by principles found in natural law. This process did not end in 1500 or even 1688. In its most familiar form, enactments that stood in accord with reason and natural justice were to be construed broadly, whereas enactments that were out of line with those dictates were to be construed strictly.[95] The latter were not to be extended beyond what was necessary to give some effect to their words. Thus, it was said that a statute dealing with alienage was "to be taken favourably, in that it doth but restore men to the law of nature."[96] No such interpretation, however, would be extended to a statute "made against natural justice."[97] The statute of limitations, for example, was regularly interpreted "against its words" in order not to allow wrongdoers to take deliberate advantage of provisions in the statute that would allow them to appropriate the lands and goods of their rightful owners.[98] Modern lawyers have become so accustomed to this result that it scarcely registers on their consciousness that these statutes were at first so interpreted to make them conform to principles drawn from the law of nature.

Sometimes arguments in favor of the enactment of new laws or repeal of existing laws were also made and expressly supported by the invocation of the law of nature. For instance, a statute from the reign of Henry VIII made it a crime for anyone to keep more than 2,000 sheep.[99] Daines Barrington, using this as an example of what he claimed to be "an immense number" of similar enactments that deserved to be repealed, argued that this particular measure was contrary to "nature and utility."[100] By the dictates of nature, he said, some lands were simply not fit for tillage, and however well-intentioned the statute may have been, it actually prohibited the only productive use that could be made of them. It was, therefore, out of line with nature's dictates. It restricted freedom without good cause. As has often been the fate of criticisms like his, nothing came of it until more than a half-century after his death. Only in 1856 was the Henrician statute erased from the statute books.[101]

Barrington did not argue that the Henrician statute should not be enforced, despite his antipathy toward it. Nor did he attempt to find a way to render it harmless through creative interpretation of its terms. He simply suggested it as a likely candidate for repeal. Clear positive law normally prevailed in practice over general arguments founded on the law of nature. That stayed his hand. Some other advocates, however, went further than Barrington was willing to go. Here and there, the English reports contain strong language qualifying the force of the words used in statutes. The statutes were "always to be expounded so as there be not a failure of justice."[102] There were said to be "many cases in the books" where the judges "have gone beyond the words" in order to align their decisions with natural justice.[103] As one English lawyer early in the seventeenth century had remarked, "[H]ow prejudicial it would be for the whole Kingdom, if that rule were infallible that no precedent or prescription, usage or custom (as some have said) should prevail against an Act of Parliament."[104] This lawyer's words seem surprising, even startling, in a land that recognized parliamentary supremacy. But they also represent a view many lawyers shared. Power was given to the judges "in respect of the inconvenience and absurdity that should otherwise follow."[105] Or as one of Sir Edward Coke's reports put it succinctly, "[T]he law, which is the perfection of reason, will never expound the words of the Act against reason."[106]

Voices were raised on the other side, it is true.[107] The evidence is not all of a piece. It may be, for instance, that statutes affecting the punishment of crime were given more literal readings than those related to private law.[108] Perhaps the gradual movement was toward conceding a more absolute authority to the legislature as time passed,[109] but the "natural law position" was far from moribund, even after 1688. English lawyers were loath to give up a belief in the authority that inhered in natural justice. Many of them proved reluctant to abandon it in favor of a regime of legislative absolutism. A measure of this reluctance is that sometimes the same lawyers seem (to us) to have been talking out of both sides of their mouths on the issue. They said that parliamentary statutes were supreme, and they also said that the rule of justice was supreme. This was, as Alan Cromartie has pointedly described it, "a culture without the modern conception of sovereignty."[110] "Arbitrary power," Edmund Burke had said, "is a thing which neither any man can hold nor any man can give."[111] This sentiment was a time-honored theme of political thought,[112] and it could also make a difference in legal practice. With it in play, the law of nature more easily affected the decision of cases at law than it does today.

A particularly fine example of the potential found within the law of nature for interpreting acts of Parliament comes from a maritime case heard in King's Bench in 1771.[113] The plaintiff had sent twenty hogsheads of tallow on a ship from Cork to Liverpool. The ship had been lost at sea, but some of the tallow had washed up on shore. There was no doubt that it had been a part of the plaintiff's shipment. The question was whether the hogsheads belonged to the king under the law of wreck or to the plaintiff instead. This was a harder case than it now seems. A thirteenth-century statute had enacted that after a shipwreck, if a man, a dog, or a cat from the ship had escaped alive, the owner of any of the shipwrecked goods could later claim the goods as his own.[114] Otherwise the goods belonged to the Crown under the law of wreck.

This statute then seemed (and now seems) quite nonsensical. Why should it matter whether a cat or a dog had survived the shipwreck? Most previous explanations—of which there were a few—had interpreted the statute pretty much as it read.[115] The king was kindly conceding some (but not all) of his rights to goods under the prerogative law of wreck. The owner of the goods might get lucky. A dog or cat might have survived. He should therefore be grateful for the statute, and if there had been no survivors, human or animal, he was no worse off than he would have been without the statute. This was the situation in the case involving the tallow; the statute appeared to stand against the plaintiff's claim, because no one—no man, no dog, no cat—had survived the ship's loss at sea. The Crown seemed to be the clear winner.

The chief justice of King's Bench, Lord Mansfield, was not satisfied with this result. It would be "contrary to the principles of law, justice, and humanity," he wrote, arbitrarily to deprive an owner of the goods that belonged to him.[116] "The very idea of it is shocking."[117] He therefore searched for a better understanding of the statute, one in accord with principles of justice. Requiring the survival of a man, a dog, or a cat, he surmised, must have had a purpose rooted in the natural law. It could not have been the product of an idle whim of the legislature or a blatant attempt to augment the king's power to enrich himself at the expense of a subject's right to his own property. Fully considered, the sensible statutory purpose must have been to provide a way of identifying the true owner of the goods. It seems to have worked this way. If a surviving dog wagged its tail or if a surviving cat purred at the approach of the claimant, then one would know that the claimant was also the owner of the shipwrecked goods. The statute had merely given examples of how such identification might happen. There could be others.[118] For Lord Mansfield, this made sense. Other animals—cattle, for instance—could not be used to identify their owners. Cows neither moo nor wag their tails when their owner approaches. This must have been what the statute intended by using the examples of the man, the dog, and the cat. So he concluded. And so the claimant prevailed.

Whatever one thinks of this ingenious chain of reasoning, it does show the potential in natural law ways of thought for the task of interpreting statutes. The judge assumed that the lawmaker had intended to enact a statute that was in line with principles of natural justice. Natural justice dictated that owners should not be deprived of their property without good cause. The judge's duty was to read the statute so that it would stand in harmony with that dictate. Lord Mansfield accordingly sought a meaning within the statute that would accord with "clear principles of justice and humanity." He found one.[119] Doing so did require him to go some distance beyond the words of the statute. But sometimes the "mind" of the legislators was what mattered, not the particular words they had chosen, and it was sensible to conclude that their "mind" had conformed to the tenets of the law of nature. This requirement might require judges to "construe statutes quite contrary to the letter," but doing so was neither an arbitrary act nor a product of misunderstanding on their part. It simply supplied what the legislators themselves would have wanted had they thought about it. Judges also assumed that their actions should stand in conformity with their own oaths to do justice.[120] In fact, that was their duty. They had sworn to it. This supposition lay behind many of the juridical "feats" that invoked the law of reason to reach results that seem very far distant from neutral readings of statutory language.

Restraints on the Exercise of Power

As it did in Lord Mansfield's decision of this maritime dispute, the law of nature served to restrain exercises of power in other cases, even cases in which power had been exercised by the king in Parliament. It was an old maxim in England that the king was under the law. *Bracton* had stated it in the thirteenth century.[121] From the Magna Carta in 1215 to the Bill of Rights in 1689 and beyond, it found expression in the positive law.[122] The maxim was sometimes invoked in decided cases to hold the king to the tenets of the law of nature. He should, for example, keep his promises.[123] He should also exercise the power to pardon in accord with his coronation oath to do justice.[124] It followed that his courts should reach results that accorded with the maxim.

Behind many such instances lay an assumption widely employed in interpreting statutes: the ruler—whether the king or Parliament—could not have meant to violate principles of natural justice in the exercise of the right to enact and enforce the law. When an untoward result was apparently dictated by a statute's words, judges might conclude that the lawmaker had simply failed to envision the perverse uses to which the words of his enactment could be put. Lack of foresight is a failing of all men, even wise and powerful men, and legislators themselves would not have wished their words to be taken literally had they been able to foresee all the purposes for which their words might be used. They had themselves entrusted the judges with the authority necessary to do justice; this authority included a responsibility to prevent injustice. This was also part of the judicial oath. In other words, in looking to the law of nature and refusing to read the words of a statute literally, it might be said that the judges were actually doing what the legislators had wanted.

As seems to have been equally true in the Continental *decisiones,* most English lawyers evinced a greater willingness to intervene against an action when the challenged exercise of power came from a person or corporate body from lower down the ranks of governmental authority than the king in Parliament. Local customs and decisions made by subordinate officials and middling sorts of corporate bodies more easily came to naught through judicial scrutiny than did the considered actions of the sovereign. For instance, an inheritance custom in a Northumbrian manor that stated if a tenant had only daughters and no sons at the time of his death, the land he held by customary tenure would pass to his oldest daughter for life and then to their male cousins in fee was held invalid under the theory that "the law of reason is the measure of both, and the lord cannot annex a condition contrary to law" to the ordinary pattern of intestate succession.[125] One test of a custom's validity was its consistency with the law of reason, and this one did not pass the test. Had Parliament enacted a similar rule, however, it would almost certainly have stood.

So it was with family settlements that attempted to create perpetual interests in land—that is, interests whose takers would not be ascertainable until a period far into the future and would prevent earlier alienation of the land. Had Parliament authorized them, as it had in the statute *De donis conditionalibus,*[126] they would have passed muster. However, in private grants, they did not. They were said to "fight against God."[127] By this martial image, critics meant simply that perpetuities were contrary to principles of natural law that God had established. Perpetuities sought "to stand in the way of the providence of God, who alone sets up and pulls down as He pleases."[128] In the nature of things, no living person can foretell or control the future. No person, therefore, should attempt to do so, and perpetuities did. From this attitude gradually arose what we now know as the Rule against Perpetuities. In time it became a strict rule of law, one to be applied relentlessly in the service of a free market in land. It had its origins, however, in a principle drawn from the law of nature. Judges sought to align the land law with nature's dictates, and one way of doing so was by invalidating perpetuities.[129] Of course, the fit between the land law and natural law was never perfect. The fee tail was the great exception in England. It allowed men to dictate what would happen long into the future. The fee tail, however, had been opened up and endorsed by an act of Parliament. It could not be "struck down" by a mere judge. Gradually effective ways were found around the restrictions on alienation that the estate tail created.[130] They restored a balance. The rules against the creation of legal perpetuities in land, which claimed no such statutory warrant and amounted to no more than private attempts to control the future, moved in the opposite direction, and in the end their invalidation became a fixed rule of law to be strictly applied.

If we can see the law of nature at work in cases involving private attempts to create perpetuities, a question that remains is whether English law ever applied principles drawn from the law of nature to invalidate statutes enacted by king and Parliament. The centerpiece of any discussion of that question must be another report written by Sir Edward Coke: his account of *Bonham's Case* (1610).[131] The amount written about the case in modern times is huge and full of contention. Its size both discourages discussion and requires it. What will be said here is confined to the perspective of this inquiry in the law of nature, justifiably so because the legal principle that no man should serve as judge in his own cause stood at the center of the case. It was an established principle of natural law.[132] For the same person to act as both party and judge ran counter to the established rule that a trial was necessarily an *actus trium personarum*. It was a self-evident invitation to bias and consequent injustice in decision. The maxim was found in the Codex (Cod. 3.5.1) as a statement of the general law, and it had also been applied in England as one part of the common law.[133]

It was, however, Coke's application of the maxim in his report of *Bonham's Case* that made it famous. Dr. Thomas Bonham, a graduate in medicine of Cambridge University, sought to practice his profession in London. The College of Physicians tried to prevent him from doing so unless he was licensed by the college first. Under letters patent issued by King Henry VIII and confirmed by an act of Parliament,[134] the college held such a privilege and monopoly, and when Dr. Bonham entered into practice after refusing to seek its license, the college acted to fine him for violation of its statutory privilege and then to imprison him for his obstinacy when he did not pay the fine. It was the ability to impose

a fine that Coke's report of the case fastened upon. The college pock-
eted half of what was collected, and this, he said, amounted to permitting it to act as a judge in its own cause. That was contrary to law. The
college was itself reaping a profit from an action it had taken as a judge.
The privilege's parliamentary confirmation did not change the result because, wrote Coke, "when an Act of Parliament is against common right
and reason, or repugnant, or impossible to be performed, the common
law will control it and adjudge such act to be void."[135] Strong words! In
the vehemence of his language and the strength of Coke's reputation,
modern commentators have seen the origins of, and even the common
law's authorization for, the practice of judicial review of legislation. American courts have been doing only what Coke's words authorized: they
treat acts of Congress as "void" if they conflict with constitutional principles of justice. From the perspective of the contemporary understanding
of the law of nature, however, *Bonham's Case* was not as dramatic or as
consequential a decision as some later commentators have made it. There
are four points of difference between it and judicial review to consider.

First, the dispute involved a grant of authority by the sovereign to a
local corporate body—just the sort of grant to a subject that had long
been regarded with particular suspicion in the courts. The question was:
Had the sovereign really meant to grant an authority that stood in conflict with basic principles of justice? Even where the words themselves
could be read that way, without some good reason, the better course was
to assume that an unjust result had not in fact been the considered in-
tention of the sovereign. Coke himself made the connection between statutes like this one and royal grants.[136] The common understanding was
that they should not be read to promote injustice or to prejudice the rights
of a third party. That had not been the ruler's considered intent. In 1610,
this was an old story. Although the decision in *Bonham's Case* did recognize the existence of a substantial power in the judiciary, it was not a
power equivalent to judicial review of general legislation.

Second, the word *void* as used in Coke's statement of the case's holding
simply meant "of no legal effect" under the circumstances. Although
there were cases where his approach could have the effect of nullifying governmental action, Coke was not necessarily asserting a broad
judicial right to determine the extent of Parliament's power. Thomas
Rutherforth (d. 1771) gives this example of the meaning of the word
void. Theft, being a wrong, confers no positive rights upon the thief. He
wrote:

> [S]ome actions, which are contrary to law, are not only wrong, but void;
> that is, the law considers them as if they never had been done, as to any
> moral effect that might have been produced by them. . . . Where the ob-
> ligation of the law is perfect, such acts as are contrary to it are void, or
> no moral effect is produced by them. The law says, Thou shalt not steal.
> The obligation is of the perfect sort; and upon that account the act of
> theft as to any effect which the possession of goods might have produced
> is void; the thief gains no property in the goods which he has stolen.[137]

In dealing with statutes, judges used *void* in this limited sense in quite
a few treatises and cases of the time, both before and after Coke employed it in *Bonham's Case*.[138]

Third, although the approach to law evident in the case now seems
inconsistent with the sovereignty of Parliament, that conclusion is not
the one lawyers versed in the law of nature would have drawn. The potential clash between courts and legislature, which is so evident to us,
was not so evident to them. Blackstone, for example, stated both views
without supposing that any contradiction between them was involved.[139]
Sir John Vaughan (d. 1674), chief justice of the Common Pleas, did much
the same.[140] The real clash was between the law of nature and the powers
of both Parliament and the royal courts. When Blackstone spoke of the
supremacy of Parliament, he did not mean that Parliament could ride
roughshod over the tenets of natural justice. When he spoke of the powers
of judges, he did not mean that they could impose their naked will on
the law. Both were bound by the laws of nature. *Bonham's Case* was one
instance where this aspect of the law had come to the fore, but it had no
special importance as a precedent. It would stretch the case out of shape
if it were to serve as sufficient historical justification for the aggressive
kind of judicial review now in use in American courts.

Fourth, the number of cases in which judges adopted such a free-
wheeling approach to statutes, one apparently based on the law of nature, was matched and very probably exceeded by cases in which judges
did just the opposite. As often as not, they resisted whatever temptation
they felt to look beyond the words of a statute to discover a "mind" formed
by the law of nature that went contrary to what the statute said. More
often they applied statutes as written. As one report put it, the judges
were refusing to correct an unjust result involving the Poor Law because
"it would be dangerous to depart from the words of the statute, and if
they once did, they should never know where to stop."[141] Refusals like

this one happened a lot. They were not unknown on the Continent.[142] Can they be reconciled with judicial respect for the superiority of the law of nature? Only with difficulty, it seems. Scholars who look for perfect consistency in judicial attitudes must look somewhere else than in the English law reports.

Scholars concerned with fundamental law's place in the English courts should also consider the legal proceedings held at Whitehall in 1616 before the highest legal and ecclesiastical authorities of the realm.[143] Like *Bonham's Case,* it involved an indirect challenge to parliamentary power, arising because the authority exercised under a parliamentary grant to the Commissioners of Sewers was challenged as contrary to the law of the land. Among its directives, in order to prevent flooding, the commissioners had ordered new banks to be erected and old banks to be torn down, requiring inhabitants to pay for the works involved and even imprisoning those who refused to pay on the grounds that they had not given their consent. Some of those who had been imprisoned—described as "certain obstinate and ill-disposed persons" in the report—objected that the exercise of these powers was contrary to the law of the land and also to basic precepts of natural justice, particularly in the respect that they had been imprisoned simply for bringing their complaints before a court of justice. Their objections, however, were swept aside. The commissioners, it was ruled, had acted in accordance with "common sense and reason" in making orders for "new works to stop the fury of the waters."[144] Those who had brought suit against them were the ones at fault. They were to remain in prison until they had taken effective action to have their suits dismissed. In reading these proceedings, it is hard not to think back to the case described in Chapter 2 involving the young man taken while climbing a ladder at night outside a maiden's house in Naples. Perceptions of the urgent needs of the community were held to justify quite draconian limitations to the scope of clear precepts of natural justice. Perhaps this is what modern proponents of natural law mean by "practical reason." At least the result seems rather more practical than principled.

The Ecclesiastical and Admiralty Courts

It is sensible to suppose that the English courts in which the *ius commune* was regularly applied would have been receptive to applying principles drawn from the law of nature, and the records of these courts in fact confirm that they were. Whether this usage contributed to a more general acceptance of natural law among common lawyers is a separate and more doubtful question, but that the principles of natural justice found a home in the civilians' corner of English legal life is certain. A late-seventeenth-century English civilian named Hugh Davis penned a treatise contending that ecclesiastical uniformity was required by the law of nature.[145] The treatise was mostly abstract theorizing, but it also stands as a sign of natural law's general acceptance among contemporary ecclesiastical lawyers. That acceptance was a given for them, and this particular author argued that they should follow it to where he led.

Natural law turned up in the court records, too. Four brief examples must suffice to make the point. They all serve to show that the law of nature had an occasional effect on the inner workings of ecclesiastical jurisdiction. The first piece of evidence comes from the fifteenth century. In England, a customary practice, one confirmed by diocesan statutes, allowed marriage to be used as a kind of penalty for repeated fornication. A man and a woman charged with an aggravated form of the offense were required to enter into a conditional contract of marriage. They each said, "If I know you carnally henceforth, I take you as my wife (husband)." Under the Western canon law as it then stood, these words were sufficient to create an indissoluble bond if the man and woman later did come together sexually. It was called "abjuration *sub pena nubendi.*" The practice was also known and used by the courts of the church in some parts of the Continent.[146] But it was subject to challenge. However useful it may have seemed at the time it was first used, by the later Middle Ages, abjuration raised more problems than it solved. It did not prevent fornication, and it was also regarded as "contrary to right and natural equity."[147] Its inclusion in diocesan statutes did not itself justify the practice, and over the course of the fifteenth century, its use was gradually abandoned. This was one way the law of nature was supposed to function: to inspire changes in the positive law, changes that would bring common practice into line with principles of justice. Here exactly that appears to have taken place.

A second example comes from a case in the diocese of Chester in the mid-1630s.[148] A man named John Ditchfield was cited to appear before the consistory court to answer a charge that he had "violated the laws of God and nature" in abusing his own father, described as "an aged and impotent man." The particulars showed that John had withheld food and lodging from his father, resulting in the father's suffering and eventual death. Apparently the son charged with misconduct offered no real defense. He was required to submit to the traditional public penance. Wearing a white sheet in his parish church, he was ordered to read out a public confession of guilt before the congregation assembled on Sunday. We cannot be sure that the confession specifically mentioned violation of the law of nature, but it was an explicit part of the charge against him, and the outcome was a confirmation of its application in court practice.

A third example arose in the context of a will contest heard in the diocese of Rochester during the second half of the fifteenth century. The testator was Richard Anstye.[149] He had several daughters, some of whom he had included as legatees under his last will and testament and some of whom he had not. The excluded daughters sought to prove that he had been *non compos mentis* when he made the document. This was a hard claim to prove as things then stood under the law,[150] but the judge of the consistory court nevertheless allowed the matter to go to arbitration. His reason was a wish that (he said) was shared by all those who were involved in the dispute "to conserve the natural affection among the daughters" toward their father, the testator. Under an assumption shaped by the law of nature, they should all take something. That was a father's duty. Arbitration would be more likely to allow this to happen than a court decree. This result illustrated a principle often discussed by jurists dealing with the law of nature. It did leave room for flexibility, but its principles mattered, and it lay within the discretion of a good judge to pay attention to them.

A fourth example involves the law of wreck, the identical subject raised by Lord Mansfield's decision in *Hamilton & Smyth v. Davis* (1771) discussed above.[151] This case was heard in an admiralty court. It involved "a poor man walking on a cliff beside the sea."[152] There he saw and took into his possession a large quantity of ambergris, a waxy and valuable substance that comes from the intestines of sperm whales.[153] The question was whether it belonged to him as finder or to the Crown (and the Admiralty) under the law of wreck. Dr. Arthur Duck, an eminent civilian, appeared on behalf of the poor man. Under the law of nature, he said, any *res nullius* became the property of the person who first took it into his possession. That was the finder, his client. The ambergris was obviously *res nullius*, having been washed up on land from the sea as it had come from the whale. His client, he said, should prevail under this principle of natural law. As so often happened in disputes involving the law of nature, however, Dr. Duck's argument was not the end of the matter. The law of nature was often subject to qualification by the positive law, and the king's advocates were not silenced by the invocation of natural law principles. They invoked the king's prerogative, long recognized by custom and judicial decision as part of English maritime law. It stood in favor of the Crown. That might seem to have determined the outcome, but in the end, the poor man's claim was not treated as a nullity, and he was rewarded. The case was compromised by awarding him a sizable annual pension to be paid out of Crown revenues—a quite sensible outcome as it must then have seemed. It cannot be said, therefore, that this controversy fully vindicated the law of nature's "constitutional" status in England. It can only be said the dispute's outcome shows that it counted for something in fact.

Conclusion

As is true of the Continental *decisiones,* evidence from the English reports demonstrates that in litigation the law of nature had a status commensurate with its place in the treatises written by common lawyers. Although described as the most fundamental of the sources of law, it occupied a subsidiary status in dealing with most practical questions. Natural law was not essential for a great many of law's tasks, almost certainly the majority among them. Specific references to the law of nature were made in the course of arguments before the courts of Common Pleas and King's Bench, but they were not everyday events. Nor were the arguments always successful when made. Its actual influence may, however, have been greater than a simple counting of citations to it indicates. The lesser number of references to authorities of any sort in the English reports than appear in the Continental *decisiones* and the relative elasticity of the phrase "law of reason" as used by English lawyers may obscure its substantive importance. Even so, it would be an exaggeration to claim that the law of nature regularly "controlled" the municipal law in England.

All the same, the law of nature did turn up in some quite unexpected places. They show how wide-sweeping natural law arguments could be. An instructive if surprising example comes from a famous case called *De modo decimandi* in Sir Edward Coke's reports.[154] The dispute involved the issuance of a writ of prohibition to prevent an ecclesiastical court from hearing a dispute in which the defendant, who had been sued there to collect tithes of wood, pleaded a custom of the county of Kent according to which no tithes of wood were due. The court held that the prohibition lay. The custom prevailed. Why? The starting point for Coke's analysis was the law of nature. The report stated that some "portion [of sustenance] is due by the law of nature, which is the law of God."[155] That would seem to have allowed the ecclesiastical suit to proceed. If natural law required payment of tithes, how could this local custom validly permit their nonpayment? However, the report continued, determination of the exact nature of payment nevertheless "appertaineth to the law of man to assign . . . as necessity requireth."[156] On this particular question the spiritual court should not ignore the law of man, even in favor of the law of God. For this proposition, Coke's report of the case cited passages from the New Testament, the *Summa theologiae* of St. Thomas Aquinas, Jean Gerson's *Regulae morales,* and Saint German's *Doctor and Student,* as well as several common law precedents. The local custom was held to prevail.

Like so many of the Continental *decisiones,* the report shows the relevance to actual legal questions of what was a quite malleable interpretation of the law of nature. The report illustrates its limitations in practice at the same time it also illustrates its presence. Some room for variation and accommodation in assessing obligations was left open to the positive law, and that room was ample enough to restrict the reach of an obligation for which a source in the law of nature existed. This was an oft-repeated situation in the English courts, as it was on the Continent. It did not mean that natural law had no actual force, only that its force turned out to be less than we sometimes think it should have been if it truly were the fundamental law of the land.

One point remains. Readers may recall that this chapter began by raising the question of whether English law was influenced in a meaningful way by Roman law and also whether English acceptance of the law of nature might have been a consequence of that influence. Faced honestly, the history of the law of nature in English law neither confirms nor refutes the argument that any such transplantation took place. There were evident English parallels to the ways in which lawyers employed the law of nature in Continental courts, but they may have been no more than that—parallels.[157] They can be explained by the widely shared belief by lawyers on both sides of the Channel that natural law was an authentic source of law. They both regarded it as a font of law, one that was meant to have consequences in practice. If so, no actual influence on the common law from without existed. Some evidence may point in the direction of seeing that kind of influence,[158] but there is no unassailable proof that it took place. Common reference to the law of nature may have been simply the result of starting out with equivalent assumptions about the sources of law.

Put differently, however, even this "minimalist interpretation" of the evidence would unite lawyers in England with those on the Continent in a sense that is important for understanding the larger history of the law of nature. They both shared a respect for it, and they both carried that respect into practice. The legal context in which this usage happened was similar, even if it was not altogether identical. Significant differences between the common law and the *ius commune* always existed, and the differences had results in determining the ways in which the law of nature exerted an impact on local law and court practice. The slighter use of natural law in dealing with procedural questions in England, for example, would have been one natural result of such a difference between existing systems of justice. Likewise, the material differences in the positive laws of inheritance that existed would have called for different ways of applying the same fundamental law.

On the more basic question of whether the law of nature had an effect on what happened in court, the similarities seem rather greater than the differences. Common approaches to the treatment of statutes and common invocations of basic principles of natural law stand out among them. Indeed many—though certainly not all—of the actual results reached through the invocation of natural law now look to have been alike on both sides of the Channel.

5

Legal Education in the United States

CROSSING THE ATLANTIC OCEAN with a view to discovering what place the law of nature occupied in the law courts of the American Republic is no more difficult than crossing the Channel from France to reach England. In some respects it is easier. The source material is plentiful. By the time the colonists cut the ties that had bound them to the English Crown, American law courts had long since come into existence. Their legitimacy was well established in the popular mind.[1] Even against a background of general mistrust of lawyers among the citizenry, the nation nonetheless embraced legal learning and the rule of law.[2] Informal reports of judicial decisions circulated widely before the American Revolution.[3] Official reports for the courts of the original thirteen states, as well as the federal courts, began publication around the time of the formation of the Republic in the 1780s, and over the course of the next fifty years, they became abundant.[4] As new states entered the Union, they too found compilers and publishers for the decisions of their judges. The field to be harvested is therefore large. The cases are there to be read.

The problem of identifying the sources by which American lawyers might have acquired a working knowledge of the law of nature nonetheless confronts all historians of the subject, just as it did in assessing the education of English lawyers, and it is no easier to solve. It arises at once when one examines the evidence relating to the founding of the new nation, and it continues into a study of later years, when the special character of American law was being formed and its law schools were founded. That American lawyers did acquire a basic familiarity with natural law becomes apparent once one takes a careful look. Indeed, scholars have long recognized this familiarity. Its place in the development of the American constitutional law has attracted able students.[5] What is less clear, however, is how it happened. The means by which ordinary American lawyers acquired a familiarity with the law of nature is not obvious. They needed more than a statement recognizing its existence if they were to apply it in practice. We must look carefully at the available evidence of what they learned.

American Independence and the Founding Fathers

The first piece of that evidence is dramatic and has long been a subject of remark. The history of the new nation opened with an emphatic assertion of the vitality of the law of nature. The War of Independence was fought under its banner. It was not the sole banner the colonists carried, but it was surely one of them. The Declaration of Independence (1776) asserted that the war was necessary to achieve for the colonists "the separate and equal station to which the Laws of Nature and of Nature's God entitle[d] them." Resistance to tyranny, defined as the denial of "certain unalienable rights" that God himself had granted to men, was said to justify the rebellion.[6]

This resistance was a theme regularly discussed in works of the natural lawyers. It had a long history. Most of that discussion favored at least a qualified recognition of this aspect of the right to self-defense, and the American patriots seized upon it to justify their actions.[7] The Federalist Papers stated the principle more than once,[8] and when the representatives from Virginia assembled to enact a constitution for themselves, the delegates began by declaring that "all men [were] by nature equally free and independent."[9] They thus asserted "an indubitable, unalienable, and indefeasible right to reform, alter, or abolish" a tyrannical government, one they concluded had long since ceased to serve the common good.

The natural law basis for this position would have impressed itself on the minds of the Americans who took the steps necessary to free themselves from British rule. Its invocation in this dramatic setting was itself a source of education in the tenets of natural law, or at the very least an invitation to investigate them. At the same time, any such investigation would have shown that the argument in favor of the right of resistance had always been subject to serious reservations. Not every individual person might lawfully assert it. The cure for tyranny might also be worse than the disease. Resistance might fail. It was sure to create disorder. Knowing whether overt conflict with a legitimate ruler was justified was therefore no easy call. Analysis could be complicated and the right answer elusive. Investigation of this theme might therefore have provided something akin to a sophisticated understanding of the law of nature for the colonists who undertook it.

By contrast with some of that sophisticated learning, the basic features of the colonists' argument were simplicity itself.[10] In a state of nature, all men had the power to defend themselves and their goods against aggression from without. It was what John Locke called "the executive power of the law of nature."[11] When they first formed themselves into society, they had ceded a large part of that power to their governors, who in turn agreed to provide an alternate and more expeditious way of securing justice for them. If the governors failed to keep that agreement, however, and if their failure was serious, sustained, and oppressive, they could be said to have forfeited their claim to the people's allegiance. By their actions, they would have betrayed the terms of the original agreement, and the people might be justified in reasserting a right to defend their persons and their property against them. Doing so was really no more than asserting a right all people had once held without qualification. The law of nature might thus come back into force and remain in force until just government had been restored.

This was a powerful sentiment, widespread among the patriots and confidently asserted. When John Adams of Massachusetts wrote to his fellow citizens in support of their right to throw off the yoke of despotic government, he cited principles of the law of nature and nations as developed by Hugo Grotius, Samuel Pufendorf, Jean Barbeyrac, John Locke, and Algernon Sidney.[12] Thomas Jefferson took much the same position, and when he was called upon to give advice to a young student of the law, it was only to be expected that he should have insisted upon the advisability of undertaking a study of the law of nature.[13] His library contained many works devoted to the subject.[14] He had carried what he had learned from them into the testing times when a war for independence was declared and fought, and he carried it forward with him into later controversies.[15]

Many among the founders of the American republic and their immediate successors expressed a common regard for the law of nature. It had called for their separation from the English monarchy, and it found a place in their own careers and works. It appeared in some of the early state constitutions they created,[16] and it was mentioned with approbation by most of the leading lights among them: John Adams (1735–1826),[17] John Quincy Adams (1767–1848),[18] Samuel Adams (1722–1803),[19] Fisher Ames (1758–1808),[20] Richard Bland (1710–1776),[21] John Dickinson (1732–1808),[22] Alexander Hamilton (1757–1804),[23] John Jay (1745–1829),[24] Rufus King (1755–1827),[25] William Livingston (1723–1790),[26] James Madison (1751–1836),[27] John Marshall (1755–1835),[28] George Mason (1725–1792),[29] Gouverneur Morris (1752–1816),[30] James Otis (1725–1783),[31] William Paterson (1745–1806),[32] Edmund Randolph (1753–1813),[33] Benjamin Rush (1749–1813),[34] William Smith Jr. (1728–1793),[35] Henry St. George Tucker (1752–1827),[36] Hugh Williamson (1735–1819),[37] James Wilson (1742–1798),[38] and George Wythe (1726–1806).[39]

If one asks how these men had come to the knowledge of the law of nature they asserted so confidently, the likely answer must be that it came from their own reading and probably also from conversations with their companions in arms.[40] No law schools existed in the colonies at the time of the American Revolution. Several colleges had been founded before 1776, it is true, but none of them possessed a separate faculty of law where the law of nature could become a regular part of the curriculum. When the subject was covered at all, it formed part of the arts curriculum.[41] This exposure might have given them a start on understanding the possibilities inherent in the law of nature. Reading Cicero on the subject would have made an impression on young minds, and so might the general lectures on law offered in American colleges. Many future lawyers passed through that experience.

Even so, the extent of this contact with the law of nature was nothing to brag about. It was almost incidental, not professional. None of the "proprietary" schools that were later begun and in which rudimentary coverage of the law of nature was provided had yet seen the light of day. To be sure, there were professional lawyers in America long before the Revolution. Twenty-two of the thirty-nine signers of the original Constitution were either professional lawyers or had received some legal training.[42] What they knew of the law of nature must have come partly from college life, partly from reading law books and talking with their fellows. We can be sure that books appropriate for its study were available in the Colonies. Lists of the contents of libraries have been compiled, and the great names of jurists tied to the subject were there to be uncovered:

works by Grotius, Pufendorf, Vinnius, Voet, Locke, Thomas Wood, Lord Kames, and others were available.[43] It is hard to arrive at a fully satisfactory explanation for what the authors of American independence knew about the law of nature, but there is little doubt that many of them did know something, and some of them knew quite a bit.

American Legal Education and Natural Law

It is of course possible that the combination of learned treatises and learned men behind the American founding was a special situation, one of limited long-term relevance to this study. Devoting prolonged attention to the Revolutionary moment may divert this narrative from its real subject: the learning available to ordinary lawyers after the Republic's existence had been secured. What opportunities did they have to learn anything about the law of nature beyond discovering the reality of its existence? Thanks to a relatively abundant secondary literature, we do know enough about the character of legal education before the rise of the university law schools to at least confront that question.

At the time of the Revolution, there were three ways to become a lawyer. Aspirants to the Bar commonly combined the three as they thought best. The formal requirements for admission to practice were perfunctory in themselves,[44] but these three avenues into the profession were not. They all required time and effort. They also seem to have been generally taken up by future practitioners in different mixtures. There was no set pattern.

The first, and probably the most prevalent, of the three was a severely practical one: entry into the office of a successful practicing lawyer as a clerk or apprentice. In that venue, young men learned the law by the performance of routine legal tasks, discussion of points of law with the lawyer and fellow clerks, and perusal of whatever books the lawyer possessed.[45] In the service of a kindly and conscientious mentor, it could add up to a satisfactory start, but with a busy or unhelpful attorney, too often it was just the reverse. Though it had its defenders at the time, there were always complaints, some of them quite loud.[46] An office clerkship could be haphazard, dreary, and lonely. The second possibility was attendance at the Inns of Court in London.[47] Whether that avenue provided adequate instruction in law, practical or speculative, was discussed briefly in Chapter 3. For a colonial student, this temporary residence in London would also have been the most difficult and expensive route to the Bar. That it was chosen by more than a few, including men who later enjoyed quite successful careers, must say something in its favor, though the attraction of life in that great city must also have diverted some young men from their studies. The third route to the Bar was private reading, and it too had obvious disadvantages. It could be slow and discouraging, particularly in the eighteenth century when *Coke on Littleton* provided the standard point of entry into the English common law. It is not a work for the faint of heart. Joseph Story's oft retold account of how, after reading through its pages "day after day with very little success, [he] sat [himself] down and wept bitterly" rings true, though he himself would recover to become its master.[48] Kent Newmyer's admirable biography of this famous American jurist rightly treats Story's early lament as proof of his strength of resolve in adversity.[49]

In the context of this study, whether or not these three avenues of entry into the profession of law in America commonly included exposure to the law of nature must be the relevant question. The first and most usual method, the law office apprenticeship, can only have done so regularly if combined with the third: perusal of the books found in the office. The second and least usual method would probably not have differed in any material way from the training discussed in Chapter 3. The last seems the most promising because it was so widely shared by fledgling lawyers and because so many contemporary works dealt with natural law. Reading would almost certainly have included some contact with ideas and legal conclusions drawn from it. Even if the books the student chose to take up were only those of the English common law, Chapter 3 demonstrated how frequently English treatises made at least passing references to natural law's existence and substance. However, even more than such partial contact with the subject, private reading on the part of American students would certainly have included a familiarity with the English writer whose influence came to dominate the study of law in the new Republic. That was William Blackstone.

Blackstone's *Commentaries* in America

Recent years have brought into the open some quite varied estimates of Blackstone's merits as a person and an expositor of the law. They range from harsh criticism to fulsome praise.[50] Whatever one thinks of his work and personal views, however, no one doubts the impact of his four-volume *Commentaries on the Laws of England* (1765–1769) on legal education in the formative years of the nation. It was a point of entry to the common law for virtually every American law student.[51] Michael Hoeflich described its publication as "a turning point in law publication" in the land, and Robert Ferguson's measured account of early American law and institutions placed it behind only the Bible in the extent of its influence on law in the new Republic.[52] Its popularity is attested by the many American editions of the *Commentaries* that were prepared and published.[53] In them, annotations and additions designed to fit the growing and changing needs of American society appeared. They were read by virtually every student of the law.

What American students of the law themselves said about Blackstone's *Commentaries* is equally persuasive of its centrality. Abraham Lincoln is reported to have remarked, "[I] never read anything which so profoundly interested and thrilled me."[54] James Kent similarly recorded the emotion of awe that his first reading of the work had instilled in him.[55] A less-gifted law student, Thomas Ruffin Jr. of North Carolina, reported to his father in 1846 that he had just finished reading the second volume of Blackstone's *Commentaries* for the tenth time.[56] If true, some of it must have stuck. Ten times is a lot. These men are but representatives, showing the measure of the influence Blackstone's treatise had on legal education in the New World. The common designation of the self-taught man as "a Blackstone lawyer" was another, indirect salute to the extent of his influence on legal education in America.

For purposes of an investigation of natural law's place in American legal education, it is not enough to take note of the success enjoyed by Blackstone's text. The question must turn to the *Commentaries* as a source of learning about natural law. What does the evidence show? There is no question that Blackstone accepted the law of nature as a valid source of law. So did virtually every lawyer. There is also no question that Blackstone invoked its authority. A computer-assisted count in the first edition of the *Commentaries* shows that Blackstone made express use of the concept of the law of nature or natural law *eo nomine* no fewer than eighty-one times.

There is, however, a question about natural law's actual influence on Blackstone's understanding of English law. A respected modern scholar, while noting the many references to natural law in the *Commentaries*, nevertheless came to the conclusion that its actual influence on the book's contents was "not exactly robust."[57] Such a disparaging comment gives reason for caution, but "robustness" in law is a hard concept to pin down, and the evidence on the other side is not easily dismissed. Blackstone made too many references to the law of nature for its relevance to law practice to be casually swept aside. He regarded the law of nature as "coeval with mankind and dictated by God himself." It was, he wrote, "binding over all the globe, in all countries, and at all times; no human laws are of any validity if contrary to [it]."[58] He noted specifically how essential its mastery by students of the common law was.[59] That point is a lesson that young American students might well have absorbed. Blackstone both stressed and illustrated it. At the very least, readers of the *Commentaries* would not have come away from reading Blackstone's text without recognizing the author's own high view of the law of nature.

These statements were generalizations, of course. What in particular would a student of the law actually have learned about possible uses of the law of nature from his reading? Using the popular American edition of the *Commentaries* published by St. George Tucker in 1803, one may easily take a look. The greater part of its Introduction reads rather like a basic manual on law used in the education of European lawyers, one that had been brought up to date to fit conditions in England and (in St. George Tucker's edition) to accord with changed circumstances in the American Republic. In the Introduction, Blackstone acknowledged God as the ultimate source of all laws; the Almighty was said to have "laid down only such laws as were founded in the relations of justice." His purpose was that "we should live honestly, should hurt nobody, and should render to everyone his due."[60] So wrote Blackstone. All human laws are founded upon "the law of nature and the law of revelation," he continued. Their true purpose was the attainment of justice.[61]

Still within the introductory section, Blackstone then dealt with the organization of human society and the initiation of human government. This coverage too was a staple of manuals on the general law, a feature that most of today's law teachers would probably dismiss as irrelevant or worse. Although Blackstone regarded as "too wild to be seriously admitted" the supposition that at some point in history there had been an actual meeting of all men then alive "in a large plain" in order to effect an organizational change to a regime of private property, he went on to recognize man's arrival at the same result by an only slightly different route. That is, he described the acceptance of the principal institutions of society as the gradual product of human experience and maturity.[62] The same thing had happened, only more slowly.

His Introduction ended with a discussion of the interpretation of specific laws and statutes that had been adopted as part of this gradual process of civilization. Some of Blackstone's examples were actually taken from Continental sources, the last dealing with a case taken from Cicero that endorsed a construction of a maritime statute not far distant from Lord Mansfield's approach in the case involving the law of wreck discussed in Chapter 4. In other words, from this Introduction an American student would have read the law of nature being praised, described, and used in a way very like that which was available to a student of Roman law on the Continent. He would not have had the *glossa ordinaria* to lead him to further illustrations of natural law's reach, but he would have seen illustrations of its potential use in practice. In St. George Tucker's additions, he would also have found illustrations of specific effects that natural law had exerted on the laws of Virginia. In them, he would also have come upon occasional dissents from Blackstone's conclusions—cases in which conditions in the new Republic called for modification of existing law.[63] However, a law student would not have seen anything to upset what Blackstone had written about the character of the law of nature.

American readers of the *Commentaries* would also have come upon the author's discussion of rights in property that had remained subject to the laws of nature—things that had been treated as *res nullius* in the Roman law and remained open to claims based upon physical occupancy. Unowned land,[64] wild animals,[65] and flowing waters (including the seas),[66] were the principal legal categories where the law of nature still applied in largely unchanged form. Rights in them could only be acquired by manucaption (or the equivalent). Otherwise they remained open to appropriation by others, just as things had stood before society's earliest organization. In the circumstances of the early American republic, where exacting governmental regulation and the march of population growth lay far in the future, these categories were not simply matters of intellectual curiosity. The famous case of *Pierson v. Post*,[67] still a staple of first-year property courses in American law schools, is a reminder of their relevance in the early 1800s. Few law students today make the connection between that famous case and the law of nature. Their counterparts in the early nineteenth century would not have missed it.

A further example of natural law's continuing relevance, one that would certainly have captured the attention of law students, appeared in Blackstone's treatment of legal wrongs in the Fourth Book. There he drew a distinction between crimes that were *malum in se* and those that were merely *malum prohibitum*, placing crimes against the law of nature (e.g., murder and arson) in the first category.[68] He also discussed the right to self-defense at some length; there were situations where the law of nature "made [the person attacked] his own protector." The criminal law was bound to respect the consequences.[69] In dealing with the law of theft, for example, he discussed the right to appropriate the property of others in cases of absolute necessity—for example, if the person who stole a loaf of bread was actually starving. His conclusion was that as a legal privilege this right was "now antiquated," but he went on to state that the purposes it once served were adequately addressed by the power to pardon bread-stealers and other criminals then vested in the English Crown.[70]

These examples of natural law's place in the common law as portrayed by Blackstone would have impressed themselves on the minds of students beginning their exploration of law. At least in appearance, they do not support the conclusion that the law of nature stated some basic goals of the law but "was not a body of axioms for everyday judicial decision making."[71] They actually support the opposite conclusion. It is true that some of the references in Blackstone's text were couched in quite abstract terms, but they were also treated as relevant to questions that arose in legal practice. How to interpret statutes, for instance, was a subject bound to come up in actual cases. Blackstone discussed it in much the same way any European natural lawyer would have. True, the examples he used also demonstrated that the law of nature was subject to modification to meet society's legitimate needs. It was removed from everyday judicial decision making in that sense. From a lawyer's point of view, however, all that this separation demonstrated was that the law of nature was not sufficient in itself to deal with many practical questions. It required the addition of positive law. That was not, however, equivalent to irrelevance. It was a basic assumption of natural law jurisprudence.

American Law Schools before 1850

Legal education in the American Republic did not stand still in the years before the Civil War. The three traditional methods remained in place, but they were joined by a fourth venue: professional law schools.[72] At the start, two different kinds of this more formal approach to legal education coexisted: the proprietary and the university law schools. The first of these was usually organized and taught by a single lawyer. The second was associated with developments in the existing American colleges.

How many proprietary schools once existed no one knows.[73] The most prominent and successful was the Litchfield Law School, begun by Tapping Reeve in 1784.[74] Litchfield is a small Connecticut town about thirty-five miles west of Hartford. In 1800, it was the fourth largest urban center in the state and a hub of local commerce. Reeve came there in 1773, quickly establishing himself as an energetic and successful practitioner. He also became a trainer of young lawyers. The number of students who found their way to his door was large by contemporary standards, and very likely it was this increase that prompted him to have a small building constructed for them next to his own house. There he could deliver a series of lectures. In other words, his law school was something like a natural outgrowth of the clerkship system of legal training. For many years it flourished. Like other schools of equivalent ambition, it offered a more systematic program of instruction in law than ordinary apprenticeship did, and the method succeeded in a measure. Students came to the Litchfield school from virtually every American state, even if not in great numbers.[75] The institution expanded modestly. Other lecturers were found. Notes from their lectures were taken by students, and some have survived. They show that the basic areas of the common law were being taught. Blackstone's *Commentaries* stood at the head of the legal works set before the students, but the library at Litchfield included others of the classic common law texts—St. German's *Doctor and Student,* for instance.[76] At the very least, students who read St. German's famous work while they were at the Litchfield institution would have been introduced to the law of nature. Very likely, the same pattern prevailed at most of the proprietary schools that opened in the years before the Civil War. The Litchfield Law School itself closed its doors in 1833. Others survived a bit longer, but none of them survived to modern times.

What replaced them, eventually driving these institutions out of legal education, was the growth of college-based schools of law. The movement started slowly. Courses dealing with moral philosophy or even natural law itself were offered in some universities even before the Revolution.[77] A more basic, if slow, change began afterward. George Wythe taught law at Virginia's William & Mary College in the 1780s. Columbia (or King's College) in New York, the University of Maryland in Baltimore, the University of Pennsylvania in Philadelphia, and the University of Transylvania in Lexington, Kentucky, all made provision for separate instruction in law in the years immediately following Independence. Harvard College in Massachusetts began to offer special instruction in law, beginning with the 1817 decision of the Overseers to "the establishment of a school for the instruction of students at law."[78]

Out of these hesitant developments eventually emerged the inevitable claims to have been "the first" among proper university law schools.[79] We need not pause to measure the validity of these claims, but it is important to note that instruction at all of the early law schools attached to universities provided students with some contact with the law of nature. That is shown by the books assigned. Very likely, more than brief mention of the subject's existence was made. If the introductory law lectures that have survived represent what was taught, it is clear that educators paid attention to principles found in the law of nature.[80] One of the reasons then given to aspiring lawyers for making the choice of university instruction in law was that it lifted the sights of students above the level of law office routine. Some of that enlargement in perspective included the law of nature. The subject did not occupy the same position it did in European universities, that certainly is true. But it would not have been ignored altogether. Only after the 1870s and the start of the movement toward the "case method" begun by Dean Langdell of Harvard Law School did the law of nature gradually fade from the immediate view of the students who studied there.[81] Identifying the date when this happened and explaining fully the reasons for it are scholarly tasks that remain to be done satisfactorily, but the law of nature's well-nigh total eclipse from the basic curriculum in American law schools had not happened before the outbreak of the Civil War.

American Legal Treatises

The argument that the law of nature was widely known among American lawyers prior to the Civil War is supported also by the treatises and other legal works they wrote during the first half of the nineteenth century. Like English lawyers, American lawyers who aspired to publish works of scholarship mixed occasional references to natural law in with their descriptions of the common law and legal practice. Just as one finds with English lawyers, a list of American lawyers who mentioned and dealt with the law of nature with respect in their own works proves to be quite a long one. It includes Joseph K. Angell (1794–1857),[82] Henry Baldwin (1780–1844),[83] William Barton (1754–1817),[84] Horace Binney (1780–1875),[85] Jesse Bledsoe (1776–1836),[86] John Bouvier (1787–1851),[87] H. H. Brackenridge (1748–1816),[88] John C. Calhoun (1782–1850),[89] Samuel P. Chase (1808–1873),[90] Daniel Chipman (1765–1850),[91] Nathaniel Chipman (1752–1843),[92] Thomas Cooper (1759–1839),[93] Nathan Dane (1752–1835),[94] John Drayton (1766–1822),[95] William John Duane (1780–1865),[96] John Duer (1782–1858),[97] John Dunlap (ca.1793–1858),[98] John Goodenow (1782–1838),[99] Frederick Grimké (1791–1863),[100] Thomas Herttell (1771–1849),[101] Francis Hilliard (1806–1878),[102] Henry Hitchcock (1791–1839),[103] David Hoffman (1784–1854),[104] Joseph Hopkinson (1770–1842),[105] Charles Humphreys (1775–1830),[106] John C. Hurd (1816–1892),[107] Charles Ingersoll (1782–1862),[108] Benjamin James (1768–1825),[109] James Kent (1763–1847),[110] Hugh Swinton Legaré (1797–1843),[111] Francis Lieber (1800–1872),[112] Samuel Livermore (1786–1833),[113] Edward Livingston (1764–1836),[114] Edward Deering Mansfield (1801–1880),[115] Luther Martin (1748–1826),[116] Daniel Mayes (1792–1861),[117] Mordecai M'Kinney (1796–1867),[118] John Barbee Minor (1813–1895),[119] Theophilus Parsons (1750–1813),[120] Josiah Quincy (1772–1864),[121] John Randolph (1773–1833),[122] William Rawle (1759–1836),[123] Tapping Reeve (1744–1823),[124] Spencer Roane (1762–1822),[125] Jesse Root (1736–1822),[126] William Sampson (1764–1836),[127] Theodore Sedgwick (1811–1859),[128] Lemuel Shaw (1781–1861),[129] Samuel Southard (1787–1842),[130] Lysander Spooner (1808–1887),[131] Joseph Story (1779–1845),[132] James Sullivan (1744–1808),[133] Zephaniah Swift (1759–1823),[134] Roger Taney (1777–1864),[135] Harry Toulmin (1766–1823),[136] Henry St. George Tucker (1780–1848),[137] James M. Walker (1813–1854),[138] Timothy Walker (1802–1856),[139] Emory Washburn (1800–1877),[140] Daniel Webster

(1782–1806),[141] Samuel Whiting (fl. 1815),[142] and Warren Woodson (1796–1868).[143] This list of lawyers is by no means exhaustive, but surely it is long enough to demonstrate the general acceptance among American lawyers of the law of nature's existence and worth.

As was true for the English evidence, the American survey did not turn up any examples of lawyers who denied the existence of the law of nature. Chapter 6 illustrates the existence of doubt among some lawyers about natural law's clarity and thus its value in litigation. Skepticism about its utility did surface from time to time in the American case law. An occasional jibe that some of its features—as in the strict prohibitions of usury—were products of "ecclesiastical superstition" also appeared in forensic debate.[144] However, these were exceptions. It would be a mistake to emphasize them and neglect the more normal praise for natural law principles. Praise was the rule in the treatises, and little of even the indirect sort of criticism that appears in some American cases is found in them.

Conclusion

Somewhat more so than for English lawyers, entry into the legal profession in the United States brought with it a general familiarity with the law of nature. The years before the founding of an American nation had seen an increase throughout the Atlantic world in the production of works devoted to explication and enlargement of natural law's scope. Works by Continental writers on the law of nature were imported, translated, and known in the New World, just as they were in England. There is too much evidence of natural law's popularity to write it off as irrelevant to the practice of law. We must look at the cases.

It bears stressing as an initial matter that during these early years of the American Republic lawyers had not thrown off the yokes of either religion or the common law. They had not relegated Christianity to the sphere of private life. Indeed, they regarded it as an integral part of their law.[145] Nor had they discarded the English law. Blackstone may have needed some revision—or at least some "updating"—to bring it into harmony with conditions in the New World, but his *Commentaries,* including their coverage of natural law, were regarded with something like reverence by American lawyers. Most of the American states also enacted statutes after the War of Independence expressly receiving the English common law.

For a history of the law of nature, the first of these two points is probably the more important. Atheism makes acceptance of the law of nature's existence and legitimacy difficult, even if its recognition may be possible in theory. In 1776 or 1850, however, there were few vocal atheists at the Bar. When Joel Prentiss Bishop came to write an introductory work for law students in the 1860s, he devoted respectful attention to the "Law of God." He repeatedly mentioned the role that divine law played in the jurisprudence of the nation.[146] This level of attention was not at all unusual. It is no source of wonder, therefore, that the law of nature should have appeared in the arguments and decisions in cases argued before American courts of law. It was widely regarded as a legitimate source of law, one that God had implanted in men's hearts. God's wisdom was also evident in the natural and created order. That it should turn up in various places in the law reports would have been no more than a logical deduction from recognition of that order's existence. Men thought it obvious. In what circumstances it appeared and how it was put to use in the American cases are the questions explored in Chapter 6.

6

The Law of Nature in American Courts

I N DRAFTING A CONSTITUTION for their nation in 1787, the delegates to the Philadelphia Convention moved away from the invocation of natural rights and natural law that had figured prominently in the Declaration of Independence. They created a document a classical jurist would have described as part of the positive, or municipal, law of the Republic. Its provisions were the work of men, most of them subject to change, rather than recognitions of the existence of God's unchangeable endowment of all his creatures with instincts, reason, and rights.[1]

Intended for a different purpose than the Declaration and meant to have the force of positive law in all aspects of national government, the Constitution did not reject the law of nature. It simply did not use language taken from it, as the Declaration had. This must have been a conscious choice. The Bill of Rights, agreed to in 1791, did move a little way toward greater coincidence with the law of nature. The guarantee of "due process of law," without which a person could not be deprived of life, liberty, or property (Amend. V), came close to statements found in natural law treatises. It is noteworthy, however, that the drafters put a guarantee of freedom of worship in terms of a prohibition against congressional action establishing religion, rather than of an affirmation of an individual right to freedom of conscience or spiritual liberty (Amend. I). Then, and for many years afterward, it was sometimes said that the constitutional provisions were "declarative of natural law,"[2] and that has always been true in a sense. They gave more definite shape to certain natural law principles. From a jurist's perspective, however, what the Constitution provided was meant to be part of the positive law of the Republic.

Some of the state constitutions adopted at the time of American independence, by contrast, included provisions that appear to have been
taken from contemporary works on the law of nature and nations.
Virginia's constitution provides a prominent example. It began with
language drawn from the law of nature, declaring "that all men are by
nature equally free and independent and have certain inherent rights."
It went on to include "the means of acquiring and possessing property"
among those rights.[3] The constitution of New Hampshire similarly
provided that all men have "certain natural, essential, and inherent
rights," stating further that among them was the right of "possessing and
protecting property."[4] Incorporation of rights associated with ownership
and protection of property provided the most frequent reminder of the
law of nature's place in America's law, but appearances of the law of
nature in that regard were not limited to such rights. Maryland's constitution, for example, declared that "monopolies are odious, contrary
to the spirit of a free government and the principles of commerce, and
ought not to be."[5] The Massachusetts "Form of Government" promised a
"certain remedy" to its citizens "to obtain right and justice freely."[6] That
provision would have been regarded in natural law thought as compensation for the citizen's surrender of a full right of self-defense.

Constitutional articles like these took principles drawn from the natural law directly into the law of the states. They did not appear in the
same form within the federal Constitution or even the subsequent Bill
of Rights. Perhaps the compromise over the issue of slavery's status that
was the price for Southern acceptance of the federal Constitution best
explains its more limited and specific character.[7] Or perhaps the federal
provisions reflected the opinion expressed by Chancellor Kent that a
strong constitution can actually be weakened by the addition of too many
"ethical and political aphorisms."[8] Whatever the reasons, there was a
marked difference between the federal Constitution's provisions and the
statements taken directly from the law of nature that were placed into
several of the state constitutions. This fact has inevitably given rise to
differences of opinion among historians about the status and relevance
of the law of nature in the history of American constitutional law.[9] Did
it leave any role for natural law at the national level?

Some of those same differences of opinion existed at the time of the
founding. A relevant question was: What part, if any, would the law of
nature play in the courts? It was a live question during the early years

of the Republic. The problem can most easily be seen in a constitutional provision that came close to a direct statement of one of the principles of the law of nature. Article I, Section 9 [3] declared, "No Bill of Attainder or ex post facto Law shall be passed." That no person should be punished or deprived of property by retroactive legislation was a staple part of nature's law. *Nulla poena sine lege.*[10] This rule was not thought, however, to rule out all retrospective legislation. The starting point for analysis was against its legality. Legislation was meant to control how men acted. By definition, a statute could not control how men acted before it had been enacted. Strictly speaking, therefore, retrospective legislation could be no law at all.[11] Sometimes, however, it turns out that legislation that deals with past acts is actually necessary, as in the creation of a statute of limitations or the grant of a pardon for offenses already committed.[12] By definition, they relate to and have an effect on what is past. The problem therefore lies in knowing on which side of the line a retrospective legislative act falls. This problem came before American courts soon enough—most notably in the famous case of *Calder v. Bull,* decided by the U.S. Supreme Court in 1798.[13] The opinions delivered in that case would have an effect on the character of judicial review of legislation in the new nation and also on many historians' understanding of the place of the law of nature in American jurisprudence.

Calder v. Bull

In 1795, the Connecticut legislature set aside a decree of a probate court in a will contest, granting a new hearing of the matter in dispute, which required deciding which of two wills was the true expression of the decedent's last wishes. The new hearing was held, resulting in an outcome that differed from the first decision, and this second proceeding was affirmed on appeal by Connecticut's supreme court of errors. The matter was then brought before the U.S. Supreme Court. The appellant's claim was that the legislature's grant of a new trial had been an ex post facto law prohibited by Article I § 10 of the federal Constitution. The case could have been disposed of by describing what the Connecticut legislature had done as a judicial act. It would then have been as though the legislature had simply acted as a further court of appeal. That was not precluded—in fact, it was encouraged—by past practice in the state, and the possibility was indeed mentioned in the opinions. However,

Justice Samuel Chase saw in the case the chance to state his own views about the limits of legislative authority, limits he thought were required by the law of nature. He did so in strident terms. His words were reminiscent of some of Sir Edward Coke's dicta in *Bonham's Case*.[14] Chase invoked the existence of "certain vital principles" of government that would "overrule an apparent and flagrant abuse of legislative power." He added that "[a]n act of the legislature (for I cannot call it a law) contrary to the great first principles of the social compact, cannot be considered a rightful exercise of legislative authority."[15] He took two common examples from the institutional literature: a law making one man a judge in his own cause and a law taking property from A and giving it to B.

Despite these principles, which might seem to have required him to invalidate the Connecticut decree, Chase nevertheless found in favor of upholding the action taken by the legislature. His reasoning was that the first probate court's decree had given the winning party only a right to acquire the property in dispute under the will and that this did not rise to the level of a "perfect and exclusive right." It thus fell short of establishing the appellant's vested right in the property bequeathed to him.[16] In other words, until his title to the goods of the decedent had been perfected, the appellant had held no right to them that the "great first principles of the social compact" would protect. Natural law's prohibitions did not extend that far.

This view now seems slightly confused, and it may be. Determining exactly what Chase meant in his invocation of the law of nature has itself given rise to controversy among historians.[17] However, his position was not unprecedented. His words mirrored almost exactly the response of European jurists to the problem of retrospective legislation. Bartolus of Saxoferrato, for example, described the question of where the line should be drawn between what could and could not lawfully be done as a "doubtful and daily one" in practice.[18] The jurists struggled with it, eventually arriving at what seems to have been a workable solution.[19] They divided civil from criminal matters and adopted a rule against legislation punishing men for crimes that had not been unlawful when they were committed. With civil legislation, the ordinary presumption against retrospective legislation was the same. However, if the legislature made it plain that its action was meant to have retrospective effect, that would be a different matter. The legislation would not necessarily violate a principle of natural justice unless it upset a "matter that was past, decided, and completed."[20] For example, a statute of limitations enacted to bar the claim of a son to recover chattels bequeathed to him in his father's will that was made after expiration of the applicable time period would survive the test. The claim would fail. The statute would rightly be applied against the son's claim because it did not bar a vested right, only an inchoate claim to recover the chattels from the father's estate. It would not be a matter "past, decided, and completed." That was, roughly speaking, the situation in *Calder v. Bull.* The Connecticut legislature's act of quashing one hearing and requiring another had only affected claims, not vested rights. This act was not, therefore, the same thing as taking A's property and giving it to B. Because it was clear that the legislature's order had been meant to cover this dispute, the ordinary presumption that legislative action only affected future conduct was overcome. The legislature's action did not, therefore, run afoul of natural law.

The other three justices whose opinions were recorded in *Calder v. Bull* did not follow Chase down this well-worn road. Justice James Iredell, in particular, took the view that the words of the Constitution were the sole proper measure for determining the case's outcome. Adoption of a written constitution that had the power of positive law thus meant a break with the past.[21] Now the relevant question would be what the Constitution required. The words in question were "[N]o state shall pass any ex post facto law." Under the common understanding of the time, Iredell held, "the true construction of the prohibition extends to criminal, not to civil cases."[22] Natural law was irrelevant to this case. He also went out of his way, as Chase himself had, to deal with the larger question of the law of nature's place in constitutional jurisprudence. "It is true," he wrote, "that some speculative jurists have held that a legislative act against natural justice must, in itself, be void."[23] But "the ablest and the purest men have differed" in determining what natural justice required; it furnished "no fixed standard" by which it could be applied. In his view, the authority of American courts in this regard was also limited. They were given the power only to determine whether the legislature had "pursue[d] the authority delegated to them" by the Constitution.[24] Under the system of government established in the United States, therefore, judges did not have the authority to invalidate legislation simply because it was "inconsistent with the abstract principles of natural justice."[25] Justice Chase had, therefore, been wrong from the start.

Although this difference in opinion had no impact on the actual outcome of the case, it could in theory have had important results in other constitutional adjudication. Iredell seemed to reject use of the law of nature, at least any use that was made in determining the validity of legislative acts. He renounced what Chase's opinion endorsed. The late David Currie described the difference of opinion between the two justices as "the opening salvo in a running battle that never has simmered down completely."[26] In his view, one shared by other commentators, the dominant view has been in line with Iredell's opinion. It rejects natural law as a practical tool to be used in judicial review of legislation. It may be said—as Currie did say—that in practice some of the U.S. Supreme Court's decisions have veered very far away from Iredell's opinion. They have moved beyond the words of the Constitution itself. Admitting this, one need not necessarily follow Currie in concluding, as he does, that the justices have been "effectively following Chase." The outcomes in some Supreme Court cases of recent vintage have had little connection with the law of nature as it was understood in the eighteenth century. Nor is it correct to ascribe the "laissez-faire excesses" of the first third of the twentieth century to the law of nature as it had been understood a century before.[27] Natural law did not authorize judges to strike down legislation because it conflicted with their own views of desirable public policy.

For immediate purposes of tracing the role played by the law of nature in early American court practice—our main task—too much should not be read into the language Justice Iredell used in the case. The essential point is the limited scope of the outcome in *Calder v. Bull*. The majority opinion did not rule out use of natural law in other contexts than that of determining the constitutional validity of legislative action. That had never been its major role in English or European court practice, as has been shown in Chapters 2 and 4, and nothing in Iredell's opinion precluded reference to it outside the sphere of constitutional adjudication. The holding in *Calder v. Bull* left that possibility open. American lawyers and judges subsequently seized the opportunity, even in cases taken before the U.S. Supreme Court.[28] The widely held opinion that the written Constitution was "not declaratory of any new law, but confirmed . . . ancient rights and principles" even left the door open for occasional consideration of natural law principles in constitutional interpretation.[29]

Moreover, at least in a technical sense, Iredell's opinion did not bind the supreme courts of the various states. The balance of opinion among state court justices seems to have taken the same view of natural law's place in American law that Iredell had.[30] They did not wish to "jump off the constitutional deep end."[31] But that choice was not unanimous. Kentucky's supreme court came close to Chase's view by holding that even if the judges could not substitute the law of nature for the Constitution, they could apply it to understand and implement constitutional guarantees.[32] California's supreme court adopted the view expressed by Justice Chase more directly in holding that an "Act for the Protection of Actual Settlers" was invalid because its provisions were "in violation of natural justice," although they were not contrary to any specific provision in the state or federal constitutions.[33]

The possibility of relying on the law of nature came to the fore in early cases of governmental "takings" of private property by right of eminent domain. The right of the government to expropriate the land of its citizens in service of the common good of the community was generally conceded in America. It had a long history in Western law.[34] The question at issue in the American courts was whether the government was under an obligation to pay for what it took. Some of the states had not enacted a constitutional requirement that compensation had to be paid to the persons from whom property was taken.[35] In these states, before the Fifth Amendment's requirement of just compensation was incorporated into law that bound the states, awards for property taken for public use had to be based on some other theory. Otherwise, no payment would be due. Where the legislative act of expropriation included no express provision requiring payment, the most prominent of the theories available was that the government's power was controlled by principles drawn from the law of nature. Natural justice required compensation for property taken. As one lawyer put it, perhaps echoing what he had read in John Locke,[36] although the laws "recognize the power of the legislature to be supreme, [they] do not admit it to be arbitrary."[37] For a state to take a citizen's property without paying for it was an arbitrary act. It followed that payment for expropriation had to be made; courts read that requirement into legislative acts of expropriation. Here natural law prevailed. It supplied an unexpressed term to the acts of a state legislature—requiring that a fair compensation be paid for property taken.

Applications of the Law of Nature

Although they loom large in public consciousness and in the views of many academic lawyers, cases involving constitutional law like those in *Calder v. Bull* have always occupied a relatively small part of legal practice. Looking beyond them permits a clearer survey to be made of natural law's place in ordinary cases found in the reports of the American state courts. Their quantity, huge even for the period before the Civil War (1861–1865), has presented the only real obstacle to drawing conclusions about the place of the law of nature in American jurisprudence. That magnitude is a result of the America's federal system, as well as a consequence of the country's growing population. Each state had its own courts. Within limits, each state was free to enact its own rules of law and practice. The magnitude of the field can be daunting to the slow-witted researcher. Computer "word searches" make the project feasible, however, even though the large numbers make it more difficult to be sure how representative the results are. What follows is an account of what the reported cases show. Most of the evidence (though by no means all) deals with private law, and in this sense it is fully in accord with what appeared in the European *decisiones* and the English reports.

General References

Two apparently contradictory impressions of the American attitude toward the law of nature emerged from judicial descriptions of it. The first and strongest testifies to the overwhelming respect normally accorded to its place in the legal system. Fulsome praise for natural law's foundational role in practice appears in many decided cases, and American judges often went quite far in expressing their admiration. The second is the reverse: criticism of natural law's perceived uncertainty as a useful guide to deciding hard cases. Some American judges, rather like Justice Iredell in *Calder v. Bull*, occasionally became impatient with its lack of specificity, and they expressed that impatience in their opinions. Even among its exponents, its lessons for immediate legal problems could sometimes seem uncertain. These critics did not dispute natural law's existence, at least openly, but they did dispute its utility.[38] That sort of workaday impatience did not figure as often in either the European *decisiones* or the English reports.

Examples of the first characteristic, unstinted praise for the law of nature, recur throughout the American reports. One federal judge described it as "of origin divine" and "obligatory upon individuals," finishing with the encomium "How great, how important, how interesting are these truths! They announce to a free people how solemn their duties are."[39] Another described it as "paramount to all other laws."[40] A California judge similarly described natural law as "an eternal rule to all men, binding upon legislatures as well as others."[41] A judge in a New Jersey case saw fit to describe it as "the only true foundation of all the social rights."[42] A Tennessee judge expressed the opinion that "all human laws depend" on "the foundations of the law of nature and the law of revelation."[43] These are but examples of many more that could be cited to show the respect commonly accorded to the law of nature by American lawyers. Like English lawyers, they often stressed the harmony that existed between natural law and positive or enacted law. The law of nature enabled equity and the dictates of reason to take effect.[44] Chapter 5's survey of early American legal literature and education took note of this sort of praise. It also showed its face in the case law.

The second view, expressing an impatience with the law of nature's actual utility in legal disputes, is found less often in judicial opinions, but it did surface from time to time, and it did have an apparent effect on the outcome of some cases. Diderot (1713–1784), the French encyclopedist, had expressed doubt about the possibility of discovering the exact consequences of the concept's principles,[45] and this source of doubt called forth an occasional echo in the courts of the New World. Some American judges pointed to apparent inconsistencies in its reach to dismiss its relevance in the case before them, noting, for example, that although usury was said to be contrary to the law of nature, the Bible itself had allowed Jews to take usury from strangers (Deut. 23:20). This being so, one New York judge concluded, usury could not be immoral or unlawful in all cases.[46] Sometimes American judges explicitly refused to enter into a controversy about natural law's reach, noting pointedly that the positive law on a question was clear and decisive.[47] And sometimes they specifically dismissed natural law as irrelevant to the task of deciding the lawsuit before them.[48] The apparent contradiction between positive law's requirement of valuable consideration in contracts and the natural law principle that men are bound to fulfill their promises, for instance, was used as an example to suggest that the law of nature did not always provide a useful tool for decision.[49] The supposedly obligatory character of a promise under the law of nature now meant little in terms of the outcome of litigation unless the promise was supported by legally sufficient consideration. In contract cases, it was said, a lawyer therefore invoked the law of nature in vain. The positive law was against it.

The great majority of comments like these were simply meant to emphasize that the positive law was normally the proper and sufficient tool for determining the outcome of a dispute. Few lawyers would have disputed that. Not all cases, however, left it at that. One annoyed federal judge saw fit to take note in his opinion that an "ingenious counsel" had resorted to repeated invocation of the law of nature in presenting his arguments. Apparently exasperated by the length and irrelevance of what he had heard, he dismissed all of it, stating that the "high sounding words" had "only serve[d] to round a period and fill up a vacuum in the argument."[50] He was impatient, not knowing where all the talk left him. He felt at sea. Of course, this impatience did not cause him, or the other American judges who had doubts about the utility of natural law, to dispute its existence. These disputes might come in time. Indeed, they did. But that was the future. For the moment, critical comments like his were but straws in the wind. Ordinarily, natural law was invoked with the expectation that it would matter.

Procedural Law

As a protection against judicial or legislative overreaching, the law of nature came to the aid of litigants in several ways. Prior chapters have dealt with some of them, showing the mixed results that followed from judicial recognition of natural law principles like the requirement of adequate citation. That was one purpose it served in European courts, and the American cases followed a similar pattern. In the course of time, this function would largely be brought within the Due Process clause of the federal Constitution, but before that happened, the law of nature served the same purpose. In 1852, for example, the U.S. Supreme Court case quashed a state proceeding in which service had been made by leaving the judicial summons at the defendant's house, apparently in accord with a state statute authorizing the practice when personal service could not be secured. This action was attacked as contrary to principles of natural justice.[51] And so it was held to be. Justice Daniel's opinion in the case made no mention of Iredell's opinion in *Calder v. Bull*. It rested on general principles of procedural fairness found in the law of nature rather than on a specific constitutional guarantee.

Several state cases also used the same principle.[52] The judges who rendered these decisions rarely rested them on the law of nature alone; they almost always cited other authorities, too—mostly decided cases. But as had been true in English and Continental courts, the law of nature was often thought important enough to include alongside authorities from the positive law. As Justice Daniel remarked after reviewing the existing case law, the legal rule he espoused "does not depend merely upon adjudged cases; it has a better foundation; it rests upon a principle of natural justice."[53] Somehow—he did not venture to say exactly how—the law of nature had an impact on the result.

Where positive law existed, making express reference to principles of natural law was not a habit practiced (nor a result uniformly reached) by all American judges.[54] What Justice Daniel did in this case was not, however, a rare occurrence. It occupied a place in many judicial opinions. It was called upon, for example, to quash divorce proceedings in states where only one of the parties was domiciled. For a state's court to enter a divorce decree against the other spouse, a person not then subject to its jurisdiction "would be void on the plainest principles of natural law" as well as contrary to prior cases.[55] The same principles were also called upon to quash proceedings in which a party purportedly bound by a prior court's proceedings had not been cited and given a chance to appear.[56] Judicial opinions like these normally cited precedents from existing case law at the same time they invoked the law of nature. As we have seen repeatedly, this was the normal pattern of decision in virtually all courts where the law of nature was expressly invoked.

The law of nature also figured in an illuminating if unusual situation, one that tested the limits of *Calder v. Bull*. It involved the permissibility of requiring an oath of those who sought admission to practice law that they had taken no part in the act of dueling. The Alabama legislature had passed an act requiring the oath. It was one way of suppressing that pernicious but seemingly ineradicable practice, and the statute was challenged as a violation of both Alabama's constitution and basic principles of natural law.[57] Objections to the oath were taken on several grounds: it required a person to testify against himself; it flouted the constitutional provision that no one could be convicted of a crime except by a jury of one's peers; it amounted to an ex post facto law involving criminal conduct; and it denied the equality of rights that was guaranteed to all free citizens of a free land.

The challenge succeeded. Conceding that no man had a natural right to practice law, the supreme court of Alabama nevertheless held that the statutory requirement of the oath was unenforceable. In so doing, the decision mentioned but skirted any question of the applicability of the holding in *Calder v. Bull*.[58] At least in some measure, its conclusions rested on natural law principles that the oath was said to violate. Imposing the oath amounted to a penalty without trial.

Enthusiasts should not exaggerate. As in the Continental *decisiones,* most challenges to legislation based solely on the law of nature failed. They were easy to make but harder to sustain. An illustrative example comes from a Massachusetts decision of 1819.[59] At a time before general incorporation statutes had become the norm, the legislature had granted a charter to a bank for a term of twenty years, apparently then a normal length of time for such grants. While that term ran, the legislature then enacted a statute that continued the existence of all corporations, including banks, for three years after the end of the original term. This extension was made for a limited purpose: to allow corporations to sue, to be sued, and otherwise to be wound up. The same statute excluded any right to continue normal banking operations during the three-year extension. The directors of the Essex bank challenged the limitation in this new statute as an abridgement of a vested right. Their counsel, Leverett Saltonstall, argued that the act was "retrospective as to the Essex Bank, [and] retrospective laws are repugnant to natural justice and, strictly speaking, are no laws."[60] He cited cases, including several from the U.S. Supreme Court, in support of that position.[61] The Massachusetts court nevertheless turned back his challenge. This was a general act, and its purpose was to allow the concerns of the bank existing while the twenty-year term ran to be "properly adjusted" at its end.[62] In the nature of things, a reasonable time was required for proper adjustments to be made, and the statute's preclusion of further banking activity during that term was fully consistent with this purpose. Indeed, the legislative extension served a beneficent purpose: "to provide that corporations should not avoid their obligations by ceasing to exist."[63]

The Massachusetts court could surely have reached the opposite result. This legislative act was undoubtedly retrospective. It changed the terms of the initial act of incorporation. In civil cases the starting point for analysis was the long-established rule that unless the statute itself was clearly intended to do otherwise, the presumption was that it did not affect fully established rights. Such a reading of the facts of this case was open to the judges. The statute at issue did not state that it extended to past acts, and the Essex Bank had a plausible claim to hold a vested right. Its incorporation for a term of twenty years was an act of the legislature. The extension might also be said to work to the detriment of the bankers by subjecting them to fresh claims. It could thus be said to be a penalty for past acts. Rejecting this argument, however, Chief Justice Parker held that the bank's charter permitted its officers to incur debts and that "the legislature . . . had a right, if it was not their duty, to provide the means of enforcing this moral obligation."[64] It made perfect sense to provide some extra time for that purpose to be accomplished. The law of nature should not be invoked in the service of iniquity, Parker thought, and to have applied the normal presumption would in practice actually have opened the door to iniquity. In his view, the legislature's action was fully justified by principles of natural justice.

American courts were customarily cautious in evaluating any interpretation, even one taken from the law of nature, where iniquity would have been the result.[65] Parker's caution recurs throughout the American law reports. It was one of the reasons that courts held, as in *Calder v. Bull,* that interpretation of natural law normally gave way to municipal law.[66] The purpose of the law of nature could be twisted by treating its precepts as if they were hard and fast rules instead of abstract and general principles. One thing judges familiar with natural law did was to make sure that this sort of twisting did not happen. The law of nature was meant to promote the well-being of human society, not its upset.

Property Law

This chapter has already taken notice of some of the guarantees of a right to own and defend private property that were found in state constitutions at the start of the American Republic. They were a strong expression of one aspect of the law of nature, and it was an aspect that mattered a great deal to the nation's founders. Of course, it was then, and is now, a contentious subject—then because of the question of slavery (surveyed below), and now because of resistance to changes in political climate that have accompanied the growth of a welfare state. The modern "law of takings" bears the scars. For the chronicler of the law of nature's place in American law, however, the subject is better traced in simpler questions involving ownership of real and personal property—in other words, by looking at the private law side of things.[67] Perhaps surprisingly for a source of law so often cited by modern critics for its broad defense of property rights, the law of nature was rarely called upon successfully to limit the validity of social legislation in the years before the Civil War. It was used in cases involving the requirement of governmental compensation for outright takings of property, but rarely extended beyond that. More often it was used to promote principles of sociability and peace. In the great majority of cases, statutes that regulated conduct and commerce were regarded as serving that legitimate purpose.[68]

A look at the cases shows, however, that the law of nature did hold a place in establishing rights in real and personal property in the New World. Except for the troublesome claims of Native Americans,[69] the land and what was on (or under) the land were open to appropriation by settlers. The law of nature was seemingly made for exactly this circumstance, and in the New World it could be applied to fill an immediate need. Its invocation had been neither so necessary nor so normal in English and European kingdoms, where land titles were more settled. There, property rights under the positive law had become fixed, better establishing who owned what than could be true in the New World. In America, there was more space for the law of nature to apply.

The clearest example of natural law's utility, one known to generations of American law students because of *Pierson v. Post*, the first case they were obliged to read in their class in Property Law, is that of animals *ferae naturae*.[70] Wild animals were *res nullius* under the law of nature, open to appropriation by the first person to reduce them to possession. In open spaces in America, this happened easily, since much land on which animals were found was itself unclaimed. On such land, successful hunters (or tamers) of wild animals acquired "a qualified property in them by the law of nature as well as the civil law."[71] So the hunter in

Pierson v. Post lost to an interloper because he had not reduced the fox to his control. That was where the law of nature drew the line.

In the more settled English conditions, a case like this was less likely to arise. Claims to capture wild animals based either upon customary right or asserted *ratione soli* by landowners—that is, claims based upon positive law—were the norm in England. These claims might prevail against the claims of hunters based upon the law of nature. Where hunters prevailed against landowners in England, as they sometimes did, the hunters themselves usually asserted rights based on immemorial usage. The availability of such claims made the law of nature less relevant in practice. Of course, the basic natural law principles were not forgotten.[72] They simply did not arise as often in practice as they would in the New World.

A second and similar American example arose in the early law of navigable waters, including the sea. The most famous case was *Arnold v. Mundy*.[73] It arose when the defendant took some oysters from the bed of the Raritan River. The owner of the adjacent land along the river, whose grant (he claimed) extended to the middle of the river, sued to recover their value. He asserted the rights of an owner of the soil. The case made its way to the supreme court of New Jersey, where one of the justices found it "as singular as it was unexpected" that a dispute over "a few bushels of oysters" should have raised "questions momentous in their nature, as well as in their magnitude." But so it did.[74] The court held that "by the law of nature, which is the only true foundation of all the social rights," as well as by the common law rightly understood, all flowing streams "for the purpose of passing and repassing, navigation, fishing, fowling, sustenance, and all other uses of the water and its products (a few things excepted) are common to all the citizens."[75] Rivers were "the great highways furnished by the great Creator for the use of the human race."[76] For this reason, the plaintiff as landowner had no valid claim to the oysters in the river until he himself had collected them. The defendant had done only what the law permitted, a permission anchored in the law of nature.

Though unusual in its facts, the New Jersey decision was not an isolated case. Nor did it deal with an unprecedented incident.[77] By the law of nature, flowing water and what was found in it were *res nullius*, open to use and appropriation by all. Undeniably there had long been exceptions—the "royal fish" in England, for instance. By custom and royal prerogative, they were the king's. But this custom never extended to the colonies, and in any event the special status of some fish only served to support the rule that by the law of nature all other fish were open to capture. So it was regularly held.[78] Today, the result of a similar court dispute over oysters or fish might actually be the same, unless the outcome had been altered by the many state and federal regulations that have come into existence.[79] A notable difference is that no mention would likely be made of the dictates of the law of nature in today's court test. In earlier times, its mention would have been quite normal.

A third example of the invocation of the law of nature in disputes over real and personal property is a more surprising one. A familiar rule of modern property law holds that in litigation, to establish a right in real or personal property, claimants must rely on the strength of their own title; they may not rely on weaknesses in the defendant's title. It is axiomatic. If the law were otherwise, no title would be secure once the property had passed out of the hands of any possessor whose title was less than perfect. Today's rule offers a way of avoiding contentious lawsuits and judicial paralysis. In the first century of the American experience, however, the same result was ascribed to the law of nature.[80] Doctrinally, the rule was connected with the principle of natural justice that no one should be deprived of his property without legal cause. The presumption of good title raised by peaceable possession helped reach that result.

To a modern critic, ascribing this presumption to the law of nature may seem a forced effort. The rule itself appears more like a principle of judicial economy, and in some of the early American cases, mentioning natural law looks more like a convenient way of allowing lawyers to make a show of learning drawn from works of Continental jurists than it does an argument requiring authority. This may be so, but in the early nineteenth century, the fact remains that the presumption was connected with a principle discovered within the natural law itself.

A fourth example is perhaps more surprising still. A long-settled rule of real property law holds that a restriction on the right of alienation may not be fastened upon a conveyance of full ownership of property—that is, a fee simple. Today the rule is normally said to rest upon a public policy favoring a free market in land.[81] In earlier days, however, the rule was more commonly said to rest upon an inconsistency between the grant of outright ownership of land and any attempt to restrict the incidents of that ownership. A grantor could not consistently do both at the same time. Today, this older rule thus appears to have been purely formal. Consequently, it has been subjected to criticism and exceptions. What has disappeared in the meantime is the connection once made between the earlier doctrine and the law of nature.

In earlier days, the identical substantive rule was often connected to natural law. Grotius held that the right to transfer the ownership of property was "of the law of nature,"[82] meaning that it formed part of the agreement by which a regime of private property had first been agreed upon. To Chancellor Kent, that agreement meant that a restraint on alienation of a fee simple was "a violent and unnatural state of things, and contrary to the nature and value of property and the inherent and universal love of independence."[83] An early Arkansas case similarly described a right to hold and transfer property held in fee simple as founded upon "a general principle of natural law."[84] Attempts to fetter its exercise actually ran counter to this principle of justice.

The exercise of a right to free alienation connected with the law of nature was also regarded as one source by which the American people had cast aside the remnants of feudalism in favor of a regime of allodial property and testamentary freedom. They had put into practice a principle derived from natural law: that attempts to fetter the ownership of land were contrary to "the very nature of property."[85] In the minds of contemporaries, the invalidation of restraints on alienation thus amounted to something more than the application of a formal rule. It was also more than a commitment to free markets in land. It was an assertion of human freedom to own property fully and freely, a freedom that was supported by their understanding of the tenets of natural law.

Laws of the Family and Succession

The law of nature played a lesser part in the family law of the United States than it did in England, although this does not mean it played no part at all. As in medieval Europe, one arena where is mattered involved kinship disqualifications that barred marriage between kin. Some ties of consanguinity were close, the closest being those between parent and child. That between brother and sister came second. These marriages were barred by the law of nature. Some ties were distant—between second cousins, for instance. Positive law might bar the latter, but the laws of God and nature did not. Many ties stood somewhere in between.

In this middle area, the United States lacked a unified system of law, and different states chose different regimes of matrimonial disqualification. What allowed them to coexist was the law of comity. It meant that forum states would ordinarily give judicial recognition to the public acts of their sister states.[86] It was not a mandatory doctrine, but ordinarily a marriage valid in the state where the parties lived and contracted together was treated as valid in other states—except, that is, if the marriage was between a man and woman whose union was barred by the law of nature.[87] Even if the marriage were valid where contracted, other states were not required to recognize the union. Principles of comity did not extend that far. Today something like the same principle still prevails, but it is said to depend only on "strong local public policy."[88] The law of nature and the law of God have disappeared.

They have also disappeared from most other areas of family law. In fact, the frequency with which the law of nature appeared in disputes over inheritance and familial relations seems always to have been less in America than in Continental Europe or England. Although there are echoes of the claim that the law of nature required parents to provide for their children in their last wills and testaments to be found among the early American cases,[89] they are relatively rare. Freedom of testation was established as a principle in the New World. The *legitim* took no place in American law.[90] A father's provision of a dowry for his daughters was a matter of choice on his part.[91] These characteristics of American law, rejecting what had been regarded as an obligation imposed by the law of nature in earlier centuries and on other continents, formed part of the same movement toward personal freedom—a movement that rejected primogeniture, tenurial guardianship, and entailed estates in land as incompatible with the creation of a nation of free men.[92]

Rejection of the limits on freedom of testation that the European jurists had derived from the law of nature did not mean, however, that it played no part whatsoever in the law of family relations in the new Republic. In fact, it was invoked. The accepted principle—that parents had a duty to care for their children by the law of nature—could make a difference in practice.[93] It was relevant, for example, in protecting the well-being of illegitimate children,[94] and it was used to help prevent an obligation owed to a child from being discharged in bankruptcy.[95] American statutes modeled upon the English Poor Laws imposed the parental duty as part of the positive law. American judges sometimes took notice of the connection between them and the law of nature, if only as a way of fortifying their imposition of a statutory duty. They held that "[t]he municipal law of the country is founded upon and enforces the precepts of natural law."[96] Therefore, a primary duty of care rested on the parents; it was morally right for the judges to act vigorously in putting that duty into force.

Today this same duty has become exclusively statutory. A commentator can say confidently that "financially able parents are statutorily required in every jurisdiction to provide support for their children."[97] In the modern cases, little attention is paid to discovering an underlying source of the requirement,[98] and when occasional academic writers have taken on that question, their explanations bear little resemblance to the reasons given in earlier centuries.[99] In fact, they sometimes seem either unaware of (or uncaring about) the close connections that once existed between their subject and the law of nature.

This kind of indifference was far from what happened in the early years of the Republic. Recognition of the law of nature in discussions of familial obligations was then almost instinctive among lawyers. Because of the existence of statutes that put the obligation into positive law form, however, it was usually mentioned only incidentally in the cases brought directly against the parents. Natural law was actually invoked more commonly in a variety of other circumstances. Most of them turn out to have involved assertions of rights by the parents, rather than claims for support brought against them. The argument was that the duty to support the child gave the parent a concomitant right to the child's person or property, a right the parent should be able to assert in court. For instance, it was relevant in child custody cases, some of which involved contests between husband and wife,[100] and others of which were brought by a parent against a stranger alleged to be detaining the child.[101] The former are particularly interesting because in more than a few of them, American judges invoked the law of nature to defeat the claims of the father against the child's mother. "[W]ith more regard to the harmony of nature," judges were able to rule emphatically that both parents held "equal rights to all the same enjoyments of life," including the children.[102] In the absence of special circumstances a child might not be restored to the father if the mother resisted. The reason given was that in nature, she had a duty and a right just as strong as the father's. The other notable feature of the cases is that some of them show American courts gradually moving away from a test dependent on the natural rights held by parents to one dependent on a judicial determination of what would serve "the best interest of the child."[103] That was the future. It would eventually eclipse any mention of the law of nature, and that direction is visible already in the first half of the nineteenth century.

Where the duty of support toward children was invoked against the parents in most of the American cases, the contested question dealt with the question of its legal reach. Particularly difficult were cases in which someone else had voluntarily furnished sustenance to a child and later sued the father to secure reimbursement. Did the father's natural law obligation extend that far? Or, put into its more common legal form, the question was: Did the law raise an implied promise to pay on the part of the parent because of the parent's natural obligation to the child?[104] The decisions on this point were not unanimous. In what seems to have been the majority, the duty was treated by judges simply as a moral obligation, sufficient as consideration to support a promise to pay for the child's necessaries but not in itself enough to create a judicially enforceable right that could be asserted against a nonconsenting father (or mother).[105] In other words, more than a duty based on the law of nature was required to give rise to a duty on the part of the parent that could later be asserted by someone who had acted on the parent's behalf.

As had long been true in the general law, the child's actions also counted in assessing the extent of the direct parental duty toward the child.[106] Leaving home out of disobedience might bring an end to it. So might the acquisition of riches by the child, though for different reasons. Under the common understanding of European jurists, the natural law had never required that such maintenance payments be made under all circumstances, and this feature was mirrored in the American cases.

The Law of Slavery

As noted at the start of this chapter, the constitutions of seven of the first American states contained declarations that all men were equally free by birth—called "free and equal clauses." They made possible frontal attacks on the institution of slavery that were more difficult with resources drawn from the law of nature alone. A few of them succeeded. But they had limited geographic scope. The institution of slavery was recognized by the positive law in the states where it mattered most, and the doctrine of *Somerset's Case*, which was generally followed in

American courts,[107] had held only that in the absence of positive law permitting slavery, the claims of a master over a slave were not enforceable. In states where slavery was part of the positive law, whether by custom or statute, *Somerset's Case* could actually point in the other direction: toward perpetuation of the institution.

There was contemporary disagreement about what the case and Lord Mansfield's opinion actually meant. Some men took its attitude to heart. In practice, the movement of Negro slaves back and forth between jurisdictions with different rules about their status also brought one inevitable result: dispute and confusion in the law. It put a strain on choice of law principles. This whole question was of the greatest moment in the history of the United States. It split the nation apart before and during the Civil War. It is also relevant to this study because, in the years before the question became a test of arms, regular use was made of the argument that slavery violated the law of nature, even though only a few lawyers contended that this violation was itself sufficient to bring an end to the institution of slavery.

The importance of the contest over slavery in American history has given rise to an enormous body of modern scholarly literature. Several studies within the field usefully discuss the law of nature's place in the great question, notably (but not only) the one written by the late Robert Cover.[108] His work is about slavery, not the law of nature. However, it deals learnedly with the case law, recognizes the place of the law of nature in the cases, and treats that subject with an uncommon recognition of both its strengths and limitations. I can do little more than praise his work and summarize the conclusions he and others have reached that are relevant to the subject of the present study.

The cases surveyed by works like Cover's demonstrate that the law of nature had an impact on the law of slavery. He himself reached that conclusion, although at the same time he regarded natural law's invocation as no more than a "tame, legalistic reflection of the driving force of the American Revolution."[109] Despite that low estimation of its effect, his book does show that it served the same purpose in American courts that it had in *Somerset's Case*. It denied any nonstatutory obligation of the courts of a free state to return a person claimed as a slave who had been brought into that same state. The force of deference to the application of natural law was even more clearly shown in the reverse situation: where a slave, leaving his home state, had gone to and acquired a domicile in a free state and then subsequently returned to the slave state from which he had come. The dominant Southern opinion in early court tests, articulated in a Kentucky case of 1820,[110] held that slavery did not "re-attach" to the former slave. "[F]reedom is the natural right of man," the Kentucky courts held, and once it had been established according to the laws of a person's domicile, only specific legislative action requiring reenslavement would suffice to overcome application of that principle in such cases.[111] In other words, the apparent result of applying the rationale in *Somerset's Case*—that the law of the forum controlled— did not apply in the reverse situation, precisely because natural law worked only *in favorem libertatis*.[112]

This way of seeing things necessarily left some holes open for the perpetuation of slavery; a temporary sojourn in the free state, for example, might not suffice to emancipate a slave who then returned to his home state. Likewise, express legislation by the state to which the freed slave returned from a free state might (and did) change the result.[113] Where statutes were enacted to perpetuate slavery in this reverse situation, positive law in effect "overruled" the law of nature. Until that took place, however, the freed slave retained his liberty despite his return. In this example, the student of the law of nature's history, assuming he can fix his attention on his chosen subject, must see a concrete legal effect made possible by the natural law.

This is not the only relevant matter produced by a survey of the evidence. That men were free by nature was an idea that, although imperfectly realized in practice, nonetheless stood as a guide to action and a reproach to societies that permitted slavery. Long centuries where slavery had been treated as a fact of life did not sanctify what was contrary to principles of morality, any more than any violation of natural justice in any system of criminal procedure would make right that system's inherent fault. Judges might not have a right to overturn settled practices, but the settled practices would still be wrong. In the climate of American life, particularly as tensions arising from expansion of the nation's territory upset the status quo apparently reached at the founding, the possibility of wider use of the law of nature opened up. Men, whom Cover called "Constitutional utopians," seized the chance.[114] So it was that Lysander Spooner (1808–1887), the reclusive but outspoken lawyer from Massachusetts, could contended that "there is and can be correctly speaking no law but natural law," and that natural law can "spare no vestige of that system of human slavery, which now claims to exist by authority of law."[115]

Most of the arguments by men who held opinions similar to Spooner's took place outside courtrooms, of course, but a few worked their way into a legal arena, especially in dealing with the constitutionally problematic Fugitive Slave Laws.[116] In them, the men who thought that the law of nature and the American Constitution should themselves be read to "outlaw" slavery encouraged more reluctant judicial allies to search for a way to go part of the distance with them. The decisions of the antebellum U.S. Supreme Court did not encourage these efforts, but the utopians were not deterred. Nor were they impressed by the arguments of slavery's defenders: that natural law principles either actually supported slavery or amounted to "unmeaning twaddle."[117] In the end they prevailed. This is not the only time in human history that ideas drawn from natural law once regarded as hopelessly utopian have ultimately won the day.

In a study of the law of nature, these great issues should not entirely overshadow the ordinary place it occupied outside the purview of constitutional law. Outside was its normal home, and even in cases involving slavery it sometimes played a prosaic but not negligible role. The law of nature was invoked, for example, to allow a right of self-defense to slaves subjected to an attack by their masters or overseers. The master was entitled to demand obedience from the slave and to punish him for refusal to carry out a lawful command, but he was not entitled to assault the slave and to put him in danger of loss of life or limb. Slaves "in common with all human beings" held "certain natural rights, and among these is that of self-protection or self-defence."[118] It was no crime for them to exercise that right. How much this meant in daily life is hard to know. The question of necessity was usually submitted to a jury. The natural law–based doctrine was, at the least, better than the alternative.

In much the same way, it was held that killing a slave could be treated as murder under the criminal law,[119] though detailed research has suggested that this doctrine of law was seldom translated into fact. In the eyes of the law at any rate, the killing was not treated simply as an invasion of the master's property interests. The slave was considered a human being. American slavery may be called chattel slavery in many respects, but the law of nature was used to keep murdered slaves from being treated as if they had actually been chattels. So was the law of nature invoked to uphold as charitable a trust established to promote the end of slavery. Slavery was, in the Massachusetts judge's opinion, "contrary to natural right and the principles of justice, humanity, and sound policy."[120] He thereby rejected the standard objection that a trust to change the law could not be upheld as charitable.

Property lawyers (old ones anyway) may also be pleased to discover a case holding that the life of a slave counted as a life in being for purposes of avoiding invalidity of a future interest under the Rule against Perpetuities—an outcome that one judge's opinion ascribed to the law of nature.[121] In the state of nature, he said, slaves were persons, and they were lives in being. The *ius gentium* had changed some things, and slaves were treated as less than full human beings for many purposes under American law, although not for all of them.[122] A few of their "natural rights" remained vigorous enough to count for something in the courts.

Statutory Construction

One of the several functions the law of nature served was to help judges in interpreting statutes. It was a guide. Statutory provisions were assumed to have been made in accord with the dictates of natural justice. That was taken to be their evident purpose. Judges were thus free, indeed urged, to read them in that light. In practice, therefore, the law of nature could lead judges to take aggressive positions, saying, for example, that "if absurd consequences, or those manifestly against common reason, arise collaterally out of a statute, [the statute] is void pro tanto."[123] In most cases, natural law's invocation led to what we would recognize as the equitable construction of legislative acts, just as it did in cases from England and the Continent. On any account of its meaning, *Calder v. Bull* had left open this avenue to justice. The assumption of beneficent legislative intent, although surely often falsified in the world of politics as it was, did open up the possibility of applying natural law principles when the wording of a statute left room for doubt.

Of the results of this assumption, the American law reports contain many examples; indeed, one of the best examples is the famous case of *Riggs v. Palmer*.[124] Although decided a few years after the period covered in this work, it deserves our attention because it illuminates with particular clarity one of the ways in which American lawyers approached statutory interpretation in the era when the law of nature served as a valid source of law. The case is all the more revealing for including a dissent that rejected the jurisprudential assumptions on which the majority opinion rested. The facts were as follows. In 1880, Francis Palmer executed his last will and testament. He made his grandson, Elmer, the chief beneficiary. In 1882, however, Francis remarried, and to prevent the possibility that his grandfather might change the terms of his will to his detriment, Elmer (a sixteen-year-old boy at the time) poisoned him. For this act he was convicted of the crime of murder and was serving his sentence in the state penitentiary at the time the case was decided. Despite his crime Elmer sought to take the property left to him under the will, invoking New York statutes that secured the right to decedents to have their testaments enforced according to their declared wishes. In the alternative, if the will were held invalid, he asserted a right to take the property as one of the heirs of his grandfather under the state's statute of Descent and Distribution.

The New York Court of Appeals rejected both of Elmer's claims. In doing so, the majority opinion cited the classic example from the *ius commune*, a court's refusal to apply the statute of the city of Bologna punishing anyone who drew blood on the city streets against a doctor who had opened a man's veins in an effort to save his life.[125] As with the Bolognese example, here it was held that the "mind" of the statutes did not reach the case. Only the words did. The result was that which Roman law endorsed (Dig. 34.9.3; 49.14.9),[126] and the New York court's opinion cited it as authority. It also called upon several works of general jurisprudence in support—among them Rutherforth's *Institutes of Natural Law,* Matthew Bacon's *Abridgement of the Law,* Pufendorf's *De jure naturae et gentium,* Domat's *Civil Law in Its Natural Order,* and Blackstone's *Commentaries.* A judge must put himself in the shoes of the legislator, these authorities advised, and he must seek to imagine what an upright legislator would have done had he been able to foresee the case at hand. That effort would surely call for a construction of the statute that excluded a murderer's claims. The New York court used language reminiscent of Sir Edward Coke's sentiments in *Bonham's Case:* "[A]ll laws . . . may be controlled in their operation and effect by general, fundamental maxims of the common law. No one shall be permitted to profit by his own fraud, or to take advantage of his own wrong."[127] These were principles drawn from the law of nature, repeatedly applied by respected authorities both within the common law and without. They applied here.

Significantly, the case attracted a dissent. Two judges who joined in it would have allowed the killer's claim. Conceding that Elmer had made himself morally unworthy of his grandfather's bounty, they regarded his conviction and imprisonment as sufficient punishment. That was all the law permitted. They also thought that if a greater remedy were called for by the facts of the case, it could only be supplied by the legislature. "[I]n the absence of such legislation here," the dissent concluded, "the courts are not empowered to institute such a system of remedial justice."[128] There could scarcely be a more poignant contrast between a regime where the law of nature served as a basic source of law and one in which legal positivism prevailed than in the contrasting opinions in this famous New York case.

The outcome of this "contest" has not proved to be a triumph for either legal positivism or the law of nature. Over the years, the obvious inequity of the dissent's position—creating what economists call a "moral hazard"—has attracted widespread academic interest,[129] as well as various suggestions for "halfway" houses, such as imposing a constructive trust on the property in the hands of the wrongdoing legatee.[130] In the end (i.e., today), the holding in *Riggs v. Palmer* has taken on a statutory form. The Uniform Probate Code contains a provision precluding inheritance by an heir or devisee who feloniously and intentionally kills the decedent in question.[131] Is this a victory for the law of nature? Yes, in a way it is. Traditionally, the law of nature was thought to provide inspiration and guidance for the creation of specific enactments of the municipal law. That has happened. But in another way, it is not. Enactment of a statute to cover the situation might today be considered the product of necessity. Without it judges might consider themselves obliged to follow the statutes literally, as indeed the two dissenters in *Riggs v. Palmer* did.

Many American cases from before the Civil War were fully in line with the judicial attitude shown in the majority opinion of this case. The enactment of statutes that caused incidental damage to citizens when put into effect—a frequent enough occurrence in any era—called forth regular challenges. A New Jersey statute authorizing the construction of a canal and dam to improve navigation, for example, was challenged in court by a claimant whose property was injured by the construction. The statute made no provision for payment to those in his position, and the state's constitution at the time contained none; the state's supreme court, however, read the legislative act to include one. The opinion asked rhetorically, "Does this act then confer . . . the right to take, injure, or destroy private property without compensation to the owners? If it does, it is unconstitutional and void as a violation of natural justice."[132] The legislature cannot have meant this to happen, the judge reasoned, and the statutory language was "adjusted" to take account of what the legislators must have intended.

It is true that not every piece of legislation, then or now, could be read to include such an intent. Not every incidental harm is compensable. And not every court then reached the same conclusion this New Jersey court did.[133] We are still struggling with the problem. What can be said from the subject's history is that two hundred years ago, the law of nature provided a fruitful source of argument about it. Natural law was then used broadly to interpret, and occasionally to invalidate, legislative acts.

Restraints on the Exercise of Power

Less emerges from a survey of the American case law relating to the use of the law of nature to restrain excesses of private and public power than is found in the English and European case law. If this result seems surprising (as it did to me), the predominant role of the U.S. Constitution in litigation, together with the outcome of *Calder v. Bull*, suggests a likely explanation: rights granted by the text of those foundational documents made recourse to the law of nature unnecessary, perhaps even slightly suspect. Specific constitutional rights, as noted at the start of this chapter, were more immediately forceful in litigation than was natural law. Constitutional rights were themselves a part—the predominant part—of the positive law. For this good reason, the law of nature took the backseat to arguments from that source of positive law.

No doubt there is a good deal of truth to this explanation, but somehow it seems too neat to be wholly convincing. It is not comprehensive or sensitive enough to the minds of contemporary lawyers to account fully for the character of judicial and lawyerly thought that is repeatedly encountered in the case law. The principle of fair dealing that lawyers took to be a part of natural law was as relevant to evaluation of governmental actions as it was to contract law.[134] It was also raised in litigation too often to be dismissed as legally irrelevant simply because of *Calder v. Bull*.

For a better appreciation of this side of American law, one can now begin with the masterful account of judicial conduct and fundamental principle in Philip Hamburger's *Law and Judicial Duty.* Most of the book deals with an earlier period than that covered in this chapter, and it has only a little to say that is directly related to the law of nature. It does, however, provide an eye-opening window on the world of American law before the triumph of legal positivism. It shows the latitude opened to judges in seeking to do right, a requirement imposed by "the obligations of their oaths, and the duty of their office."[135] They acted to rein in acts of injustice, sometimes even when those acts had been authorized by society's governors. Judges had taken an oath to do so. In fulfilling it, they were acting as continuators of both a common law and a civil law tradition.

Something of that spirit lived on after the adoption of the U.S. Constitution and the decision in *Calder v. Bull.* One minor but representative instance involved an ordinance in the city of Savannah in Georgia that restricted the purchase of a larger quantity of fish in the public market than was necessary to feed one's family. Alfred Haywood violated the ordinance and was fined $30, which he refused to pay, instead challenging the ordinance itself. His case rested on several arguments, among which was the contention that the ordinance was contrary to a natural law principle of freedom in commercial life. In the event, he was successful. He did not have to pay the fine. It is not certain which of Haywood's arguments carried the most weight, but the judge who wrote the opinion saw fit to state that "Free Trade is destined to become . . . the permanent and paramount policy of the world."[136] He added, "And I rejoice that it is so."[137]

Other cases of a similar nature are there to be found in the nineteenth-century American reports.[138] Natural law's principle of self-preservation was invoked, for example, to assert the relevance of the privilege against self-incrimination in purely civil matters.[139] It was invoked to limit the scope of powers to pardon crimes held by the executive.[140] Cases requiring public authorities to compensate owners for the loss of property taken by eminent domain, already described, are also a reminder that the force of natural law in curbing abuses of governmental power was not spent.[141] Natural law was used to require governmental officials to abide by ordinary principles of fairness in litigation—to take no prejudicial step against a citizen without citing him, for example.[142] It also helped judges to separate questions of power from those of right, allowing them to conclude that where natural rights came into play, "the protection of such a right from violation by superior force must always turn the scale," at least unless it had been specifically foreclosed by legislative fiat.[143] Remarkably, therefore, natural law held its own in this arena. The frequency of such uses of the law of nature was somewhat less in the United States than is found in the Continental *decisiones* or in the English reports, but it had not vanished by the time the Civil War began.

Conclusion

The presence of so many arguments and decisions invoking the law of nature in the American reports makes a case for its influence. How strong that case is overall must nevertheless remain a matter of opinion. The affirmative case will certainly not survive submersion in the acidic baths prepared by most proponents of the movements of legal realism and law and economics.[144] The actual extent of its influence, when weighed against other kinds of arguments, must also be a matter of doubt. What can be said with some confidence, however, is that the American usage comes close to matching in substance and frequency the evidence drawn from the European and English case law. If the law of nature can be said to have helped shape the law there, it helped shape the law of the United States. An American lawyer, arguing before the U.S. Supreme Court in 1819, contended that the law of nature "everywhere forms a part, and the best part, of the municipal code."[145] That was hyperbole, no doubt, spoken in service to a client's interests. But it could then be said without self-consciousness or fear of ridicule.

Recognizing the prevalence of this sentiment and the similarity in the usage of the law of nature on both sides of the Atlantic does not, however, fully capture one feature of American usage that did diverge from the European experience. It was a willingness to invoke natural law for purposes that stretched and sometimes surpassed its scope as understood by European jurists of the Natural Law School. It led some lawyers to cite the law of nature in broader circumstances than a Continental jurist would have.[146] This tendency may possibly be a sign of uncertainty about the character of the law of nature, and it certainly was a sign of the need American lawyers felt to fill gaps and uncertainties in the legal system of their new Republic. They sometimes sought to expand the traditional boundaries of natural law.

Examples of apparent confusion or overreaching in applying the law of nature are to be found among the reports—not with great frequency, perhaps—but more often than is true for the Continental *decisiones*. In one American case the bond of marriage was said to be made indissoluble by the law of nature.[147] In another, decided the next year (though in a different state), the right to a divorce on the grounds of cruelty was also said to be "founded in the well-recognized law of nature."[148] These might both be described as "creative" uses of the laws of nature. The standard position within the traditions of the *ius commune* held that unions between men and women were a part of the law of nature but that questions of an existing marriage's dissolution were matters of positive civil or divine law.[149] These American lawyers either did not know or chose to ignore that particular *communis opinio*.

In a similar way, a strong protection for vested rights in land could be and was in fact attributed to the law of nature, as in protecting titles to land against forcible seizure or retrospective legislation.[150] On the other side, it was said in a case from Kentucky that the doctrine of adverse possession, by which those rights were lost in favor of a possessor without title, also had its "foundation in the law of nature."[151] Of course, these cases could be reconciled with natural law's precepts. Both opinions laid stress on the importance of the preservation of peace in the world. Men are social creatures, and peace among them can best be secured by the establishment of settled land titles.[152] Invocations of natural law, one might say, could work toward that goal in different ways. Even so, these were two seemingly different expressions of how that happened. It is revealing to see both positions attributed to the law of nature.

Human liberties, like a right to freedom of testation, were also tempting concepts for making a connection with principles of natural law. These liberties were asserted, albeit often with modesty, as having been "derivable from the law of nature," or "built upon the law of nature," or "consistent with the precepts of nature."[153] Lawyerly imagination was doubtless on show in these cases. The right to make a will directing what should happen to a man's property after his death was, for example, a difficult right to connect with a real state of nature. It could scarcely have existed before society's organization. It was not required to hold society together. However, it might plausibly be said to follow from a natural law's premise that "every man has a natural right to the fruits of his own labor,"[154] and American lawyers sometimes made this argument. They even advanced the position that a right to take property by inheritance was somehow guaranteed by natural law.[155] In these cases, these lawyers seem actually to have meant no more than that their argument was supported by "law of nature, that is, in simpler phrase, by the rules of good sense, by the rules of conduct acknowledged to be suitable and beneficial to all men."[156] That appeal made a kind of practical sense; somehow an argument was improved by invocation of the law of nature. There was an easy connection to make and to put before a judge.

A researcher sees this usage particularly frequently because the early American reports often contain the arguments of counsel as well as the judge's opinion. They show what one would expect: that arguments made on the basis of natural law were more often advanced by counsel than they were accepted by judges. The same is true in the Continental *decisiones*. The tendency to inject every reason one can conjure up into a brief or oral argument is a tempting one for lawyers in any era, and lawyerly desperation may best explain more than a negligible percentage of the references to the law of nature that appeared in the American reports.

That being said, one can still admire the ingenuity of its invocation by a Missouri lawyer in support of his argument that an easement by necessity had been created in favor of his client. An easement of necessity is created when a grant of land surrounded by the lands of others (including the grantor's own) is made, and access to the land being granted is feasible only by traveling over the grantor's own property— hence the easement. The landlocked parcel is worthless without it. This limited right to use the grantor's contiguous property for access that arises is treated as a necessary but unstated part of the original grant, and in a Missouri case from 1848, the plaintiff's lawyer also claimed that its existence followed from principles of the law of nature. He asserted the connection with natural law four times before adding that "[i]f not a principle of natural law, [it was] at least one which could not long be omitted in the code of a civilized people."[157] In the case from which these words are taken, the decision ultimately went in favor of this lawyer's client— rightly so, most modern lawyers would agree. The same substantive rule exists in today's law. We simply have found a different reason for it.

Conclusion

T HIS HAS BEEN A limited exploration of natural law's history, one confined to a specific arena and also one restricted in time. It has not sought to challenge the conclusions of existing historical accounts of natural law theory. It has not attempted to trace the rise of human rights. Except for producing some evidence to show what it was actually like to live under a legal regime where the existence and validity of the law of nature were more widely acknowledged than they are today, this book may be of little relevance to those fields of study.

What relevance it does have, however, probably serves to confirm their value. Although it says little about the theories and complex traditions of natural law as worked out by St. Thomas Aquinas and those who followed his teachings, this book seeks to show that natural law theory could lead—in fact, did lead—to practical results. Aquinas himself must have expected that they would. Perhaps the results were not exactly what natural law's modern advocates have hoped for, but they were real results all the same.

This study's purpose has been only to investigate what natural law meant in practice at a time when it was widely accepted as a fundamental source of law. That investigation has, I think, produced evidence that modestly advances our understanding of the development of Western legal tradition, and it does appear to challenge the conclusions of historians who have dismissed the law of nature as irrelevant to what happened in the world. Such dismissals have not been rare. Even an able scholar like Forrest McDonald concluded that outside the field of international law, natural law occupied no place in the lives of European men and women; it was, he thought, "entirely alien to matters of concern

within a single kingdom, empire, or commonwealth."[1] That opinion is
not supported by the evidence, at least the evidence presented in these
pages.

Exactly how large a place it occupied in practice within any particular system of government and its legal arm is open to debate, but that
it had no relevance whatsoever to the daily events of human life or to
the everyday concerns of practicing lawyers is not. This survey of the
relevant evidence, incomplete as it surely is, proves that natural law was
carried into practice in the courts of each of the three geographical areas
surveyed. Its importance may be doubted; its presence should not. At
least six specific conclusions about its use emerge from a consideration
of the evidence. Each of them calls attention to a different aspect of what
the law of nature meant in practice.

First, in all three geographical areas surveyed, future lawyers learned
something about the basic characteristics of the law of nature as part of
their early training. In what they studied at universities or what they
learned from private study, most lawyers came to the world of practice
having read and heard its basic tenets set out before them. The details
and the exact sources of that knowledge are not always easy to discern.
The evidence often fails us. However, most beginning lawyers did know
that the law of nature was a valid source of law and that the positive
law was meant to be in harmony with it. Among other things, they had
become familiar with some of its general principles during their early
training. They knew, for example, that men should keep their promises,
but they also knew that abstract principles like this one had often been
abridged or varied in human experience, as, for example, in affecting
the extent to which gratuitous promises would be enforced in courts
of law.

Long before they came into direct contact with clients and courts,
therefore, they would have understood that the law of nature provided
a starting point for the formulation of the positive law and also that it
admitted a variety of results in practice. Not all its tenets had been (or
could be) put to immediate use. But it did provide a measuring stick by
which the positive law could be interpreted and evaluated. Most lawyers would also have gained a modest familiarity with the enormous
body of learned literature on the subject. It is certainly true that European lawyers would have had a fuller knowledge of the treatises and
texts than would many English barristers or lawyers on the American

frontier. Even in remote corners of the New World, however, the study of Blackstone's *Commentaries* would have brought some familiarity with the law of nature to lawyers at the start of their careers.

Second, once launched in their careers, some lawyers brought what they had learned about the law of nature into their professional lives. They used it. Evidence from cases decided in all three of the areas and time periods covered in this book confirms the assumption that most lawyers will use what they know when it fits their needs and also that the law of nature did sometimes fit their needs. How frequent or effective its invocation was overall is not altogether easy to describe. Most litigated disputes concern the proof of facts, not points of law.[2] Even where legal doctrine mattered, reliable statistics cannot be compiled. The character of natural law—a foundation of all law but not the source of hard and fast rules—only complicates the question. We are on firm ground, however, in saying that its authority was invoked, although only in a minority of the cases found in the reports.

We can also conclude that the use of natural law appeared more often in some areas of the law than in others. Where principles of morality were at stake in litigation, one typically finds natural law invoked and treatises to it cited. However, it also appeared in many detailed and mundane questions related to family law and the law of inheritance. Even the rules of the law of procedure and proof were touched by it, and it was also relevant in dealing with problems of statutory interpretation. Commercial law occasionally raised points drawn from it. Even so, reference to the law of nature would not have been an everyday affair for most lawyers. Where the positive law had put the abstract principles of the law of nature into specific form and added sanctions to it, the need to recur to first principles in litigation could disappear. Positive law was sufficient. That is what the jurists assumed should happen, and, in fact, it is what did happen.

Third, the law of nature was a common possession of lawyers in the world of Western jurisprudence. In the course of investigating European, English, and American case law, remarkably few points of difference related to the applications and teachings of the law of nature emerged. A few did. Some change over the course of time did occur. However, it was less than I expected. This consistency is remarkable and, at first sight, surprising. The English common law was not identical in its basic institutions to those of most Continental systems of law. The political beliefs of the American colonists were very different from those that prevailed in medieval France or Spain. Yet, the law of nature was used in much the same ways in the times and places examined in this investigation of the case law.

Of course, it is true to say that the law of nature was a general source of law; it was open to some quite important variations created by the positive law. It is also true that some things did not change very much—for example, the necessity of citation before judicial determination or the need for parents to care for their young. Still, the shared substance of the learning drawn from the law of nature and put into practice in the courts merits recognition. It should probably be no surprise that treatises written by a jurist from a European land were carried into England and America or that they were translated for English speakers. The law of nature served as one force for what is now called "legal integration." Students of comparative legal history might take note. When lawyers in sixteenth-century Italy or nineteenth-century Virginia discussed points of practice connected to the law of nature, they were speaking a common language.

Fourth, in actual cases the law of nature was almost always treated as a source of positive law, not as a rival or alternative to it. This way of looking at law was clearly stated in the Continental treatises, and in the great majority of litigated cases, natural law did serve to interpret statutes or local customs and to answer difficult or unanswered questions. Its normal use was not to invalidate existing positive law. The fact that an institution was contrary to the law of nature did not in itself make the institution unlawful. There were circumstances in which the law of nature might be used to challenge the actions of a ruler or legislator. The possibility was admitted, and the historical record, including what this survey has shown, does contain examples in which the invocation of natural law was used to question governmental acts—sometimes successfully. They were not frequent, however, and most of them rested on the assumption that society's governors could not actually have meant to have their acts turned into a source of wickedness. The insights of "public choice" theories of legislative action lay far in the future.

An unfortunate accident of the dominance of the modern practice of judicial review in American courts has been to suggest that "striking down" legislative acts was the main purpose natural law was meant to serve. The American case of *Calder v. Bull* has also had the unhappy "side effect" of suggesting that courts were faced with an either/or choice. One choice was the Constitution, and the other was the law of nature; the majority of the courts chose the former. In reality, however, they were always meant to work together. The American Constitution stated rules of positive law, some of which were derived from the law of nature or were at least consistent with it. Lawyers who made reference to both natural and positive law in submissions to courts of law were not confused. They were relying on traditional learning. It taught that the two laws were in harmony and should be used together. The American Constitution would have been regarded as one instance where the two had been so fused.

Fifth, throughout its history, the law of nature has been a modest force for good. At least that is my opinion of what its acceptance meant in practice. It was not a cure-all, but it did promote the cause of justice. It helped to cement principles of right and wrong in the minds of lawyers and consequently in the decisions made in courts of law. That no person should be condemned unheard is a valuable legal rule. That swindlers should restore gains made by fraud is a workable and fair principle of law. That parents should care for their children is not a matter of serious dispute. That penalties in criminal law should be proportional to the degree of the criminal's fault is a healthful reminder of the limits to which a "War on Crime" can aspire. Maybe it is true that these statements are "just common sense," as others have suggested to me. The law of nature was nonetheless the vehicle through which these principles became established as law. It was given as the reason they were applied in courts, and some of them would not have seemed quite so obvious at the time they were introduced as they now do to us. Natural law served as a useful vehicle in securing many results we now regard as self-evident.

Sixth, the history of natural law's use in courts does suggest that it would be a mistake to claim too much for it. Its practical limitations have been a theme that runs through every part of this book, and it is a theme compelled by the evidence. In some ways, it is nonetheless a surprise. Many of the treatments found in today's literature about natural law do at least appear to claim more for it than it actually delivered. It did not abolish slavery. It did not end judicial torture. It did not require payment of a "living wage." It did not prevent the oppression of native peoples in the Americas. It did not prevent what by our lights seem to have been serious miscarriages of justice. In myriad ways, natural law appears not to have lived up to its promise.

A fuller examination of the law of nature found in legal treatises would of course also have predicted something like these facts of legal life. That the natural law could be amended and diminished both by the law of nations and by the positive law was an accepted part of Western jurisprudence. This often happened. The results of the interactions among the three sources of law found in the Roman Law Digest can be seen in the case law from European, English, and American courts. On balance, it appears to me that the law of nature did serve the cause of justice, but an American judge from Virginia surely had it right when he wrote, "Whatever may be the extent of the obligations of natural law, no system of municipal law has ever enforced them in all their consequences."[3] He would certainly have agreed with the eighteenth-century English writer who held that it "must be allowed" that "the civil power can put such restraints and limitations upon the Law of Nature as are for the common good of society."[4] That statement was actually not much different from something Thomas Aquinas had written centuries before. He noted that the more one descended into details and consequences, the more qualifications one was forced to admit.[5] A general acceptance of this admission in practice everywhere set limits on natural law's effective reach.

NOTES

BIBLIOGRAPHY

INDEX

Notes

Preface

1. E.g., *Natural Law: Historical, Systematic and Juridical Approaches*, A. N. García, M. Šilar, and J. M. Torralba eds. (2008), 379–467; although this book is called "juridical," it does not discuss a single case. Charles P. Nemeth, *Aquinas in the Courtroom* (2001), 179–200, discusses some modern judicial decisions but mostly to criticize them from a Thomistic point of view. Other examples are Klaus Luig, "Der Einfluß des Naturrechts auf das positive Privatrecht im 18. Jahrhundert," in: *Römisches Recht, Naturrecht, nationales Recht* (1998), 151–67; and Thomas C. Kischkel, "Das Naturrecht in der Rechtspraxis: Dargestellt am Beispiel der Spruchtätigkeit der Gießener Juristenfakultät," *Zeitschrift für neuere Rechtsgeschichte* 20 (2000), 124–47.

Introduction

1. Introduction, in: *Early Modern Natural Law Theories: Contexts and Strategies in the Early Enlightenment*, T. J. Hochstrasser and P. Schröder eds. (2003), p. ix.
2. See, e.g., Souter, J. in dissent in Alden v. Maine, 527 U.S. 706, 773–75, 781 (1999); John Hart Ely, *Democracy and Distrust* (1980), 87; Hans Thieme, *Das Naturrecht und die europäische Privatrechtsgeschichte* (1954), 7; David Lieberman, *The Province of Legislation Determined: Legal Theory in Eighteenth-Century Britain* (1989), 224–336.
3. Michael B. Crowe, *The Changing Profile of the Natural Law* (1977); Brian Tierney, *The Idea of Natural Rights: Studies on Natural Rights, Natural Law and Church Law, 1150–1625* (1997).
4. John Finnis, *Natural Law and Natural Rights*, 2d ed. (2011); Robert P. George, *In Defense of Natural Law* (1999).
5. E.g., Hadley Arkes, *Constitutional Illusions & Anchoring Truths: The Touchstone of the Natural Law* (2010); Knud Haakonssen, *Natural Law and Moral*

Philosophy: From Grotius to the Scottish Enlightenment (1996); Javier Hervada, *Natural Right and Natural Law: A Critical Introduction* (1990); Russell Hittinger, *The First Grace: Rediscovering the Natural Law in a Post-Christian World* (2003); Jean Porter, *Ministers of the Law: A Natural Law Theory of Legal Authority* (2010); Brian Tierney, *Liberty and Law: The Idea of Permissive Natural Law, 1100–1800* (2014); Lloyd Weinrib, *Natural Law and Justice* (1987).

6. See works in prior note; also useful are: A. P. d'Entrèves, *Natural Law: An Introduction to Legal Philosophy,* 2d ed. (1970); Merio Scattola, "Before and After Natural Law: Models of Natural Law in Ancient and Modern Times," in: *Early Modern Natural Law Theories,* above note 1, at 1–11; Christopher Wolfe, "Thomistic Natural Law and the American Natural Law Tradition," in: *St. Thomas Aquinas and the Natural Law Tradition: Contemporary Perspectives,* John Goyette et al. eds. (2004), 201–02.

7. Ennio Cortese, *La norma giuridica: Spunti teorici nel diritto comune classico,* 2 vols. (1962–1964).

8. E.g., Brian Bix, *Dictionary of Legal Theory* (2004), 142–44; Knud Haakonssen, "Natural Law," in: *Encyclopedia of Ethics,* L. C. Becker ed. (1992), 884–90; D. J. Ibbetson, K. Luig, and J. Fleming, "Natural Law," in *Oxford International Encyclopedia of Legal History,* Stanley Katz ed. (2009), IV, 214–20.

9. See, e.g., Tadeusz Guz, "Gott als der Urheber des Naturrechts," in: *Das Naturrecht und Europa,* T. Guz ed. (2007), 149–79; Gaines Post, "The Naturalness of Society and the State," in: *Studies in Medieval Legal Thought* (1964), 494–561.

10. H. Grotius, *De iure belli ac pacis,* Prol. 6–9. Modern research into human behavior under conditions of lawlessness has served to confirm the absence of a direct clash between them. See Paul Robinson, "Natural Law and Lawlessness: Modern Lessons from Pirates, Lepers, Eskimos, and Survivors," *Illinois L. Rev.* (2013), 433–506.

11. See Brian Tierney, "Natura id est Deus: A Case of Juristic Pantheism?" *J. History of Ideas* 24 (1963), 307–22.

12. The Huntress, 12 F. Cas. 984, 986 (D. Maine 1840) (No. 6,914) (by Ware, J. citing Pothier's treatise on contract law in support).

13. *Summa theologiae,* 1a2ae. 95, 2 (Blackfriar's ed.), 104–05: "Si vero in aliquo a lege naturali discordet, jam non erit lex, sed legis corruptio." See also H. Grotius, *De iure belli ac pacis,* Bk. II, c. 2, tit. 5: "Lex enim civilis quanquam nihil potest praecipere quod ius naturae prohibet, aut prohibere quod praecipit."

14. See generally Richard Ross, "Distinguishing Eternal from Transient Law: Natural Law and the Judicial Laws of Moses," *Past & Present* 79 (2012), 79–114.

15. See, e.g., J. van den Sande, *Decisiones Frisicae,* Lib. I, tit. 9, def. 2.

16. See, e.g., Patrick Brennan, "Persons, Participating, and 'Higher Law,'" *Pepperdine L. Rev.* 36 (2009), 475–90, at 484–87.

17. See, e.g., Pauline Westerman, *The Disintegration of Natural Law Theory: Aquinas to Finnis* (1998); Ralph McInerny, "The Principles of Natural Law," *American J. of Jurisprudence* 25 (1980), 1–15; Russell Hittinger, *A Critique of the New Natural Law Theory* (1987). I have been aided in understanding the issues involved by reading William May, "Contemporary Perspectives on Thomistic Natural Law," in: *St. Thomas Aquinas and the Natural Law Tradition*, above note 6, *at* 113–56; and Michael Crowe, *The Changing Profile of the Natural Law* (1977), 246–90.

18. F. Merlino Pignatelli, *Controversiarum forensium*, Cent. I, c. 53, no. 2 (citing *Summa theologiae* 1a2ae, qu. 70, art. 1); G. de Cabedo, *Practicarum observationum*, Dec. 79, no. 2 (citing *Summa theologiae* 1a2ae, qu. 96, art. 5).

19. *De Jure praedae*, Proleg. (nine "rules" and thirteen "laws").

20. See John Witte Jr., *Law and Protestantism* (2002), 92–93, 123–27, 130–34, 139–40, 150–52, 158–61; John McNeill, "Natural Law in the Teaching of the Reformers," *J. of Religion* 26 (1946), 168–82.

21. E.g., G. B. Almici, *Institutiones iuris naturae et gentium*, Proem., no. 8 (admitting the use of the works of Protestant jurists); J. F. Finetti, *De principiis juris naturae*, Lib. II, c. 8: "Quamquam Pufendorii opus de jure naturae et gentium omnino contemnendum non sit"); see also Robert Feenstra, "L'influence de la Scolastique espagnole sur Grotius en droit privé," in: *La Seconda Scolastica nella formazione del diritto privato moderno*, Paolo Grossi ed. (1973), 377–402.

22. See Johann Sommerville, "Selden, Grotius, and the Seventeenth-Century Intellectual Revolution in Moral and Political Theory," in: *Rhetoric and Law in Early Modern Europe*, Victoria Kahn and Lorna Hudson eds. (2001), 318–44, at 320; Anthony Pagden, *The Languages of Political Theory in Early-Modern Europe* (1987), 3–6.

23. E.g., Merio Scattola, "Before and After Natural Law," in: *Early Modern Natural Law Theories*, above note 1, at 12–22.

24. Peter Riesenberg, "The Consilia Literature: A Prospectus," *Manuscripta* 6 (1962), 3–22.

25. See the discussion of the manuscript sources in A. Fliniaux, "Les anciennes collections de 'Decisiones Rotae Romanae,'" *R.H.D.* 4 (1925), 61–93, 382–410; Gero Dolezalek and Knut W. Nörr, "Die Rechtsprechungssammlungen der mittelalterlichen Rota," in: Coing, *Handbuch* I, 849–56. There was, however, also prior movement in the same direction elsewhere; see Dirk Hierbaut, "The Spokesman in Medieval Courts: The Unknown Leading Judges of the Customary Law and Makers of the First Continental Law Reports," in: *Judges and Judging in the History of the Common Law and Civil Law*, P. Brand and J. Getzler eds. (2012), 192–208.

26. See, e.g., Mario Ascheri, *Tribunali, Giuristi e Istituzioni dal medioevo all'età moderna* (1989), 86–87, 211–35; Gero Dolezalek, "Quaestiones motae in Rota: Richterliche Beratungsnotizen aus dem vierzehnten Jahrhundert," in: *Proceedings of the Fifth International Congress of Medieval Canon Law,*

S. Kuttner and K. Pennington eds. (1980), 99–114; Dolores Freda, *La Dottrina dei Lawyers* (2009), 1–25; Marco Nicola Miletti, *Stylus Judicandi: le Raccolte di "Decisiones" del regno di Napoli in età moderna* (1998), 103–54; Serge Dauchy and Véronique Demars-Sion, *Les recueils d'arrêts et dictionnaires de jurisprudence (XVI–XVIIIe siècles)* (2005).

27. Warden v. Greer, 6 Watts 424, 426 (Pa. 1837).
28. E.g., *Co. Lit.* *92a: "Lex spectat naturae ordinem."
29. See André Pellicer, *Natura: Étude sémantique et historique du mot latin* (1966).
30. I have taken to heart the warning by John Phillip Reid, *Constitutional History of the American Revolution* (1986), 92–94 (pointing to the tendency on the part of some historians to emphasize natural rights as a result of "carelessness" in assuming that any reference to "nature" in the sources was a reference to the law of nature).

1. Legal Education in Continental Europe

1. See Paul Brand, *The Origins of the English Legal Profession* (1992), 106–19.
2. Antonio García y García, "La enseñanza del derecho en la universidad medieval," in: *En el Entorno del derecho común* (1999), 101–05; Peter Weimar, "Die legistische Literatur und die Methode des Rechtsunterrichts der Glossatorenzeit," in: *Zur Renaissance der Rechtswissenschaft im Mittelalter* (1997), 3–43.
3. See Manlio Bellomo, *Aspetti dell'insegnamento giuridico nelle università medievali: I, le "Quaestiones disputatae"* (1974).
4. Helmut Coing, "L'insegnamento del diritto nell'Europa dell'Ancien Régime," *Studi Senesi*, 82 (1970), 179–93; E. M. Meijers, *Études d'histoire du droit* (1959), III, 68–79; Boudewijn Sirks, "Bijnkershoek as author and elegant jurist," *T.R.G.* 79 (2011), 229–52.
5. See the examples given in Martin Bertram, "Kirchenrechtliche Vorlesungen aus Orléans (1285–7)," in: *Kanonisten und ihre Texte (1234 bis Mitte 14. Jh.)* (2013), 413–33, at 424–33; and Giulio Vismara, "Vita di studenti e studio del diritto nell'Università di Pavia alla fine del cinquecento," *Archivio storico Lombardo* 90 (1966), 425–81.
6. A. Wijffels, *Qui millies allegatur: Les allegations du droit savant dans les dossiers du Grand Conseil de Malines (causes septentrionales, ca. 1460–1580)* (1985), II, 467–878.
7. Marguerite Duynstee, *L'enseignement du droit civil à l'université d'Orléans du début de la guerre de Cent ans (1337) au siège de la ville (1428)* (2013), 51–54.
8. See Robert Villers, "L'enseignement du droit en France de Louis XIV a Bonaparte," *L'educazione giuridica* 1 (1975), 101–14; R. Feenstra and C. J. D. Waal, *Seventeenth-Century Leyden Law Professors and their Influence on the Development of the Civil Law* (1975), 15–44; Coing, "L'insegnamento," above note 4, at 191–92.

9. See Michael Stolleis, *Geschichte des öffentlichen Rechts in Deutschland* (1988), I, 277–84. For developments in France, see, e.g., A. de Curzon, "L'enseignement du droit français dans les universités de France aux XVIIe et XVIIIe siècles," *R.H.D.* 44 (1919), 209–69, 305–64; and Hervé Leuwers, "La Faculté de droit de Douai et la formation juridique et citoyenne," in: *Enseignement et droit* (1998), 85–118, at 96–97. See also Philippe Meylan, *Jean Barbeyrac (1674–1744) et les débuts de l'enseignement du droit dans l'ancienne Académie de Lausanne* (1937); Georges Martin, *L'enseignement du droit en Bretagne jusqu'en 1725* (1910), 125–28. See also Francisco Carpintero, "*Mos italicus, mos gallicus* y el Humanismo racionalista," *Ius commune* 6 (1977), 108–71, at 121–50.

10. See, e.g., Jan Schröder, *Recht als Wissenschaft: Geschichte der juristischen Methode vom Humanismus bis zur historischen Schule (1500–1850)* (2001), 167–87; Maria Gigliola di Renzo Villata, *Formare il Giurista: Esperienze nell'area Lombarda tra sette e ottocento* (2004), 1–105.

11. Paul F. Grendler, *The Universities of the Italian Renaissance* (2002), 430–43, 472 (concluding that legal education in the Italian universities "remained fundamentally the same from the age of Bartolo until that of Napoleon").

12. E.g., François Rabelais, *Gargantua et Pantagruel*, Liv. 3, cc. 39–40, explaining why the texts and commentators supported deciding cases by a toss of the dice.

13. Hastings Rashdall, *The Universities of Europe in the Middle Ages*, F. M. Powicke and A. B. Emden eds. (1936), III, 168.

14. See generally Peter Stein, *Roman Law in European History* (1999), 97–101; Biagio Brugi, *Per la storia della giurisprudenza e delle università italiano* (1921), 11–35; Ian Maclean, *Interpretation and Meaning in the Renaissance: The Case of Law* (1992), 65–66, 85; Charles McClelland, "The Aristocracy and University Reform in Eighteenth-Century Germany," in: *Schooling and Society*, Lawrence Stone ed. (1976), 146–73, at 147–50; Patrick Arabeyre, "De quelques oeuvres issues de l'enseignement du droit canonique dans les universités françaises du XVe siècle et da la première moitiè du XVIe siècle," in: *Proceedings of the Thirteenth International Congress of Medieval Canon Law*, Peter Erdö and Sz. Anzelm Szuromi eds. (2010), 669–91; Edward Peters, "The Sacred Muses and the Twelve Tables: Legal Education and Practice," in: *Law as Profession and Practice in Medieval Europe: Essays in Honor of James A. Brundage*, K. Pennington and M. H. Eichbauer eds. (2011), 137–51.

15. See James Gordley, *The Jurists: A Critical History* (2013), 32–45.

16. Ibid., 156–64.

17. See S. Stelling-Michaud, *L'université de Bologne et la pénétration des droits romain et canonique en Suisse* (1955), 47–75.

18. The texts are conveniently collected and their meaning discussed in Rudolf Weigand, *Die Naturrechtslehre der Legisten und Dekretisten von Irnerius bis Accursius und von Gratian bis Johannes Teutonicus* (1967), 8–121.

19. See, e.g., the evidence presented in Gerald Strauss, *Law, Resistance, and the State: The Opposition to Roman Law in Reformation Germany* (1986), 31–37.

20. See Caccialupus, *De modo studendi,* Docum. VIII (advice given to law students that each "[t]andem quaerat veritatem et aequitatis et iusticiae sit amator"); see also James A. Brundage, *Medieval Origins of the Legal Profession* (2008), 248–54; Jaques Paquet, "Aspects de l'université médiévale," in: *Universities in the Late Middle Ages,* J. Ijsewijn and J. Paquet eds. (1978), 15–25.

21. Odofredus of Bologna, in *University Records and Life in the Middle Ages,* Lynn Thorndike ed. (1944, repr. 1971), 66–67; Woldemar Engelmann, *Die Wiedergeburt der Rechtskultur in Italien* (1939), 172–89; Gero Dolezalek, "Wie studierte man bei den Glossatoren?" in: *Summe—Glosse—Komentar: Juristisches und Rhetorisches in Kanonistik and Legistik,* F. Theisen and W. E. Voss eds. (2000), II, 55–74.

22. See Inst. 1.2.1; *gl. ord.* ad id, v. *hic educatio;* and Dig. 25.3.5.7.

23. *Gl. ord.* ad Dig. 25.3.5.7, v. *iuste* (distinguishing a child born to a concubine from one born as a consequence of an adulterous affair).

24. E.g., J. Mynsinger, *Apotelesma,* Proem. § Summa, no. 1, beginning with an exhortation to hard work; A. Vinnius, *Commentarius,* Lib. I, tit. 1–2, beginning with definitions of the basic sources of law.

25. See, e.g., J. P. Surdus, *Tractatus de Alimentis,* Tit. I, quaest. 1–42, which appears to treat every conceivable relationship where the obligation might exist.

26. E.g., CUL MS. Dd.2.35 (law lectures from the University of Bologna from the early sixteenth century); it is filled with reference to commentators on Roman law.

27. This is stated in Caccialupus, *De modo studendi,* Documen. VII: "Confiteor quod Bartolus omni tempore omni personae utilis et necessarius est," going on however to qualify that strong endorsement because of the brevity and obscurity of some of his exposition.

28. *Commentaria* ad Dig. 1.1.3, no. 6: "[E]t tamen ius naturale est ut benefacienti benefaciamus" (citing Dig. 5.3.25.11 in support).

29. Ibid., nos. 6–7.

30. Ibid., ad Dig. 1.1.9, and also ad Dig. 1.3.8.

31. Ibid., ad Dig. 4.6.20, explored in detail in Yan Thomas, "Rechtsfiktion und Natur bei den Kommentatoren des Mittelalters," in: *Recht zwischen Natur und Geschichte,* F. Kervégan and H. Mohnhaupt eds. (1997), 9–10.

32. E.g., U. Huber, *De Ratione juris docendi et discendi diatribe* (2010), 8.

33. G. Riccio, *Praxis aurea,* Resol. 422, no. 2 (citing the principles of natural equity and charity that also applied in the context of a family).

34. See "Notes Taken at the Lecture of Some Civilian," Cambridge Univ. Library, MS. Dd.5.78.2, f. 9v; E. Speckhan, *Quaestiones et decisiones,* Cent. I, quaest. 17.

35. A variant of the problem, dealing with relations between brothers, is found in A. Trentacinque, *Consilia,* Cons. XIII, nos. 17–18.

36. See Leonard Boyle, "The Curriculum of the Faculty of Canon Law at Oxford in the First Half of the Fourteenth Century," in: *Pastoral Care, Clerical Education and Canon Law, 1200–1400* (1981), no. xiv.

37. D.a. D. 1, c. 1: "Humanum genus duobus regitur, naturali videlicet iure et moribus."

38. E.g., Paucapalea, *Summa,* 4–8; see generally R. Weigand, *Naturrechtslehre,* above note 18, 140–259; Orazio Condorelli, "Carità e diritto agli albori della scienza giuridica medievale," in: *Diritto canonico e servizio della carità,* J. Miñabres ed. (2008), 41–103, esp. 51–79.

39. See the discussion and references to literature in Christoph Bergfeld, "Katholische Moraltheologie und Naturrechtslehre," in: Coing, *Handbuch* II/1, 999–1015.

40. Inst. 1.1: "[I]urisprudentia est divinarum atque humanarum rerum notitia."

41. *Isidori Hispalensis Episcopi Etymologiarum sive Originum Libri* X, W. M. Lindsay ed. (1911), Lib. V, cc. 2–6.

42. Ibid., c. 2.

43. E.g., *gl. ord.* ad D. 1 c. 7, v. *ius naturale,* included citation of Dig. 25.4.1, Inst. 1.2.1, Inst. 4.1.1, and Dig. 1.2.3, as well as to other canonical texts.

44. *Gl. ord.* ad D. 1 c. 5, v. *quod religioni conveniat,* acknowledging also that some things might be contrary to the laws of nature but nonetheless consistent with the tenets of the Christian religion (e.g., the Virgin birth).

45. E.g., *Summa angelica,* v. consuetudo, no. 3.

46. X 1.4.11; see Jean Gilissen, *La Coutume* (Typologie des sources du Moyen Âge Occidental, Fasc. 41) (1982), 30–31; Udo Wolter, "Die 'consuetudo' im kanonischen Recht bis zum Ende des 13. Jahrhunderts," in: *Gewohnheitsrecht und Rechtsgewohnheiten im Mittelalter,* G. Dilcher et al. eds. (1992), 104–14.

47. See, e.g., J. Clarus, *Practica criminalis,* tit. Usura, no. 3: "[U]surae sunt omni iure prohibitae et in primis quidem de iure naturali."

48. See, e.g., Panormitanus, *Commentaria* ad X 1.4.11, no. 3.

49. E.g., *Summa angelica,* v. consuetudo, no. 2: "Finis iuris canonici est felicitas animae, . . . finis iuris civilis est bonum publicum."

50. Panormitanus, *Commentaria* ad X 1.4.11, no. 3: "[H]ic notabiliter dicit Innocentius consuetudo potest augere, diminuere et distinguere ius divinum," giving as an example the biblical injunction "in ore duorum vel trium stat omne verbum," which was limited by civil law "in multis casibus." See also Cortese, *La norma giuridica,* I, 111–14.

51. See, e.g., D. Arumaeus, *Decisionum et sententiarum,* Lib. I, dec. 1, nos. 14, 19 (applying natural law precepts to argue a case involving money discovered in the wall of a house recently purchased by the finder).

52. R. Cumberland, *Treatise of the Laws of Nature,* C. II §§ 23–24, comparing the brain size of animals and human beings.

53. See, e.g., G. S. Wilkinson, "Altrutism and Cooperation in Bats," in: *Recent Advances in the Study of Bats*, M. B. Fenton et al. eds. (1987), 299–323; Marc Hauser et al., "Give unto Others: Genetically Unrelated Cotton-Top Tamarin Monkeys Preferentially Give Food to Those Who Altruistically Give Food Back," *Royal Society Proceedings: Biological Sciences* 270 (2003) 2363–70.

54. E.g., J. Damhouder, *Praxis rerum criminalium*, C. 91, nos. 99–108 (including, among others, storks, lions, elephants, and turtles).

55. Dig. Proem. 15 *(Tanta)*.

56. *Gl. ord.* ad Dig. 1.1.1, v. *quod natura* (distinguishing what animals do by instinct and human beings by the use of reason (as part of a fourfold division).

57. See, e.g., D. Tuschus, *Conclusiones*, Lit. I, concl. 592, nos. 1–3.

58. *Gl. ord.* ad Dig. 1.1.1, v. *omnium animalium*.

59. See Gaines Post, *Studies in Medieval Legal Thought: Public Law and the State, 1100–1322* (1964), 8–12.

60. This paragraph follows from the conclusions in J. G. Heineccius, *Methodical System*, Lib. I, c. 1 §§ 13–14. See also Brian Tierney, *Liberty and Law: The Idea of Permissive Natural Law, 1100–1800* (2014).

61. *Gl. ord.* ad Inst. 1.1.1, v. *alterum non laedas*.

62. See T. Sanchez, *De matrimonii sacramento*, Lib. II, disp. 5, no. 3. It appears that dispensations were "sometimes (very seldom)" permitted when the couple was related in the second degree of affinity; see Kirsi Salonen, *The Penitentiary as a Well of Grace in the Late Middle Ages: The Example of the Province of Uppsala 1448–1527* (2001), 107.

63. Inst. 1.2.2: "Usu exigente et humanis necessitatibus gentes humanae iure quaedam sibi constituit." See also Cortese, *La norma giuridica*, I, 73–86.

64. *Gl. ord.* ad id, v. *nam usu*.

65. A. Vinnius, *Commentarius*, Tit. II, c. 2, no. 3.

66. On this theme, see generally Bernd Franke, *Sklaverei und Unfreiheit im Naturrecht des 17. Jahrhunderts* (2009).

67. See *gl. ord.* ad D. 47, c. 8, v. *commune*.

68. *Summa theologiae*, 1a2ae, qu. 94, art. 4.

69. Lib. II, c. 11, tits. 1–5.

70. E.g., R. Cumberland, *Treatise on the Laws of Nature*, Introduction § 2. For discussion, see Stephen Buckle, *Natural Law and the Theory of Property: Grotius to Hume* (1991), 4–16.

71. See, e.g., Edward J. Murphy, "Contract Law and Natural Law," in: *Common Truths: New Perspectives on Natural Law*, Edward McLean ed. (2000), 219–35.

72. See the discussion in Reinhard Zimmermann, *The Law of Obligations* (1990), 767–70.

73. Inst. 2.6.pr.

74. Alain Wijffels, "La bonne foi en droit savant médiéval: *bona fides-mala fides* dans les consilia d'Alexander Tartagnus (Imolensis)," in: *La bonne foi* (Centre de recherches en histoire du droit et des institutions) 9 (1998), 23–51.

75. Some of the perplexities this has caused are explored in J. D. M. Derrett, "Justice, Equity and Good Conscience," in: *Changing Law in Developing Countries,* J. Anderson ed. (1963), 114–53.

76. See also *gl. ord.* ad Cod. 1.17.1.

77. The substance of this paragraph is taken from Jan Hallebeek, "Developments in Mediaeval Roman Law," in: *Unjust Enrichment: The Comparative Legal History of the Law of Restitution,* E. J. H. Schrage ed., 2d ed. (1999), 59–120.

78. See D. J. Ibbetson, "Unjust Enrichment in England before 1600," in *Unjust Enrichment* (prior note) at 121–48.

79. Peter Birks, *The Foundations of Unjust Enrichment* (2002), 3–23.

80. Moses v. Macferlan (1760), 2 Burr. 1005, 1008, 97 E. R. 676, 678 (opinion of Lord Mansfield).

81. See, e.g., J. L. Watts, *The Making of Polities: Europe, 1300–1500* (2009); Gaines Post, *Studies in Medieval Legal Thought* (1964); Myron Gilmore, *Argument from Roman Law in Political Thought 1200–1600* (1941).

82. See, e.g., Joachim Rückert, "Natürliche Freiheit—Historische Freiheit—Vertragsfreiheit," in: *Recht zwischen Natur und Geschichte,* F. Kervégan and H. Mohnhaupt eds. (1997), 305–37.

83. Jean-Jacques Rousseau, *The Social Contract,* G. D. H. Cole trans. (1950), 3.

84. Gerald Stourzh, "The Modern State: Equal Rights, Equalizing the Individual's Status and the Breakthrough of the Modern Liberal State," in: *The Individual in Political Theory and Practice,* Janet Coleman ed. (1996), 303–27, esp. 312–14.

85. Lowrie J. Daly, *The Medieval University 1200–1400* (1961), 140–44; Rashdall, *The Universities of Europe,* above note 13, III, 156–57; Nancy Siraisi, *Arts and Sciences at Padua: The Studium of Padua before 1350* (1973), 29.

86. See Lawrence Stone, "The Size and Composition of the Oxford Student Body, 1580–1910," in: *The University in Society,* L. Stone ed. (1974), I, 3; C. T. Allmand, "The Civil Lawyers," in: *Profession, Vocation and Culture in Later Medieval England,* C. H. Clough ed. (1982), 155–80.

2. The Law of Nature in European Courts

1. See Heinrich Gehrke, "Deutsches Reich: Rechtsprechungssammlungen," in: Coing, *Handbuch* II/2, 1343–72; and Udo Wagner, "Niederlande: Rechtsprechungssammlungen," ibid., 1399–1417.

2. Klaus Luig, "Der Einfluß des Naturrechts auf das positive Privatrecht im 18. Jahrhundert," in: *Römisches Recht, Naturrecht, nationales Recht* (1998), 151–67.

3. E.g., P. Farinacius, *Decisiones,* Pt. II, dec. 81.

4. E.g., Jürgen Heideking, "The Law of Nature and Natural Rights. Die Positivierung von Naturrecht im America des ausgehenden 18. Jahrhunderts," in: *Naturrecht, Spätaufklärung, Revolution,* O. Dann and D. Klippel eds. (1995), 48–60.

5. S. Vaz Barbosa, *Principia et loci commu*n*es,* Lib. I, no. 50: "Iure suo nullus privandus est absque culpa sua" (citing Dig. 48.19.26; Cod. 9.47.22; X 1.2.2; X 3.11.2; and Sext. 5.12.22).

6. D. Arumaeus, *Decisionum et sententiarum,* Lib I, dec. 1, no. 14: Quod nullius in dominio est, id occupanti naturali ratione conceditur. See also Dig. 41.1.3.

7. V. Bondino, *De iure controverso,* Collect. 12, no. 88: describing the statute's authors as "memores iusticiae et rationis," and citing also J. Menochius, *De praesumptionibus,* Lib. II, praes. 1, no. 35.

8. A. Sola, *Commentaria,* Cap. XII, lib. 2, nos. 1–2, but also including citation to the works of many other jurists.

9. J. Accarisius, *Decisiones,* Dec. 8, no. 27–28 (1639): "cum scribentes citationem juri naturali imo et divino adscribant," citing works by Baldus, Vantius, and Borellius.

10. See, e.g., G. Dunozetus, *Decisiones,* Dec. 80: "ut in terminis similis statuti decidit Rota . . . 27 junii 1607." See also H. Magonius, *Decisiones,* Dec. 123, citing prior decisions of 1561 and 1567 that had determined a point of law about the time of day of the crime's commission. For discussion and further illustration, see Ulrike Muessig, "Superior courts in early-modern France, England and the Holy Roman Empire," in: *Judges and Judging in the History of the Common Law and Civil Law,* P. Brand and J. Getzler eds. (2012), 209–33.

11. See David Strauss, "Common Law Constitutional Interpretation," *U. Chicago L. Rev.* 63 (1996), 877–935.

12. Inst. 1.11.4: "adoptio enin naturam imitatur." For typical discussion, see, e.g., L. Balbus, *Observationes,* Cent. VI, dec. 510.

13. See, e.g., the development of rules concerning the introduction and contents of *articuli* and *interrogatoria* as used in the examination of witnesses, as they are described in Yves Mausen, *Veritatis Adiutor: La procédure du témoignage dans le droit savant et la pratique française (XIIe–XIVe siècles)* (2006), 219–51.

14. E.g., A. Trentacinque, *Consilia,* Pt. I, cons. 1, nos. 3–8, dealing with the proclamations of princes; Id., Pt. II, cons. 18, nos. 2–4, dealing with sworn contracts tending to the detriment of third parties.

15. See generally K. W. Nörr, *Naturrecht und Zivilprozess* (1976); Susanne Lepsius, "Summarischer Syndikatsprozeß: Einflüsse des kanonischen Rechts auf die städtische und kirchliche Gerichtspraxis des Spätmittelalters," in: *Medieval Church Law and the Origins of the Western Legal Tradition,* Wolfgang Müller and Mary Sommar eds. (2006), 252–74.

16. Some doubts were also clarified by the papal decree "Saepe contingit" placed in the *Corpus iuris canonici:* Clem 5.11.2.

17. B. Stracca, *De mercatura,* Dec. 104, no 18: "defensionis facultas nemini est deneganda," citing Cod. 10.1.10 and Extrav. Com. 2.3.1 in support. A similar example is M. Mendes de Castro, *Practica Lusitana,* Lib. III, c. 22 §§ 1–3.

18. H. Grotius, *De iure belli ac pacis*, Lib. II, c. 1 § 3; F. Suárez, *Tractatus de legibus*, Lib. II, c. 17, no. 6.

19. See Ian Brownlie, *International Law and the Use of Force by States* (1963), 214–30.

20. E.g., U. Locatus, *Iudiciale inquisitorum*, v. *citatio*, no. 2: "Citatio est divini naturalis canonici et civilis iuris."

21. F. Claperius, *Decisiones*, C. 35, quaest. 2, no. 1: "nam citatio est prima ac potissima pars iudicii sine qua tollitur defensio de iure naturali inducta."

22. O. Zuccaro, *Decisiones criminales*, Dec. 6, no. 6.

23. F. Mantica, *Decisiones*, Dec. 12 (1587).

24. J. Ayliffe, *Parergon*, tit. Of a Citation, no. 5.

25. J. B. Ventriglia, *Praxis rerum notabilium*, Annot. VIII § 1, nos. 1–17. See also P. Wehner, *Dubiorum seu quaestionum*, v. *citatio;* Panormitanus, *Consilia*, Cons. 99, no. 1.

26. P. Wehner, prior note, no. 3: "extra enim hos tres casus, est omnino prohibita talis citatio per edictum."

27. E.g., where a person not cited knew about the obligation from other sources, he lost the ability to complain; see P. Farinacius, *Decisiones*, Pt. II, dec. 244.

28. E.g., F. Albizzi, *Decisiones S.R.R.*, Dec. 8, nos. 8–12 (appealing to the *stylus curiae* to allow its omission).

29. M. Phaebus, *Decisiones*, Dec. 3, nos. 12–13.

30. F. Albizzi, *De inconstantia in judiciis*, Quaest. IV, no. 1.

31. E.g., a citation that did not state the place where the defendant was to appear was held invalid because it was contrary to "defensionem de iure naturali competentem." G. Dunozetus, *Decisiones*, Dec. 219, no. 2.

32. E.g., J. B. Fenzonius, *Annotationes*, C. 195, no. 27, upholding the requirement of fresh citation "tanquam aequiorem et humaniorem."

33. M. Mantova Benavides, *Praxis iudiciariae centuria*, Cas. XV; P. M. Wehner, *Dubiorum seu quaestionum*, v. *citatio* (pp. 69–75); O. R. Seraphinus, *Decisiones aureae*, Dec. 564, no. 2.

34. *Practica criminalis*, Quaest. 94, no. 3: "[A]ppellatio est species defensionis quae est de iure naturali, et consequenter a lege seu statuto tolli posse non debet."

35. *Practicarum conclusionum*, Lit. S, concl. 465, no. 3: "Odiosum dicitur statutum tollens appellationem, quia removet defensionem." See also O. Zuccaro, *Decisiones civiles*, Dec. 43, nos. 12–13.

36. See Dig. 49.1.6, 13, 15 (appeal allowed even if defendant acquiesced in the sentence; it was not necessary that the cause for the appeal be specified exactly).

37. Peter Landau, "Die kirchliche Justizgewährung im Zeitalter des Reform in den Rechtssammlungen," in: *La giustizia nell'alto Medioevo (secoli IX-XI)* (1997), 427–56.

38. J. P. Fontanella, *Cathaloniae Decisiones*, Dec. 120.

39. Ibid., no. 9: "quasi aperientes de novo oculos."

40. See L. Mathaeu y Sanz, *Tractatus de re criminali*, Contr. II, nos. 1–65.
41. Sext 2.15.5, v. deferendum: "non enim fuit inventum ut esset iniquitatis defensio sed innocencie praesidium."
42. See S. Scaccia, *De iudiciis causarum*, Lib. I, cap. 97, no. 62.
43. Ibid. (making clear, however, that he himself was not satisfied with this solution).
44. G. A. Marta, *Tractatus de clausulis*, Cl. 12, no. 7; L. Matthaeu y Sanz, *Tractatus de re criminali*, Contr. II, no. 65; C. Urceoli, *Decisiones*, Dec. 1, no. 2.
45. E.g., J. de Sesse, *Decisiones*, Dec. 91, nos 38–39: "Sed licet de iure haec procedunt, de consuetudine tam servatur contrarium." See also J. Clarus, *Practica criminalis*, Quaest. 94, no. 1: "Et ita de consuetudine servatur;" J. Mynsinger, *Observationes*, Cent. IV, obs. 41, no. 3: T. J. Reinharthus, *Selectae observationes*, Lib. I, obs. 16, no. 1. See also the conclusion in Roy Garré, *Das Gewohnheitsrecht in der Rechtsquellen- und Methodenlehre des späten ius commune in Italien (16–18. Jahrhundert)* (2005), 269–71.
46. One was "recourse to the superior" that served many of the same purposes as an appeal; see, e.g., O. R. Seraphinus, *Aureae decisiones*, Dec. 495, nos. 2–3: "Recursus ad superiorem succedit loco appellationis."
47. F. Monaldus, *Consilia*, Cons. 119, no. 1: "Dico nulli dubium esse iudicem cogere debere filium ad dandum alimenta patri egenti si in ea facultate est."
48. See F. Lanfranchi, "Ius exponendi e obbligo alimentare nel diritto romano-classico," *Studia et Documenta Historiae et iuris* 6 (1940), 46–53; Olga Tellegen-Couperus, "Father and Foundling in Classical Roman Law," *J.L.H.* 34 (2013), 129–38, at 135.
49. See, e.g., A. Valascus, *Decisiones*, Consult. 182, and the Scandinavian example, in Lars Ivar Hansen, "The Field of Property Devolution in Norway during the Late Middle Ages," in: *Disputing Strategies in Medieval Scandinavia*, Kim Esmark et al. eds. (2013), 247–77.
50. N. Boerius, *Decisiones Buredegalenses*, Dec. 127.
51. G. L. Riccio, *Praxis aurea*, Resol. 28, no. 2: "Natura autem nullam constituit differentiam inter legitimos et illegitimos."
52. E.g., N. A. Gizzarelli, *Aureae decisiones*, Dec. 47: citing the obligation "equitate quadam a natura insita cum brutis omnibus communi."
53. E.g., J. B. Fenzonius, *Annotationes*, ca. 140, nos. 6–7: "nam naturalis est coniunctio inter patrem et filium; natura autem nullam constituit differentiam inter legitimos et illegitimos."
54. Contrast Panormitanus, *Consilia*, Cons. 63, no. 4, taking the view that it was only part of the positive law with C. Pellegrino, *Decisiones*, Dec. 116, no. 3, holding that to restrict the child's right would be "odiosum legi naturali et civili." See also F. Tortus, *Annotationes*, Prael. 105–06, taking the position that the legitim "non debetur de iure naturali sed de iure civili suadente naturali ratione."

55. See *Capella Tholosana,* Quaest. 437, and gloss thereto, holding the more common opinion to be that the child's share could be diminished by statute but not eliminated entirely, as this would be "contra omnem legem naturalem. Et ista est communis conclusio de equitate canonica." See also Charles Reid Jr., *Power over the Body, Equality in the Family* (2004), 165–74.

56. See, e.g., F. Merlino Pignatelli, *Controversiarum forensium,* Cent. II, ca. 38, no. 14, upholding the statute because it was tied to natural law and did not touch the substance of the marriage. Similar is O. R. Seraphinus, *Aureae decisiones,* Dec. 811. Apparently contrary is C. Barzius, *Decisiones,* Dec. 29, no. 9.

57. E.g., J. de Sesse, *Decisiones,* Dec. 26, giving both sides and ending with a description of customary practice in Aragon, which was for parents to give 5s. to sons in place of *alimenta.*

58. J. Mangilius, *De imputationibus.*

59. E.g., A. de Gamma, *Decisiones,* Dec. 11, no. 8: distinguishing a right to inherit from a right to *alimenta,* because "suadet evidens ratio nam si quoad alimenta praestanda idem ius naturale respicit."

60. See, e.g., A. Capycius, *Decisiones,* Dec. 2, nos. 3–6; V. de Franchis, *Decisiones,* Dec. 618, no. 3: J. Ludovicus, *Decisiones,* Pt. II, dec. 76, nos. 9–11. See also Tellegen-Couperus, "Father and Foundling," above note 48, at 135: "The right of children to their parents' inheritance was stronger than the parents' right to dispose freely of their property."

61. See Dig. 22.54, 9 and DD. ad id; J. Clarus, *Practica criminalis,* Quaest. XIV, no. 5.

62. M. Phaebus, *Decisiones,* Dec. 23, no. 9 (arguing that it would be to suppose the impossible to deny the son this right).

63. E.g., U. Locati, *Opus iudiciale inquisitorum,* Cas. V; G. L. Riccio, *Praxis aurea,* Resol. 310, no. 7; L. Postius, *Decisiones,* Dec. 54, nos. 17–20.

64. See the thoughtful treatment by Mario Ascheri, "Le fonti e la flessibilità del diritto comune: il paradosso del *consilium sapientis,*" in: *Legal Consulting in the Civil Law Tradition,* M. Ascheri, Ingrid Baumgärtner & Julius Kirshner eds. (1999), 11–53.

65. D. Arumaeus, *Decisionum et sententiarum,* Lib. I, dec. 6, no. 6: "Ars iuris civilis imitatur naturam, [Inst. 1.11.1] et ideo vult devolvere successiones ad instar fluminum." See also *gl. ord.* ad Dig. 4.2.8, v. *magis,* dealing with the greater natural strength of descending ties of kinship.

66. J. Brunnemannus, *Decisionum centuriae V,* Cent. I, dec. 75.

67. C. Marzimedici, *Decisiones,* Dec. 49. A similar example is found in L. Postius, *Decisiones,* Dec. 27, no. 2, involving the legal rights of a married woman to control dotal property.

68. O. Zuccaro, *Decisiones civiles,* Dec. 10. It involved a suretyship agreement in which the first brother had stood surety for the second and had been made to pay the principal debt.

69. E.g., M. Mantova Benavides, *Praxis iudiciariae centuria*, Cas. LXVIII.
70. E.g., M. A. Blancus, *Practica criminalis*, pp. 113–18, nos. 3–9: "[D]efensio est inducta a natura et cuilibet competit, etiam brutis."
71. Ibid., nos. 21–23.
72. Ibid., nos. 37 and 59. See generally, J. B. Caccialupus, *De debitore suspecto et fugitivo* § 3, no. 7.
73. See J. Grivel de Perigny, *Decisiones*, Dec. 43, nos. 20–25, acknowledging opinion to the contrary but upholding his own as the *communis opinio;* A. Capycius, *Decisiones*, Dec. 58, no. 2, limiting the right to assertions of the falseness of the plaintiff's initial utterance.
74. E.g., A. Spirelli, *Decisiones*, Dec. 45, no. 21.
75. T. Grammaticus, *Decisiones*, Dec. 36, nos. 50–59: "[I]n criminalibus defensio tolli non possit, . . . nam iuris naturae est ut in crimine quis se defendat."
76. G. A. Tesauro, *Quaestionum et decisionum*, Lib. I, quaest. 80, no. 1: "quia bona de iure naturali et iure gentiium primaevo commnia erant et indignum esset hominem . . . morti traditum [esse]." A second example is M. Giurba, *Consilia*, Cons. 63, nos. 13–14.
77. H. a Laurentiis, *Decisiones Rotae Avenionenis*, Dec. 15, no. 5: "Deinde quod non potest princeps defensionem tollere, quae est iuris naturalis . . . praesertim ubi agitur de vita hominis ad Dei similitudinem creati."
78. E.g., M. Berlich, *Decisiones*, Dec. 79 (allowing crimes against the law of nature to be considered in fixing penalties even if their prosecution was barred by the passage of time).
79. M. A. Chamocho Cantudo, *Sodomía: El crimen y pecado contra natura o historia de una intolerancia* (2012), 77–116.
80. See, e.g., N. Boerius, *Decisiones Burdegalenses*, Dec. 301; J. B. Díaz de Luco, *Practica criminalis canonica*, C. 103.
81. Andreas Roth, "Crimen contra naturam," in: *Natural Law and the Laws of Nature in Early Modern Europe*, Lorraine Daston and Michael Stolleis eds. (2008), 89–103.
82. See, e.g., J. Damhouder, *Praxis rerum criminalium*, C. 98; M. Muta, *Decisiones*, Dec. 86; N. Everhardus, *Consilia sive Responsa*, Cons. LXVII, but more lenient treatment in the case of clerical offenders (perpetual imprisonment) seems to have been envisioned.
83. P. Caballus, *Resolutionum criminalium centuriae*, Cent. I, cas. 129, no. 2.
84. J. Brunnemannus, *Decisionum centuriae V*, Cent. V, dec. 95.
85. J. Grivel de Perigny, *Decisiones*, Dec. 23, no. 12.
86. J. Papon, *Recueil d'arrests*, Lib. XXII, tit. 7, no. 1. A similar case involving attempted sodomy with a fellow prisoner is found in L. Peguera, *Decisiones*, Dec. 75.
87. He was sentenced to be burned alive along with the animal involved.
88. See generally David Chauvet, *La personalité juridique des animaux jugés au moyen âge* (2012).

89. P. Caballus, *Resolutionum criminalium*, Cas. 200, no. 4: "non solum homini ratione vetitum esse sed et ex instinctu naturae animalia quaedam irrationalia id abhorrere et a tali coitu se abstinere."

90. Compare E. Speckhan, *Quaestiones et decisiones*, Cent. I, quaest. 84 (arguing against punishing the animal). See also M. A. Chamocho and R. Manchón, "Le crime de sodomie dans l'opuscule Latin *Ad peccatorem sodomitam*," in: *Droit et Moeurs*, M. A. Chamocho ed. (2010), 295–316, at 309–11.

91. Heinbard Steiger, "Die Freiheit der Meere und das Naturrecht," in: *Naturrecht und Staat in der Neuzeit: Diethelm Klippel zum 70.Geburtstag*, Jens Eisfeld ed. (2013), 11–37.

92. N. Everhardus, *Consilia sive responsa*, Cons. III, no. 10: "[N]on debent huiusmodi nova et inconsueta telonia vel vectigalia imponere nisi subsistente iusta et legitima causa, cum sit odiosa iuri naturali et libertati contraria." See also F. Marcus, *Decisiones*, Quaest. 40, 490.

93. A. Sola, *Commentaria*, Cap. XII, lib. 2, nos. 1–2.

94. See *Theologians and Contract Law: The Moral Transformation of the Ius Commune (ca. 1500–1650)* (2012).

95. X 5.19.4 provided the *locus classicus* for this prohibition. Roman law was rather more flexible; see, e.g., Dig. 22.1.17.

96. Panormitanus, *Commentaria* ad X 5.19.rubr. "contra naturam rerum quoniam pecunia germinat pecuniam quae tamen naturaliter non est apta germinare." See also Diana Wood, *Medieval Economic Thought* (2002), 84–87. The question was controversial, however; see J. B. García, *Un Siglo de moral económica en Salamanca, 1526–1629* (1985), 75–77.

97. See John T. Noonan Jr., *The Church that Can and Cannot Change: The Development of Catholic Moral Teaching* (2005), 134–37.

98. See, e.g., James Davis, *Medieval Market Morality: Life, Law and Ethics in the English Marketplace, 1200–1500* (2012), 213–15; John T. Noonan Jr., *The Scholastic Analysis of Usury* (1957); Reiner Franke, *Die Entwicklung des (Darlehens-) Zinses in Frankreich* (1996), 17–90; Diego Alonso-Lasheras, *Luis de Molina's "De Iustitia et Iure": Justice as Virtue in an Economic Context* (2011), 125–83.

99. Raymond de Roover, "Scholastic Economics: Survival and Lasting Influence from the Sixteenth Century to Adam Smith," *Quarterly J. of Economics* 69 (1955), 161–90, at 173; Christian Zendri, "L'usura nella dottrina dei giuristi umanisti: Martin de Azpilcueta (1492–1586)," in: *Credito e usura fra teologia, diritto e amministrazione*, Diego Quaglioni et al. eds. (2005), 265–90.

100. See, e.g., Gerard Noodt, *The Three Books on Interest-Bearing Loans and Interest* (2009), C. 11, dealing with loans at interest and the principles of Christianity.

101. E.g., J. Clarus, *Practica criminalis*, v. *usura*, no. 3: "[U]surae sunt omni iure prohibitae, et in primis quidem de iure naturali. Et est communis opinio."

102. E.g., M. Bellone, *Decisiones Rotae Genuae*, Dec. 193, no. 8; J. Brunnemannus, *Decisionum centuriae V*, Cent. I, dec. 78; B. Cavalcanus, *Decisiones*, Pt. II, dec. 13, nos. 30–31; O. R. Seraphinus, *Decisiones aureae*, Dec. 599, no.3.

103. E.g., A. Tartagni, *Consilia*, Lib. I, cons. 57, no. 1.

104. See, e.g., J. F. McGovern, "The Rise of New Economic Attitudes—Economic Humanism, Economic Nationalism—during the Later Middle Ages and the Renaissance," *Traditio* 26 (1970), 217–53.

105. So stated by J. Gibalini, *De usuris*, Lib. I, cap. 7, art. 8, cons. 3, no. 30: "Quia tamen contrariam esse consuetudinem in Italia plerique testantur."

106. J. Meichsner, *Decisiones*, Tom. I, lib. 1, dec. 12.

107. G. A. Tesauro, *Novae decisiones*, Dec. 57, containing a long discussion of the subject with many citations to the learned literature.

108. F. Merlino Pignatelli, *Controversiarum forensium*, Cent. I, ca. 75; G. Wynants, *Decisiones*, Dec. 88, no. 10; J. B. Coccini, *Decisiones*, Dec. 468.

109. B. Cavalcanus, *Decisiones*, Pt. II, dec. 13, nos. 30–31; he was, however, required to restore at least some part of the usurious profits.

110. See, e.g., D. de Soto, *De iustitia et iure*, Quaest. I, art. 5.

111. E.g., *Codex Fabrianus*, Lib. IV, tit. 8 (ascribing the prohibitions against usury to the canon law alone).

112. F. Costantini, *Decisiones*, Dec. 3 (1608); see also B. Gattus, *Consilia*, Cons. 6, no. 66.

113. See the examples found in F. Amendola, *Additiones*, Dec. 9.

114. D. Mevius, *Decisiones*, Pt. III, dec. 70, no. 1: "[Monopolia] aut commerciorum libertati quam natura fovet adversa . . . [et] noxiam damnat jurisprudentia gentium communis." See also Raymond de Roover, "Monopoly Theory Prior to Adam Smith: A Revision," *Quarterly J. of Economics* 65 (1951), 492–524.

115. See H. P. Haberkorn, *Decisiones*, Dec. 44.

116. Its possibilities are nicely explored by Orazio Condorelli, "Norma juridica y norma moral: justicia y *salus animarum* según Diego de Covarrubias," in: *Razón Práctica y Derecho*, J. C. Cruz ed. (2011), 49–86.

117. V. Bondino, *De iure controverso*, Colluct. 8, c. 1, no. 21.

118. J. Brunnemannus, *Decisionum centuriae V*, Cent. I, dec. 78: "quia aequitati juris naturalis et canonici [est] conforme ut haeres ad damna a defuncto data restituenda teneatur."

119. See M. Bellone, *Decisiones Rotae Genuae*, Dec. 193.

120. Jan Hallebeek, *The Concept of Unjust Enrichment in Late Scholasticism* (1996). See also Karl Weinzierl, *Rückgabepflicht nach kanonischem Recht* (1932); Decock, *Theologians and Contract Law*, above note 94, at 514–19.

121. F. Mantica, *Decisiones*, Dec. 307, no. 1: "Nam hoc statutum est odiosum et contra ius commune et ideo strictissime est intelligendum."

122. *De iure belli ac pacis*, Bk. II, c. 2, tit. 5: "Lex enim civilis quanquam nihil potest praecipere quod ius naturae prohibet, aut prohibere quod praecipit."

123. Aquinas, *Summa theologiae*, 1a2ae 95, 2.

124. Ibid., 1a2ae 96, 4: "Et huiusmodi magis sunt violentiae quam leges, quia, sicut Augustinus dicit, lex esse non videtur quae iusta non fuerit."

125. *Gl. ord.* ad Cod. 1.9 (22).2, v. *quoties.*

126. See Edward Corwin, *The "Higher Law" Background of American Constitutional Law* (1928).

127. Stefan Vogenauer, *Die Auslegung von Gesetzen in England und auf dem Kontinent* (2001).

128. See, e.g., John Killoran: "Aquinas and Vitoria: Two Perspectives on Slavery," in: *The Medieval Tradition of Natural Law,* H. J. Johnson ed. (1987), 87–101.

129. E.g., F. Tortus, *Annotationes,* tit. *Summarum,* no. 128; J. B. Ventriglia, *Praxis rerum notabilium,* Annot. XXXVI; C. A. de Luca, *Decisiones Rotae Marchiae,* Dec. 14; see generally Garré, *Das Gewohnheitsrecht,* above note 45, at 255–71.

130. See, e.g., Maurizio Fioravanti, "Constitutionalism," in: *History of the Philosophy of Law in the Civil Law World, 1600–1900,* D. Canale, P. Grossi, and H. Hofmann eds. (2009), 289–90.

131. See Wim Decock, "The Judge's Conscience and the Protection of the Criminal Defendant: Moral Safeguards against Juridical Arbitrariness," in: *From the Judge's Arbitrium to the Legality Principle,* G. Martyn, A. Musson, and H. Pihlajamäki eds. (2013), 69–94.

132. O. Cacheranus, *Decisiones,* Dec. 88, nos. 2–4: "contra ius divinum et humanum rationique naturali adversus non deberet valere," and "ubi non est culpa ibi regulariter non debet esse poena."

133. See also F. Claperius, *Decisiones,* Ca. 14, quaest. 1: "grave enim est non solum legibus sed etiam naturali aequitatae contrarium pro alienis debitis molestari."

134. Ibid., no. 25: the rule against the validity of "statuta . . . iniqua et iniusta procedit quando sint sine causa . . . secus si cum causa, tunc enim aequa et iusta sunt." Another example of arguments pro and con is found in J. Thomingius, *Decisiones,* Dec. 26.

135. Ibid., nos. 30–31.

136. F. Chartarius, *Decisiones rotae Genuensis,* Dec. 121, no. 15: "Non obstat quod statutum intelligi debeat prout iacet quia debet tamen intelligi ne absurdum contineat et ne via malitiis et calumniis litigantium aperiatur."

137. See Gaines Post, "The Naturalness of Society and the State," in: *Studies in Medieval Legal Thought* (1964), 494–561.

138. Karl Llewellyn, "One 'Realist's View of Natural Law for Judges," in *Jurisprudence: Realism in Theory and Practice* (1962), 111–15.

139. E.g., A. Leoncillus, *Decisiones,* Dec. 49, no. 21: "Durum hoc est sed ita lex scriptum est et quod non omnia quae sunt a nostris maioribus constituta ratio reddi potest, et quod rationes legum inquiri non oportet. See also P. Christianaeus, *Practicarum quaestionum,* Lib. I, tit. 14, dec. 62 (criticizing judges for disregarding statutes "under the pretext of doing equity").

140. J. Brunnemannus, *Decisionum centuriae V,* Cent. I, dec. 95, no. 2: "[S]tatuta non secundum corticem verborum sed secundum rationem accipienda sunt." See the analysis in: Ian Maclean, *Interpretation and Meaning in the Renaissance: The Case of Law* (1992), 142–58.

141. E.g., C. Barzius, *Decisiones,* Dec. 97, nos. 35–36: "[R]atio sit sicut anima et spiritus legis, verba autem sint sicut corpus et superficies, ratio legis est quae ipsam legem regulat." See also Cortese, *La norma giuridica,* II, 317–20.

142. G. B. Coccini, *Decisiones,* Dec. 70 (1602), "Verborum enim significatio debet ad intellectum sanum bonum civilem et vitio carentem applicari."

143. A. Gaill, *Practicarum observationum,* Lib. II, obs. 33.

144. G. A. Tesauro, *Novae decisiones,* Dec. 34, no 3: "[T]estamenti factio iuris naturalis est . . . [et] statutum iura naturalia tollere non potest." The more common opinion, at least as I understand it, was that testamentary disposition of property was part of the law of nature only in the sense that the urge to foster the fortunes of one's progeny was a natural desire. See, e.g., S. de Praetis, *De ultimarum voluntatum interpretatione,* Lib. I, interp. 2, sol. 2, nos. 9–10. See also D.p. C. 13 q. 2 c. 7, helpfully explored in Jan Hallebeek, "Dispositions *ad pias causas* in Gratian's *Decretum,*" in: *Der Einfluss religiöser Vorstellungen auf die Entwicklung des Erbrechts,* R. Zimmermann ed. (2012), 79–102.

145. Ibid., justifying the prohibition, at least where it was possible to make an inter vivos transfer. See the discussion of French, German, and American law in: Jens Beckert, *Inherited Wealth,* Thomas Dunlap trans. (2008), 21–82.

146. D. Mevius, *Decisiones,* Pt. III, dec. 38, nos. 4, 16. See also Oliver Schihin, "Zwischen gelehrtem Recht und territorialer Praxis: Einige Aspekte der Leibeigenschaftstheorie von David Mevius," in: *David Mevius (1609–1670),* Nils Jörn ed. (2007), 81–96.

147. Mevius, *Decisiones,* prior note: "nec ad iniqua, impia [aut] improba."

148. E. Speckhan, *Quaestiones et decisiones,* Cent. I, quaest. 97, no. 21: "quod libertas venandi sit juris naturalis et gentium ideoque per principem tolli eam non posse." See also J. Ludovicus, *Decisiones,* Pt. I, dec. 31, no. 4 (upholding a statute restricting the carrying of weapons but limiting it to defensive weapons).

149. Ibid., no. 27: "Hoc est iure naturali permissivo . . . [et] multa sint iure naturae licita quae inspecta reipublicae utilitate et iuxta aequissimum communitatis regimen per legem humanam prohiberi possunt."

150. Mario Ascheri, *The Laws of Late Medieval Italy (1000–1500): Foundations for a European Legal System* (2013), 330–33.

151. E.g., A. Tartagni, *Consilia,* Lib. I, cons. 52, no. 2: "si assumeremus verba secundum propriam significationem statutum contineret absurditatem vel iniquitatem, nam tunc accipientur verba secundum impropriam et non secundum propriam significationem."

152. E.g., the "descending theme" of government as developed by Walter Ullmann; see his *Principles of Government and Politics in the Middle Ages,* 2d ed. (1966), 296–305.

153. R. I. Moore, *The Formation of a Persecuting Society: Power and Deviance in Western Europe, 950–1250* (1987).

154. E.g., rights involving marriage and the family, as described in Reid, *Power over the Body,* above note 55, at 7–12, 25–68.

155. K. Pennington, *The Prince and the Law, 1200–1600: Sovereignty and Rights in the Western Legal Tradition* (1993). See also J. A. Fernández-Santamaría, *Natural Law, Constitutionalism, Reason of State and War* (2005), 349–91.

156. B. Tierney, *Religion, Law, and the Growth of Constitutional Thought 1150–1650* (1982).

157. G. de Cabedo, *Practicarum observationum,* Dec. 75, no. 1: "Rex obligatur ex contractu inito cum subdito."

158. E. Speckhan, *Quaestiones et decisiones,* Cent. I, quaest. 72, no. 25: "Non est princeps supra leges, sed leges supra principem." See also Cortese, *La norma giuridica,* I, 143–81.

159. G. de Cabedo, *Practicarum observationum.* Dec. 75, no. 3: "Denique ex causa, id est ob enorme preiudicium coronae vel propter bonum publicum." See also Jane Black, *Absolutism in Renaissance Milan: Plenitude of Power under the Visconti and the Sforza 1329–1535* (2009), 11–29.

160. E.g., J. P. Surdus, *Decisiones,* Dec. 1, no. 18: holding against the prince in such a case, "licet possit non tamen voluit."

161. A. Gaill, *Practicarum observationum,* Lib. II, obs. 58, no. 1: "distinguendum utrum disponat vel statuat aliquid contra ius naturale vel gentium an vero contra ius positivum"; C. van Neostadius, *Decisiones,* Dec. 15: "non potest uti jure et plenitudine potestatis cum diceretur ea abuti"; F. Roccus, *Responsorum legalium,* Resp. 49, nos. 2–3: "Nec etiam princeps de plenitudine potestatis a contractu recedere valet, enim plenitudo non extenditur ad ius naturale"; see also J. Mynsinger, *Observataiones,* Cent. IV, obs. 8, nos. 2–7 (various opinions are given and discussed).

162. S. Rovitus. *Consilia cum decisionibus,* Cons. 3, no. 2: "[C]rimen laesae maiestatis non tollet ea quae sunt de iure naturali seu gentium primaevo sed ea tantum quae sunt de mero iure civili."

163. E.g., N. Everhardus, *Consilia sive responsa,* Cons. LVIII, no. 50, dealing with papal grants and commands.

164. E.g., *Codex Fabrianus,* Lib. I, tit. 11 § 1 (that the prince "nec voluuisse unquam credendus est quod iuste velle non potuit").

165. F. Mantica, *Decisiones;,* see above note 121. See also the parallel case of the jurists' treatment of papal actions in Kenneth Pennington, "Pro peccatis patrum puniri: A Moral and Legal Problem of the Inquisition," *Church History* 47 (1978), 137–54.

166. M. de Afflictis, *Decisiones,* Dec. 24, no. 7: "cum sit fundata super iure naturali et divino," citing Joannes Andreae in support.

167. See Michael Wilks, *The Problem of Sovereignty in the Later Middle Ages: The Papal Monarchy with Augustinus Triumphus and the Publicists* (1963), 288–327.

168. J. Altogradi, *Controversiae forenses,* Contr. 91.

169. Ibid., no 13.

170. Ibid., no. 7: "[S]i tales concessiones facere potest extraneis, multo magis id ei licere debet in favorem consanguineorum, quia et praecepto iuris naturalis immo divini prima charitas incidit a se ipso."

171. The question was discussed clearly and at some length by Panormitanus, *Commentaria* at X 2.1.12, nos. 8–9. See also F. Marcus, *Decisiones,* Quaest. 1321 (involving the papal power to amend the rule requiring two witnesses for the proof of a fact).

172. See the balanced assessment by Paul Hyams, "Due Process versus the Maintenance of Order in European Law: The Contribution of the *ius commune,*" in: *The Moral World of the Law,* Peter Coss ed. (2000), 62–90.

173. F. Merlino Pignatelli, *Controversiarum forensium,* Cent. II, c. 37: "Naturae humanae vitio adscribendum."

3. Legal Education in England

1. See Paul A. Brand, *The Origins of the English Legal Profession* (1992), 106–19; Alexandra Braun, *Giudici e accademia nell'esperienza inglese* (2006), 43–63.

2. This chapter excludes solicitors and attorneys, who learned their profession by a system akin to apprenticeship. See Robert Robson, *The Attorney in Eighteenth-Century England* (1959), 52–67; C. W. Brooks, *Pettyfoggers and Vipers of the Commonwealth* (1986), 151–81.

3. See J. H. Baker, "Oral Instruction in Land Law and Conveyancing, 1250–1500," in: *Learning the Law: Teaching and the Transmission of Law in England 1150–1900,* J. A. Bush and A. Wijffels eds. (1999), 157–73, esp. 172–73.

4. E.g., James Whitelocke, later J. K. B. See *Liber Famelicus of Sir James Whitelocke,* Camden Society 70, John Bruce ed. (1868), 13–14.

5. E.g., Thomas Egerton, later Lord Ellesmere, who studied at Oxford in the 1550s, did not take a degree, but the evidence from his notes and papers shows that he studied the civil law as well as classics and history while a student. He later cited precedents from it. See also Louis Knafla, *Law and Politics in Jacobean England* (1977), 39–40; Mark Curtis, *Oxford and Cambridge in Transition 1558–1642* (1959), 154–55; D. S. Bland, "Rhetoric and the Law Students in Sixteenth-Century England," *Studies in Philology* 54 (1957), 498–508.

6. The subject is entertainingly and well described by D. J. Ibbetson, "Ghosts of the Past and the English Common Law," in: *History in Court: Historical Expertise and Methods in a Forensic Context,* Alain Wijffels ed. (2001), 111–32.

7. F.N.B. *78.

8. Wilfrid Prest, "Legal Education of the Gentry at the Inns of Court, 1560–1640," *Past & Present* 38 (1967), 20–39; Thomas Evans, "Study at the Restoration Inns of Court," in: *Learning the Law,* above note 3, at 287–302.

9. See David Lemmings, "The Student Body of the Inns of Court under the Later Stuarts," *B.I.H.R.* 58 (1985), 149–66.

10. Baker, *Introduction,* 161–62; "The Third University 1450–1550: Law School or Finishing School?" in: *The Intellectual and Cultural World of the Early Modern Inns of Court,* J. E. Archer, E. Goldring, and S. Knight eds. (2011), 8–24; *Legal Education in London, 1250–1850,* S.S. Lecture of 2005 (2007). See also William Holdsworth, *Essays in Law and History,* A. L. Goodhart and H. G. Hanbury eds. (1946), 25–26 (contrasting the "efficient legal education" offered at the Inns before the Civil War with its "collapse" afterward); and M. C. Mirow, "The Ascent of the Readings: Some Evidence from Readings on Wills," in: *Learning the Law,* 227–54 (refuting the conclusion that the Readings had ceased to be effective in the seventeenth century).

11. See, e.g., the evidence relating to the contributions of Gerard Legh, in: Paul Raffeld, "The Inner Temple Revels (1561–62)," in: *The Intellectual and Cultural World,* prior note, 32–50, esp. 40–44; But cf. W. Prest, "The Learning Exercises at the Inns of Court 1590–1640," *J. Society of Public Teachers of Law* 9 (1967), 301–13.

12. W. Prest, *Legal Education,* above note 8, 24–25; W. C. Richardson, *A History of the Inns of Court: With Special Reference to the Period of the Renaissance* (1975), 101–166.

13. An example is Thomas Kebell (d. 1500), described in E. W. Ives, *The Common Lawyers of Pre-Reformation England* (1983), 57–59. See also Baker, *Legal Education in London,* above note 10, 18–19.

14. See J. H. Baker, "Oral Instruction in Land Law and Conveyancing, 1250–1500," in: *Learning the Law,* above note 3, 157–60.

15. See J. H. Baker, Introduction, *Readings and Moots at the Inns of Court in the Fifteenth Century, Volume II,* S.S. 105 (1990), pp. lxxvvii–cx.

16. See Robert Keilway, *Relationes quorundam casuum selectorum tempore Henrici VII* (1633), nos. 27, 116, 120. On the authorship of this text by John Caryll (d. 1523), see *Readings and Moots,* prior note, 74–75.

17. See *St. German's Doctor and Student,* T. F. T. Plucknett and J. L. Barton eds., S.S. 91 (1974), 12–20, 32–39. See also Edward Coke, "First Reading on Fines" in: *Three Law Tracts* (repr. 1982), 225 (describing English laws as "unwritten laws, but divinely cast into the hearts of men and built upon the irremovable rock of reason").

18. Many examples from the Middle Ages are found in Stanley Cunningham, "Albertus Magnus on Natural Law," *J. Hist. of Ideas* 28 (1967), 479–502.

19. See, e.g., "Moot on Justification of Self-Defence," in: *Notebook of Sir John Port,* J. H. Baker ed., S.S. 102 (1986), 107–08.

20. See, e.g., *"Prerogativa Regis" Tertia lectura Roberti Constable de Lyncolnis Inne anno 11 H. 7,* S. E. Thorne ed. (1949).

21. J. H. Baker, *Readers and Readings in the Inns of Court and Chancery,* S.S. Supp. Ser. 13 (2001). It contains a list of the Readings that have been printed, at 605–12. See also Margaret McGlynn, *The Royal Prerogative and the Learning of the Inns of Court* (2003), 1–72.

22. Robert Callis (d. 1624), *Reading upon the Statute of Sewers* (1685), 24: "And the Laws of this Realm . . . have fetched their Pedigree from the Law of Nature"; Francis Bacon, *Reading on the Statute of Uses, A.D. 1600,* J. Stephens ed. (1892), 399, 410; Robert Gynes, Reading on 2 Edw. VI, c. 13 (1568) (stressing conformity between divine law and the common law, as described in Ian Williams, "The Tudor Genesis of Edward Coke's Immemorial Common Law," *Sixteenth Century J.* 43 (2012), 105–09; David Jardine, *A Reading on the Use of Torture in the Criminal Law of England* (1837), 59 (arguing that judicial torture was "opposed to the fundamental principles of reason and law"). See also Baker, *Readers and Readings,* 238–39.

23. Thomas Fitzwilliam's "Reading on the Statute of Merton" (1465), in: *Readings and Moots at the Inns of Court,* I, S. E. Thorne ed. S.S. 71 (1954), 38–60; Robert Brooke, *Reading upon the Statute of Limitations: 32 H. 8, cap. 2* (1647).

24. E.g., Richard Hall's "Reading on the Statute of Gloucester" (I. T. 1481), in: *Readings and Moots,* 147–48, 154–55 (repeatedly using the concept of reason to construe the statute's treatment of the law of costs); John Grene's "Reading on the Statute of Marlborough" (1499), in: *Notebook of Sir John Port,* J. H. Baker ed., S.S. 102 (1986), 163 (question of allowing escape by prisoners known to be innocent of the crime for which they were arrested); James Dyer's "Reading on the Statute of Wills" (M. T. 1552), in: *Three Learned Readings Made upon Three Very Usefull Statutes* XVIII, no. 19 (1648), 62 (legality of conveyance of land to second son after "some unnatural act of ingratitude to the father" by the elder son); Thomas Frowyk's "Reading on Prerogativa Regis," chs. 1–3 (I. T. 1495), in: Margaret McGlynn, *The Royal Prerogative and the Learning of the Inns of Court* (2003), 261–94, at 278–79 (discussion of the extent of the king's rights under primer seisin).

25. See T. Williams, *The Excellency and Praeheminence of the Law of England* (1680).

26. It is printed in B. H. Putnam, *Early Treatises on the Practice of the Justices of the Peace in the Fifteenth and Sixteenth Centuries,* in: *Oxford Studies in Social and Legal History*(1924), 286–414.

27. Ibid., 333–35; compare Matthew Hale, *Historia Placitorum Coronae,* C. 40, pt. 2 (1736), I, 484.

28. Ibid., 307; compare Edmund Dudley's "Reading on Quo Warranto" (1486/1487), in: *John Spelman's Reading on Quo Warranto (1519),* J. H. Baker ed., S.S. 113 (1997), 54–55.

29. Norman Doe, *Fundamental Authority in Late Medieval English Law* (1990). See also J. W. Gough, *Fundamental Law in English Constitutional History* (1955), 12–29; S. B. Chrimes, *English Constitutional Ideas in the Fifteenth Century* (1936), 214–18; F. E. Dowrick, *Justice According to the English Common Lawyers* (1961), 46–72; Robert Jefferson, "The Uses of Natural Law in the Royal Courts of Fifteenth-Century England" (Unpublished PhD dissertation, University of Utah, 1972).

30. *Fundamental Authority,* prior note, at 176. See also J. W. Tubbs, *The Common Law Mind* (2000), 71–128.

31. See, e.g., Smith v. Hancock (1648), Style 137, 82 E. R. 592 (both terms being used to describe the principle that no man should be a judge in his own cause).

32. Y. B. Trin 9 Edw. IV, pl. 9, f. 14 (1469).

33. Y. B. Mich. 20 Hen. VII, pl. 20, f. 10b (1504).

34. Y. B. Mich. 11 Hen. VII, pl. 35, f. 11b (1495).

35. E.g., Y. B. Pasch. 12 Edw. IV, pl. 22, f. 8b–9b (1472).

36. See, e.g., Sir William Capell's Case (Chan. 1494), in: *Notebook of Sir John Port*, J. H. Baker ed., S.S. 102 (1986), no. 8, 13–14.

37. See Louis Knafla, "The Law Studies of an Elizabethan Student," *Huntington Library Q.* 32 (1969), 221–40, esp. 231.

38. See Holdsworth, *H.E.L.*, XII, 86–87.

39. See Holdsworth, *H.E.L.*, VI, 600–03.

40. See Bracton, *De legibus*, f. 2.

41. See, e.g., 1 Bl. Comm. *41: "[B]eing co-eval with mankind and dictated by God himself, [the law of nature] is of course superior in obligation to any other." See also Chapter 5.

42. The range and nature of these general treatments are discussed in Julia Rudolph, *Common Law and Enlightenment in England, 1689–1750* (2013), 30–40.

43. *Enchiridion legum: Speculum juris anglicani*, C. 1 (1673).

44. *The English Lawyer, Describing a Method for Managing of the Laws of this Land* (1631), 149–62, esp. 153.

45. *Direction or Preparative to the Study of the Law*, C. 1 (1829). Similar is Thomas Wood, *An Institute of the Laws of England* (1722), 4.

46. *Studii legalis ratio, or Directions for the Study of Law* (1667), 10 ("very Reason and the order of nature" should direct study of the law).

47. *The Faithful Councellor: Or the Marrow of the Law in English* 2d ed., C. 1 (1675).

48. For the many editions, see *Legal Bibliography of the British Commonwealth of Nations* [Sweet & Maxwell], 2d ed. (1955), 24–26.

49. *Free Parliaments* (1731), 51 (taking note of the beneficial effects of "that Law of Nature, implanted in every Man's Mind").

50. "Epieikeia et table generall a les annals del ley" (1609), p. iii (defining his subject in terms of the law of nature).

51. "Law Lectures on the Liberty of the Subject, 1616," British Library, Harl. MS. 4841, f. 47: "Le ley de nature, customes et statutes sont le matter et forme dont nostre ley."

52. "Case of the Post-Nati," in *Works of Francis Bacon* (1854), II, 169: "[A]s the common law is more worthy than statute law, so the law of nature is more worthy than them both." See, however, the more negative characterization of Bacon's description in Daniel Coquillette, *Francis Bacon* (1992), 288–91.

53. *The Compleat Arbitrator: Or the Law of Awards and Arbitraments*, C. 2 § 6 (1770), 26 (voiding bonds to marry entered into under compulsion because "it is

so agreeable to the Laws of Reason and the Laws of God, that Marriage should proceed from a free Choice").

54. *A Treatise of Equity*, C. 1 § 2 (1793–1794) (describing the foundation of all laws as "natural justice and equity" and stating that it "corrects and controls them when they do amiss," citing Grotius and Pufendorf). See also D. J. Ibbetson, *Historical Introduction to the Law of Obligations* (1999), 216–19.

55. *Observations on the More Ancient Statutes*, 4th ed. (1775), 559 (arguing that "natural justice" requires interested parties to be given an opportunity to defend their interests).

56. *Examen legum Angliae, or the Laws of England Examined by Scripture, Antiquity, and Reason* (1656), 5–6 (complaining that the moral law "principally grounded upon the Law of Nature" was insufficiently enforced in England).

57. *Droit le Roy: Or Rights and Prerogatives of the Imperial Crown of Great Britain* (1786), 19, 31 (attempting to show that the powers of English monarchs were limited by the laws of God and nature only).

58. *The English Lawyer: Shewing the Nature and Forms of Original Writs, Processes and Mandates, of the Courts at Westminster* (1732), 161: "The Common Law Herein Imitating the Law of Nature, Preserving Its Vigour by Rotation and Circuity." See, however, the same author's *Institutio legalis: Or an Introduction to the Study and Practice of the Laws of England* (1732), 33–35 (mentioning only the general common law, local custom, statute law, and decided cases, which he described as *responsa prudentium*).

59. *Britton*, Lib. I, c. 32, F. M. Nichols ed. and trans. (1865), I, 194 (Law of nature compared with institution of slavery that was introduced "par constitucioun des gentz").

60. *Enchiridion Legum: A Discourse Concerning . . . Laws in General and in Particular . . . the Laws of England*, c. 1 (1673), 10 (the Law of Nature is "next to the Divine Law in excellency, antiquity, immutability, and severity").

61. William Burge, *Commentaries on Colonial and Foreign Laws* (1907), III, 1 (the institution of marriage said to be based upon natural law).

62. *Essay on the Legality of Impressing Seamen* (1777), 10 (a reference to the "independence and liberty of men in a state of nature").

63. *Reading upon the Statute of Sewers* (1685), 24 ("And the Laws of this Realm . . . have fetched their Pedigree from the Law of Nature").

64. See his short treatise or lecture "Of Copieholds," Cheatham's Library, Manchester, MSS. A.2.23, f. 52 and A.3.99, first 13 folios (custom described as being "allowed by the lawes of God, the lawes of nature, the lawe of nations, and by the private lawes of everye countrye").

65. *Laws against Popish Recusants*, Stat. 5 Eliz. c. 1 § 14 (1680), 47 (persons attained under statute of Praemunire still entitled to protection against other persons under the Law of Nature, which is *indelibelis & immutabilis*, something that the Parliament could not take away").

66. *Co. Lit.* *11b (listing the Law of Nature as one of the "divers Laws within the Realm of England"). See also the more cautious characterization of Allen D. Boyer, *Sir Edward Coke and the Elizabethan Age* 85–87 (2003); J. W. Tubbs, *The Common Law Mind: Medieval and Early Modern Conceptions* 163–65 (2000); Harold Berman, "The Origins of Historical Jurisprudence: Coke, Selden, Hale," 103 *Yale L.J.* (1994), 1651, 1691–93.

67. *Treatise on Obligations and Contracts* (1818), 4 (distinguishing obligations based upon "equity or natural law" from those that were "purely civil").

68. *Star Chamber Cases* (1641), 50 (due process in trials of foreign litigants said to be secured by the law of nature).

69. *Considerations on Criminal Law* (1772) (devoting Bk. I, c. 6 to exposition of the place of the law of nature in the law of crimes).

70. *The Countrey Justice,* C. 1, 1st ed. (1618) (speaking of the common laws as "receiving principally their Grounds from the Law of God and Nature").

71. *Les Reports des cases & Matters en Ley . . . en Ireland* (1674), Preface: "Law of Nature, Which Is the Root and Touchstone of All Good Laws."

72. *The English Lawyer* (1631), 191 (endorsing and giving examples of the force of the law of nature in practice).

73. *Origines juridiciales,* C. 2, 3d ed. (1666), 3 (approving Lord Ellesmere's view that the common law was grounded upon the Law of God and the Law of Nature).

74. *Principles of Penal Law* (1775), 35–36 (considering the compatibility of the penalty of transportation of convicted felons with the law of nature).

75. *Certaine Observations Concerning the Office of the Lord Chancellor,* Pt. II, c. 7 (1651), 111 (cases in Chancery involving foreign merchants to be determined *secundum legem naturae*).

76. *Patriarcha, or The Natural Power of Kings* (1680), 3 (that government by kings was ordained by the scriptures, ancient practice, and the Law of Nature).

77. *Lord Nottingham's Chancery Cases,* Vol. 2, no. 643, D.E.C. Yale ed., S.S. 79 (1961), 484–85 (parental obligation to provide for children under natural law used to justify the common law's rule that title to land descends but does not ascend).

78. *Law or a Discourse Thereof in Four Books,* Bk. 1, c. 1 (1759), 3–4 (defining the Law of Nature as "fixed in man's nature which ministreth common principles of good and evil").

79. *Fleta,* Lib. III, c. 2, H. G. Richardson and G. O. Sayles eds. S.S. 89 (1972), 2 (law of possession and ownership of things acquired under natural law).

80. See *The Governance of England,* c. 4, Charles Plummer ed. (1885), 117 (kings do wrong if they do "any thynge ayenst the lawe of God or ayenst they lawe off nature"). He was also the author of a work devoted to the subject, *De natura legis naturae,* printed in *Works of Sir John Fortescue,* Thomas Lord Clermont ed. (1869). See also E. F. Jacob, "Sir John Fortescue and the Law of Nature," *Bull. John Rylands Library* 18 (1934), 359–76.

81. *Report of Some Proceedings on the Commission for the Trial of Rebels in the Year 1746,* 2d ed. (1791), 273–74 (right to plea in self-defense "founded in the law of nature").

82. *The Lawiers Logike, Exemplifying the Praecepts of Logike by the Practice of the Common Lawe,* 1st ed. (1588, repr. 1969), 2 (law and logic "must be conformable unto those sparkes of naturall reason . . . appearing in the monuments and disputations of excellent authors").

83. *The Law of Evidence by a Late Learned Judge* (1760), 143 (stating rule against self-incrimination and adding "in this we do certainly follow the Law of Nature").

84. *Epiekeia: A Dialogue on Equity in Three Parts,* D.E.C. Yale ed. (1953), 108 (endorsing the view that "in matters doubtfull" courts should "restore thereupon to the lawe of Nature which is reason and the grownde of all lawes").

85. *History of the Pleas of the Crown,* I:1, c. 8 (1736), 51 ("The law of nature, and also necessity" as a source of pleas of self-defense in criminal homicide cases).

86. *A Treatise Concerning Statutes or Acts of Parliament,* c. 5 (1677), 53: "Reason hath been so forcible against the words of Statutes that even in the Prince's Prerogative, the words of Statutes have been controlled."

87. *The Grounds of the Lawes of England* (1657), p. xiii (discussing rules "drawn from the secondary law of nature and reason").

88. *A Treatise of the Pleas of the Crown,* Lib. II § 28, 8th ed. (1824), 540 (prior royal pardon ineffective to render lawful an act that is malum in se "as being against the law of nature").

89. See Philip Hamburger, "Revolution and Judicial Review: Chief Justice Holt's Opinion in *City of London v. Wood,*" 94 *Columbia L. Rev.* (1994), 2091–2153, at 2092–93.

90. *A New Law Dictionary* 2d ed. (1732), s.v. Law: "[A]ll is founded on the Law of Nature or Reason and the revealed law of God."

91. *Works of that Grave and Learned Lawyer Judge Jenkins upon Divers Statutes,* s.v. *Parliament* (1648) (Acts of Parliament against reason or repugnant or impossible to be performed are void).

92. *Essay on the Law of Bailments* 2d ed. (1798), 10 (conformity of rules of liability of bailees conformable with rules of natural reason). See D. J. Ibbetson, "Sir William Jones and the Nature of Law," in: *Mapping the Law: Essays in Memory of Peter Birks,* Andrew Burrows and Lord Rodger eds. (1996), 619–39.

93. *Archeion or A Discourse upon the High Courts of Justice* (1635), 95 (that the "Law of Humanity, Reason and Nature" has preserved mankind from the "shipwreck" of Adam's Fall).

94. *Les Tenures de Monsieur Littleton,* chs. 209, 212 (1581), 46–47 (prescriptive usage "si ceo soit encounter reason ceo ne doit ester allowe devant Judges").

95. *Consuetudo vel Lex mercatoria* (1636), 308 (utility of "the principles which are taken from the law of God and Nature").

96. *Short Treatise of the Lawes of England with the Jurisdiction of the High Court of Parliament* (1644), 9–11: "You shall understand that all humane lawes are either the law of Nature, or Customes, or Statutes."

97. *Treatise on the Law of Insurance* (1805), 238 (endorsing the view under the law of nature that to be validly insured, an object must have been in existence at the time the insurance was issued).

98. "A Dialogue Concerning Heresies," Lib. IV, c. 14, in: *Complete Works of St. Thomas More* (1981), IX, 415: "nature, reason and goddys beheste byndeth."

99. *Treatise on the Study of the Law* (1797), 49 (recommendation to study the law of nations, "which is party founded on the law of nature, and partly positive").

100. *Treatise of the Laws for the Relief and Settlement of the Poor* (1805, repr. 1978), Lib. I, c. 15, 144–46 (applying principles of "natural justice" to provisions of the Poor Laws).

101. *A Discourse of the Poor* (1753), 19–20 (citing Cicero approvingly, for the proposition that reason was a foundation of law and an Act of Parliament without reason was "void as contrary to a Principle of Justice").

102. *The Grounds and Maxims of the English Laws,* c. 1, 6th ed. (1792): "The common law is grounded on the rules of reason."

103. *An Essay on the Law of Usury* (1797), 3–4 (seeking to show the falsity of the traditional view that the taking of any interest from a loan was prohibited by the law of nature).

104. "History of the Common Law," British Library, London, Harl. MS. 1572, fols. 11v-12 (role of "a natural instinct" implanted in every creature by "the God of nature").

105. *Observations upon Some of His Majesty's Late Answers and Expresses* (1642), as discussed in J. W. Gough, *Fundamental Law in English Constitutional History* (1955), 85–86.

106. *A Profitable Book, Treating of the Laws of England,* 15th ed. (1827), pp. xiii–xiv (discussing movement away from communally held property in a state of nature).

107. *Studii legalis ratio, or Directions for the Study of Law* (1667), 10 (argument that "very Reason and the order of nature" should direct study of the law).

108. Sharington v. Strotten, 1 Plowd. 298, 75 E.R. 454 (K.B. 1565), and in *Commentaries or Reports of Edmund Plowden* *304 (1816): "[W]e ought not to think that the Founders of our Law were remiss in searching after the Law of Nature, or that they were ignorant of it."

109. *Investigation of the Native Rights of British Subjects* (1784), 18 (allegiance to the monarch said to be "founded upon the law of civilized nature").

110. *Essay upon the Law of Contracts and Agreements* (1823), 101 (lack of enforceability of contracts "contrary to the law of God and Nature").

111. *Explanation of the Old Oath of Legeance* (1641), 171 (allegiance and duty to the prince "are part of the Law of Nature, whereto all Nations have consented").

112. Speech in House of Lords (1766), quoted in Ernest Barker, *Traditions of Civility* (1948, repr. 1967), 317 (appeal to "the natural law of mankind and the immutable laws of justice").

113. *Brief Animadversions on the Fourth Part of the Institutes of the Lawes of England* (1669), 97: "Because the Law (guided by nature and reason) cannot feign or allow things that are against nature, reason, nor admit of fictions that are contradictory to each other, yea false and impossible."

114. *De pace regis et regni* (1609), Pref. (need for positive criminal laws to augment "the lawes of God, of nature or reason").

115. "Reading on Visus Francplegii" (1976), Pref., as described in J. H. Baker, v. Rodes, in: *New Oxford Dictionary of National Biography* (2004) (Preface on the relevance of the law of nature to English law).

116. *Doctor and Student*, Dial. I, c. 2, T. F. T. Plucknett and J. L. Barton eds. S.S. 91 (1974), 13: "And this law ought to be kept as well among Jewes and gentyles as amonge crysten men. And this is the law which among the learned in English law is called the law of reason."

117. *Table Talk of John Selden*, v. Law of Nature, F. Pollock ed. (1927), 69–70 (God as the ultimate source of the law of nature). Selden was also author of a treatise on the subject: *De jure naturali et gentium juxta disciplinam Ebaeorum* (1st ed. 1640); see G. J. Toomer, *John Selden: A Life in Scholarship* (2009), II, 490–562.

118. *Declaration of the People's Natural Right to a Share in the Legislature* (1776), 235–37 (Parliamentary acts contrary to the law of nature are to be "HOLDEN FOR NONE") (caps in original).

119. *Epitome of All the Common and Statute Laws* (1656), 683, cited in Nancy L. Matthews, *William Sheppard, Cromwell's Law Reformer* (1984), 5.

120. *Jura populi Anglicani* (1701), 30–31 (Right of the people to petition the government for redress of grievances founded on the law of nature). See Hamburger, "Revolution and Judicial Review," above note 89, at 2102.

121. "Larger Work on Tythes," C. 22, in: *The English Works of Sir Henry Spelman*, 2d ed. (1717), 110–11 (the Law of Nature as source of legal obligations to give offerings to God and, by implication, to the clergy).

122. *Les Plees del Coron*, Lib. II, c. 1 (1567), 53–54 (section "De Justice" using language taken from civil law sources based on the law of nature to describe the character of English justice).

123. *Regestrum Practicale, or the Practical Register*, v. Impossibility, 4th ed. (1707), 395: "For the Common Law is not contradictory in any thing to the Law of Nature, but agrees with it in all things."

124. *Le Digest des briefs originals*, Lib. I, tit. *De alienagenis*, no. 19 (1687) (describing the regular use of "ley de nature" in Chancery.

125. Harrison v. Doctor Burwell (1670), in *Reports and Arguments of that Learned Judge Sir John Vaughan*, 1st ed. (1677), 226–27 (definition of transgressions

when men "violate laws coeval with their original being" and referring to Selden's treatment of natural law as "given in the beginning to all Mankind"). See J. Gwynn Williams, "Sir John Vaughan of Trawscoed, 1603–1674," *National Library of Wales J.* 8 (1953), 121, 140–41.

126. *Symboleography,* Pt. II, tit. *Of the Chancerie* § 2 (1627), 174 (giving examples of general rules given that "by the Law of Nature itself, better and more rightfull cannot be given").

127. *Essays Ecclesiastical and Civil* (1706), 45 (in defense of liberty of conscience in religious matters, tit. Law of Nature; and that the "Law of Reason is to do things as near as we can like unto God").

128. *The Excellency and Praeheminence of the Law of England* (1680), 9: "The Law of Nature, which is the Parent of all good Lawes in the World."

129. *The Body of the Common Law of England* (1655), Pref. (asserting that the common laws of England are "subject to be altered by two other Laws, viz. the statute-law and the law of Reason [which] many times controles the Common Law").

130. *Systematical View of the Laws of England as Treated of in a Course of Vinerian Lectures* (1792–1793), I, 2 (assertion that the laws of England "secure and inforce" the natural rights of individuals).

131. *Eunomus: Or Dialogues Concerning the Law and Constitution of England,* Dial. I § 17 3d ed. (1791), 33: "The law of nature not only should be studied as the ground of the great and fundamental laws in all societies, but because the state of nature itself does still subsist in many respects."

132. *Some Considerations on the Law of Forfeiture for High Treason* (1795), 13–18 (attempt to show that forfeiture was consistent with the law of nature even though it could penalize the innocent).

133. "Tract on Law and Especially the Law of England," British Library, London, Stowe MS. 159, fols. 303v-04 (describing the Lawe of Reason as "written in the hartes of all men").

134. My search found no mention of natural law in Francis Buller (d. 1800), *Introduction to the Law Relative to Trials at Nisi Prius* (1772); William Scroggs (d. 1683), *Practice of Courts-Leet and Courts-Baron* (1701); or Richard Hutton (d. 1639), *The Diary of Sir Richard Hutton,* W. R. Prest ed. (1991).

135. See "Memoirs and Correspondence," C. 3, in: *Works of Jeremy Bentham,* John Bowring ed. (1843), X, 63.

136. "The History of the Law of Nature: A Preliminary Survey," *J. Soc. Comparative Legislation,* n.s. II (1900), 418–33, at 430. For similar characterizations, see Roscoe Pound, *The Development of Constitutional Guarantees of Liberty* (1957), 74; C. H. S. Fifoot, *History and Sources of the Common Law* (1949), 300–01.

137. Pollock, "History of the Law of Nature," prior note, at 430. See also the slim and patronizing treatment of the subject found in John Chipman Gray, *The Nature and Sources of the Law,* 2d rev. ed. (1921), 130–31.

138. "English Law and the Renaissance," in: *Select Historical Essays of F. W. Maitland,* Helen M. Cam ed. (1957), 145–48.

139. D. J. Ibbetson, "Natural Law and Common Law," *Edinburgh L. Rev.* 5 (2001), 4–20; Michael Lobban, *History of Philosophy of Law in the Common Law World, 1600–1900* (2005), 62–63, 93–94, 141–42; see also Julia Rudolph, *Common Law and Enlightenment in England, 1689–1750* (2013), 164–200.

4. The Law of Nature in English Courts

1. For the more positive view, see Reinhard Zimmermann, "Der europäische Charakter des englischen Rechts," *Zeitschrift für europäisches Privatrecht* 1 (1993), 4–51. For the more negative view, see J. H. Baker, *Introduction to English Legal History*, 4th ed. (2002), 27–29. Both "sides" admit the existence of counterexamples; see the thoughtful treatment in H. Patrick Glenn, *On Common Laws* (2005), 97–108.

2. See, e.g., D. J. Ibbetson, "Civilian and Canonist Influence on the Writ of *Cessavit per Biennium*," in: *Laws, Lawyers and Texts: Studies in Medieval Legal History in Honour of Paul Brand*, S. Jenks, J. Rose, and C. Whittick eds. (2012), 87–100; Thomas McSweeney, "Property before Property: Romanizing the English Law of Land," *Buffalo L. Rev.* 60 (2012), 1139–99; David Seipp, "The Reception of Canon Law and Civil Law in the Common Law Courts before 1600," *Oxford J. Legal Studies* 13 (1993), 389, at 406–12.

3. See the discussion by Lord Hope in R. (Jackson) v. Attorney-General [2006] 1 A.C. 262.

4. 1 *Bl. Comm.* *1(b); Waltham v. Sparkes (1695), 1 Ld. Raym. 41, 91 E.R. 924–25.

5. *Countrey Justice*, 1st ed. (1618), c. 1.

6. *Treatise on the Laws and Customs of the Realm of England Commonly Called Glanvill*, VII: 1, G.D.G. Hall ed. (1993), 71.

7. The academic literature on this subject is well discussed in Frank Roumy, *L'Adoption dans le droit savant du XIIe au XVI siècle* (1998).

8. Adoption of Children Act, 16 & 17 Geo. V, c. 29 (1926).

9. Eeles v. Lambert (1647), Style 37, 73, 82 E.R. 512, 540; see also "Laws" (ca. 1695), 3 Salk. 221, 91 E.R. 788: "Laws are divided into arbitrary or natural laws, the last of which are essentially just and good and bind everywhere and in all places where they are observed."

10. Rex v. Boreston & Adams (Exch. temp. Car. I), Noy 158, 160, 74 E.R. 1119, 1120.

11. Omychund v. Barker (1744), 1 Atk. 22, 33, 26 E.R. 14, 23. See also James v. Price (1773), Lofft 219, 220, 98 E.R. 619, 621; Jones v. Randall (1774), 1 Cowp. 37, 39, 98 E.R. 954, 955.

12. See Norman S. Poser, *Lord Mansfield: Justice in the Age of Reason* (2013), 214–16.

13. Sir William Elvis v. Archbishop of York et al. (1619), Hob. 315, 316, 80 E.R. 458, 459.

14. *The Speech of the Right Honourable Lord Mansfield in the House of Lords, February 4, 1767, in the Cause between the City of London and the Dissenters* (1774),

12, 22–23. See also David Lieberman, *The Province of Legislation Determined* (1989), 124–26.

15. Sharington v. Strotton (1564), 1 Plowd. 298, 304, 75 E.R. 454, 463.

16. E.g., Collingwood v. Pace (Exch. Ch. 1663), 1 Keb. 585, 589, 83 E.R. 1126, 1128 (interpreting a statute as one that restored men to the law of nature).

17. Manby v. Scot (1661–1662), 1 Keb. 69, 363, 83 E.R. 816, 996: "There being no presidents we must resort to the law of Nature." See also Calvin's Case (1609), 7 Co. Rep. 1, 14a, 77 E.R. 379, 393; "Le Case del Union," (1606), Moo. K.B. 790, 792, 72 E.R. 908, 909. For analysis, see Keechang Kim, *Aliens in Medieval Law* (2000), 172–73.

18. This was acknowledged in Ex parte Hopkins (Chan. 1732), 3 P. Wms. 152, 24 E.R. 1009; Englefield's Case (Exch. 1591), 7 Co. Rep. 11b, 12b, 77 E.R. 428, 430.

19. Rex v. Thorp (1695), Comb. 456, 457, 90 E.R. 589; see also Fursaker v. Robinson (1717), 1 Eq. Cas. Abr. 123, 21 E.R. 929; Atkins v. Hiccocks (Chan. 1737), West T. Hard. 114, 117, 25 E.R. 849, 850–51.

20. See A. W. B. Simpson, *History of the Common Law of Contract* (1975), 118–22; and "The Penal Bond with Conditional Defeasance," *L.Q.R.* 82 (1966), 392–422.

21. E.g., Sir William Capell's Case (Chan. 1494), in: *Notebook of Sir John Port*, J. H. Baker ed., S.S. 102 (1986), no. 8, 13–14; see also Holdsworth, *H.E.L.*, V, 220–23.

22. *Table Talk of John Selden*, v. Equity, no. 2, F. Pollock ed. (1927), 43. A more favorable comparison of Chancery with a shoemaker's shop is found in William West, *Symboleography* (1618), Pt. II, tit. Of the Chancerie § 11.

23. See generally J. F. Stephen, *History of the Criminal Law of England* (1883), I, 122–26, III, 263–666; an example is Rex v. Simpson (1715), 1 Str. 44, 93 E.R. 375, a case involving criminal proceedings for theft of deer under the statute of 3 Will.& Mary, c. 10 (1691).

A darker picture of the reality is painted in F. Dalholwala, "Summary Justice in Early Modern London," *E.H.R.* 121 (2006), 796–822. Other statutes that came close to the European pattern were those that established "courts of equity and conscience" in specific places. However, they established procedural rules of much greater specificity than their Continental equivalents; see, e.g., 3 Jac. I, c. 15 (1606).

24. This subject is discussed, with citation to contemporary legal sources in my "Natural Law and the Trial of Thomas More," in: *Thomas More's Trial by Jury*, H. A. Kelly ed. (2011), 53–70.

25. See, e.g., John Fortescue, *De Laudibus Legum Anglie*, S. B. Chrimes ed. (1949), 46–52; William Lambarde, "Charge to Quarter Sessions (1591)," in: *William Lambarde & Local Government*, Conyers Read ed. (1962), 104–05.

26. See, e.g., J. Clarus, *Practica criminalis*, Lib. V, Quaest. 64; J. Damhouder, *Praxis rerum criminalium*, cc. 35–41. The question at issue was almost always whether torture had been lawfully authorized; see, e.g., A. Trentacinque, *Consiliorum seu Responsionum*, Pt. II, cons. 36.

27. Rex v. Cleg, 1 Str. 475, 93 E.R. 643.
28. W. Fulbecke, *Parallele,* Dial. X, pp. 58, 62: "parcel of the Law of Nature."
29. E.g., Rex v. Dilliston (1690), 1 Show. K.B. 83, 85–86, 89 E.R. 465, 467 (dealing with the property holdings of infants; application of a rule calling for forfeiture of their rights was said to be "excused by the law of reason"); Bolton v. Throgmorton (1682), Skin. 55, 90 E.R. 27 (on need for a hearing before ruling on a person's rights to chattels); Hill v. Bunning (1660), 1 Sid. 17, 18, 82 E.R. 943, 944 (per Bridgeman, C. J.).
30. Rex v. University of Cambridge, or Doctor Bentley's Case (1723), Fort. 202, 204, 92 E.R. 818, 819.
31. Rex v. University of Cambridge (1723), 8 Mod. 148, 163–64, 88 E.R. 111, 120.
32. Regina v. Dyer, (1703), 1 Salk. 181, 91 E.R. 165; Rex v. Weston (1715), 10 Mod. 279, 280, 88 E.R. 728; Rex v. Angell (1734), Cas. T. Hard. 124; 95 E.R. 78.
33. See, e.g., Michael Nolan, *Treatise of the Laws for the Relief and Settlement of the Poor* (1805), I, c. 14.
34. E.g., Babington's Case (1616), Moo. K.B. 918, 72 E.R. 996. See the aggressive use of the principle in "Of Oaths before an Ecclesiastical Judge Ex Officio" (1607), 12 Co. Rep. 26, 12 E.R. 1308.
35. See also the same principle, in a slightly different setting, in Wilson v. Rogers (1746), 2 Str. 1242, 93 E.R. 1157.
36. See, e.g., A. Capycius, *Decisiones,* Dec. 2, nos. 1–6 (dealing with primogeniture's effect on the *legitim*); C. Pellegrino, Praxis [et] D*ecisiones,* Dec. 116, no. 12 (discussing the English custom in the context of the rights to inheritance of daughters); J. Ludovicus, *Decisiones,* Pt. II, dec. 76, no. 9 (treating the English "statute" of primogeniture as *odiosum*).
37. As, for example, the contrary custom of the province of York or the City of London; see, e.g., Savil v. Savil (Chan. 1634–1635), 1 Chan. Rep. 78, 21 E.R. 512.
38. As, for example, under the Poor Laws; see Rex v. Inhabitants of Hyworth (1716), 1 Str. 10, 93 E.R. 352.
39. See, e.g., J. Godolphin, *Orphan's Legacy,* Pt. I, c. 5, no. 3; for further evidence on the point, see my "*Legitim* in English Legal History," *Illinois L. Rev.* (1984), 659–74.
40. 43 Eliz. I, c. 2 § 6 (1601).
41. See, e.g., Waltham v. Sparkes (1694), Skin. 556, 557, 90 E.R. 250; also found in 1 Ld. Raym. 41, 91 E.R. 524.
42. Rex v. Munden, 1 Str. 190, 93 E.R. 465. A statute had imposed such a duty in the case of one's own parents, but the court refused to extend it to a wife's parents, holding that the act "can be extended no farther than the law of nature went before."
43. *Co. Lit.* 12a; 2 *Bl. Comm.* *220.

44. E.g., Sharington v. Strotton (1564), 1 Plowd. 298, 305, 75 E.R. 454, 464: "[A] consideration proceeding from nature is a sufficient consideration in our law." The result was said to be "grounded upon the consideration of nature." See also Grisley v. Lother (1614), Hob. 10, 80 E.R. 161; Duchess of Albemarle v. Earl of Bath (Chan. 1693), 2 Freem. 193, 195, 22 E.R. 1155, 1152.

45. Sir George Curson's Case, (Ct. of Wards 1607), 6 Co. Rep. 75b, 77a, 77 E.R. 369, 371.

46. Fawkner v. Watts (Chan. 1741), 1 Atk. 405, 408, 26 E.R. 257, 259 (case involving marriage portions and advancements, in which it was said that "every father and mother, by the law of nature, is under an obligation to maintain their own children, but yet this may be varied by circumstances").

47. Kentish v. Newman (Chan. 1713), 1 P. Wms. 234, 24 E.R. 368.

48. J. Godolphin, *Orphan's Legacy*, Pt. I, c. 1, no. 1: They "had their origination from the *jus gentium* as the product of the *jus naturale*." See also J. Page, *Jus fratrum: The Law of Bretheren* 3: "[F]athers have, by the Law of Nature, a free power to dispose of their estates and children."

49. 2 *Bl. Comm.* *10; see also Cod. 1.2.1; Hog v. Lashley (1792), 6 Brown 550, 592, 2 E.R. 1259, 1288.

50. See Peter Landau, "La libertà di testare nella storia del diritto tedesco del tardo medioevo e della prima età moderna," *Rivista internazionale di Diritto Comune* 6 (1995), 29–47. A modern analysis is Shelly Kreizer-Levy, "Mandatory Nature of Inheritance," *Amer. J. of Jurisprudence* 53 (2008), 105–31.

51. Butler v. Butler, (Chan. 1743), 3 Atk. 58, 60, 26 E.R. 836, 837: Coles v. Hancock (Chan. 1680–1681), 2 Chan. Rep. 210, 21 E.R. 659.

52. Rex v. Boreston and Adams (Exch. temp. Car. I), Noy 158, 160–61, 74 E.R. 1119, 1120–21.

53. See Adam Hofri-Winogradow, "Parents, Children and Property in Late 18th Century Chancery," *Oxford J. Legal Studies* 32 (2012), 741–69.

54. E.g., Anon. (ca. 1570), Cary 5, 21 E.R. 3: "Upon nudum pactum there ought to be no more help in chancery than there is at the common law."

55. See, e.g., Bretton v. Bretton (Chan. 1662), Nelson 63, 21 E.R. 790; Pett v. Pett (1700), 1 Ld. Raym. 571, 572, 91 E.R. 1281, 1282.

56. 2 *Bl. Comm.* *210; T. Rutherforth, *Institutes*, Lib. I, c. 7, no. 10; Martin ex dem. Tregonwell v. Strachan and Harrison (1744), 1 Wils. K.B. 66, 69, 95 E.R. 495, 497. See also D. Arumaeus, *Decisiones*, Dec. 6, no 6: "Ars iuris civilis imitatur naturam . . . et ideo vult devolvere successiones ad instar fluminum."

57. Plowden's Queries, no. 35, 75 E.R. 860 (a devise of land to the grantor's wife for life, with remainder to her "next of blood" in a case where the woman had been previously married and was survived both by a son of that marriage and a son by the second marriage should go to the second son because only he was also of the blood of the testator).

58. Att'y Gen. v. Lady Downing (Chan. 1767), Wilm. 1, 25, 97 E.R. 1, 10.

59. Collingwood v. Pace (1663), 1 Keb. 535, 83 E.R. 1097, 1098; see also Bosanquett v. Dashwood (Chan. 1734), 2 Eq. Cas. 246, no. 26, 22 E.R. 209; Anon. (ca. 1570), Cary 5, 21 E.R. 3.

60. This point is well made in Daniel Boorstin, *The Mysterious Science of the Law* (1996), 44–61.

61. Butler v. Gastrill (Chan. 1721), Gilb. Rep. 156, 160, 25 E.R. 110, 112.

62. See Edward Cardwell, *Documentary Annals of the Reformed Church of England* (1844), I, 316–20.

63. Somerset v. Stewart (1771–1772), 20 St. Trials 1, Lofft 1, 98 E.R. 499. See also Forbes v. Cochrane (1824), 2 Barn. & Cress. 448, 471, 107 E.R. 450, 459; Baker, *Introduction*, 475–76; William Wiecek, "Somerset: Lord Mansfield and the Legitimacy of Slavery in the Anglo-American World," *Univ. of Chicago L. Rev.* 42 (1974), 86–146.

64. Alan Watson, *Slave Law in the Americas* (1989), 122–24.

65. An English example is Moore v. Hussey (1610), Hob. 93, 99, 80 E.R. 243.

66. Somerset v. Stewart, Lofft at 19, 98 E.R. at 510; a statement in slightly longer form, but indistinguishable in principle, is found in 20 St. Tr. at 92. See also Rex v. Inhabitants of Thames Ditton (1785), 4 Dougl. 300, 99 E.R. 891.

67. E.g., O. Cacheranus, *Decisiones,* Dec. 88, no 25, describing *statuta odiosa* as those enacted without adequate good reason *(causa);* L. Censius, *Decisiones,* Dec. 49, nos. 11–15: "nam certum est prohibitionem alienationis ut odiosum stricte intelligendum est." Opinions about the scope of the category could differ; see, e.g., B. Cavalconus, *Decisiones,* Dec. 41, nos. 49–50, treating as *odiosum* a Florentine statute permitting Doctors of Law to undertake the role of notaries and proctors.

68. E.g., M. de Afflictis, *Decisiones,* Dec. 24, no. 7: interpreting a statute expansively because it was "universalis procedens tam de iure naturali quam divino."

69. Chamberline v. Harvey (1696), 5 Mod. 182, 190, 87 E.R. 596, 600.

70. Smith v. Gould (1706), 2 Ld. Raym. 1274, 92 E.R. 338; Smith v. Brown & Cooper, 2 Salk. 666, 91 E.R. 566. *Contra* Butts v. Penny (1677), 2 Lev. 201, 83 E.R. 518. See George van Cleve, "Somerset's Case and Its Antecedents in Imperial Perspective," *L.H.R.* 24 (2006), 601–45, at 613–23.

71. F.N.B. *167; see J. H. Baker, "Personal Liberty under the Common Law of England," in: *The Origins of Modern Freedom in the West*, R. W. Davis ed. (1995), 178–202; Ruth Paley, "After Somerset: Mansfield, Slavery and the Law in England, 1772–1830," in: *Law, Crime and English Society, 1660–1830*, Norma Landau ed. (2002), 165–84.

72. See W. J. Zwalve, "*Sola scriptura*, An Essay in Comparative Legal History on 'Obligacions' in Thirteenth-Century France and England," *T.R.G.* 80 (2012), 85–128.

73. Compare, for example, Pillans v. Van Mierop (1765), 3 Burr. 1664, 97 E.R. 1035, with Rann v. Hughes (1778), 4 Brown 27, 2 E.R. 18. See also the

treatment in Simpson, *History of the Common Law of Contract,* above note 20, at 488, concluding that "[t]he doctrine of consideration is indeed intensely moralistic . . . [and it] has as its function in relation to the commercial world the imposition of decent moral standards."

74. James Gordley, "Natural Law Origins of the Common Law of Contract," in: *Towards a General Law of Contract,* John Barton ed. (1990), 367–465.

75. See the essays in: *Unjust Enrichment: the Comparative Legal History of the Law of Restitution,* 2d ed., E. J. H. Schrage ed. (1999).

76. Goram v. Sweeting (1670), 2 Wms. Saund. 200, 85 E.R. 964, 966.

77. Alderson et al. v. Temple (1768), 4 Burr. 2235, 2239, 98 E.R. 165, 167. A similar case is Hodgson v. Richardson (1731), 1 Black. W. 463, 465, 96 E.R. 268, 269; Woodford v. Multon (1601), Cary 13, 21 E.R. 7. See also Constantin Willems, *Actio Paulina und Fraudulent Conveyances* (2012) (discussing connections with the development of English law on the subject).

78. Tonson v. Collins (1761), 1 Black. W. 321, 323, 96 E.R. 180, 181; Millar v. Taylor (1769), 4 Burr. 2303, 98 E.R. 234. The argument was rejected and the right held purely statutory by the House of Lords, in Donaldson v. Becket (1774), 2 Brown 129, 1 E.R. 837 (1774). See Trevor Ross, "Copyright and the Invention of Tradition," *Eighteenth-Century Studies* 26 (1992), 1–27.

79. Rex v. Trinity-House (1662), 1 Keb. 300, 301, 83 E.R. 958; see also Herbert v. Laughluyn (1636), Cro. Car. 493, 79 E.R. 1025; Wyatt v. Thompson (1794), 1 Esp. 252, 170 E.R. 347.

80. See the discussion in Simpson, *History of the Common Law of Contract,* above note 20, at 528–32; the case is reported in Aleyn 26, 82 E.R. 897, and Style 47, 48, 82 E.R. 519, 520.

81. See Style at 48, 82 E.R. at 520.

82. (1628), Palm. 548, 81 E.R. 1214, also reported *sub nom.* Williams v. Lloyd (1628), Jones W. 179, 82 E.R. 95.

83. E.g., Sanderson v. Warner (1622), Palm. 291, 293, 81 E.R. 1087, 1089.

84. See the comments and bibliography in David Hawkes, *The Culture of Usury in Renaissance England* (2010), 187–94.

85. James Davis, *Medieval Market Morality: Life, Law and Ethics in the English Marketplace, 1200–1500* (2012), 65–68, 213–15.

86. The most important was 21 Jac. I, c. 17 (1624), in its effect setting the rate permitted at 8 percent. See generally, Eric Kerridge, *Usury, Interest and the Reformation* (2002).

87. Lloyd v. Williams (1771), 3 Wils. K.B. 250, 254, 95 E.R. 1039, 1041.

88. (1602) 11 Co. Rep. 84b, 77 E.R. 1260. Two other printed reports of the case also exist: Moo. K.B. 671, 72 E.R. 830, and Noy 173, 74 E.R. 1131.

89. "The Argument, Decision, and Reports of Darcy v. Allen," *Emory L.J.* 45 (1996), 1261–1328; See also Raymond de Roover, "Monopoly Theory Prior to Adam Smith: A Revision," *Quarterly J. of Economics* 65 (1951), 492–524; Stephen White, *Sir Edward Coke and "The Grievances of the Commonwealth," 1621–1628* (1979), 116–23.

90. 11 Co. Rep. at 88b, 77 E.R. at 1266.

91. E.g., D. Mevius, *Decisiones*, Pt. III, dec. 70, no. 1, speaking of monopolies as "libertati quam natura fovet adversa."

92. 11 Co. Rep. at 87a, 77 E.R. at 1264.

93. 21 Jac. I, c. 3 (1624).

94. T. F. T. Plucknett, *Statutes and their Interpretation in the First Half of the Fourteenth Century* (1922), 57–65; S. E. Thorne, "Introduction," *A Discourse upon the Exposicion and Understandinge of Statutes* (1942), 68–92.

95. See Stefan Vogenauer, *Die Auslegung von Gesetzen in England und auf dem Kontinent* (2001), II, 743–45, 751–53.

96. Collingwood v. Pace (Exch. Ch. 1663), 1 Keb. 585, 589, 83 E.R. 1126, 1128.

97. Gilmore v. Shuter (1678), Jones T. 108, 84 E.R. 1170.

98. See, e.g., Heath v. Henley (Chan. 1663), Nelson 75, 21 E.R. 793; Sheldon v. Weldman, 1 Chan. Cas. 26, 22 E.R. 676 (1663). Judicial treatment of the Statute of Frauds has followed the same path, though there has never been equivalent agreement about its proper interpretation. See, e.g., William Roberts, *Treatise on the Statute of Frauds* (1805), pp. xi–xxvii.

99. 25 Hen. VIII, c. 13 (1533–1534).

100. *Observations on the More Ancient Statutes* (1775), 561.

101. 19 & 20 Vict. c. 64.

102. 2 Co. Inst. 23. See also Stradling v. Morgan (Exch. 1560), 1 Plowd. 199, 208, 75 E.R. 305, 319: "[Y]et we ought to construe such general words to stand with reason and not in such manner as to confound all order and usage."

103. Edwards v. Freeman (Chan. 1727), 2 P. Wms. 435, 443, 24 E.R. 803, 806.

104. See "Jurisdiction of the Court of Chancery Vindicated" (temp. Jac. I), 1 Chan. Rep. 1, 3, 21 E.R. 576.

105. Reniger v. Fogossa (Exch. Ch. 1560), 1 Plowd. 1, 9, 75 E.R. 1, 15.

106. Magdalen College Case (1615), 11 Co. Rep. 66b, 70a, 77 E.R. 1235, 1240.

107. The question is explored in J. H. Baker, *OHLE, Volume VI, 1483–1558* (2003), 76–81.

108. Anthony Musson, "Criminal Legislation in Late Medieval England," in: *From the Judge's Arbitrium to the Legality Principle,* G. Martyn, A. Musson, and H. Pihlajamäki eds. (2013), 33–47, at 41.

109. See, e.g., Nightingale v. Bridges (1690), 1 Show. K.B. 135, 89 E.R. 496.

110. Alan Cromartie, "The Rule of Law," in: *Revolution and Restoration,* John Morrill ed. (1992), 55–69, at 56.

111. See his "Speech in the Impeachment of Warren Hastings (1788), in: *The Works of the Right Honourable Edmund Burke* (Boston 1826–1827), VII, 110.

112. E.g., Katherine Chambers, "'When We Do Nothing Wrong, We Are Peers,' Peter the Chanter and Twelfth Century Political Thought," *Speculum* 88 (2013), 403–26.

113. Hamilton & Smyth v. Davis (1771), 5 Burr. 2732, 98 E.R. 433.

114. 3 Edw. I (Westm. 1), c. 4 (1275). The larger subject of claims to wreck, which is complicated, is explored in Rose Melikan, "Shippers, Salvors, and Sovereigns: Competing Interests in the Medieval Law of Shipwreck," *J.L.H.* 11 (1990), 163–82, at 171–78. Several readings on the statute were given; see J. H. Baker, *Readers and Readings in the Inns of Court and Chancery* (2000), p. xi.

115. See *John Spelman's Reading on Quo Warranto Delivered in Gray's Inn (Lent 1519),* J. H. Baker ed., S.S. 113 (1997), 26–42; "William Fleetwood's Treatise," no. 120, in: *Hale and Fleetwood on Admiralty Jurisdiction,* Michael Pritchard and D. E. C. Yale eds., S.S. 108 (1992), 248–54.

116. 5 Burr. at 2738; 98 E.R. at 436.

117. Ibid.

118. 5 Burr. at 2739, 98 E.R. at 437.

119. Lord Mansfield's general approach to statutory interpretation is more fully explored in James Oldham, *English Common Law in the Age of Mansfield* (2004), 31–34; C.H.S. Fifoot, *Lord Mansfield* (1936), 221–25.

120. Stradling v. Morgan (Exch. 1560), 1 Plowd. 199, 205–06, 75 E.R. 305, 315; In the Matter of Cavendish (1587), 1 And. 152, 158, 123 E.R. 403, 406.

121. *Bracton, De legibus,* f. 5b. For its contemporary understanding and application, see Charles McIlwain, *Constitutionalism: Ancient and Modern* (1940, repr. 1975), 76–83; D. E. C. Yale, " 'Of No Mean Authority': Some Later Uses of Bracton," in: *On the Laws and Customs of England: Essays in Honor of Samuel E. Thorne,* M. S. Arnold et al. eds. (1981), 383–96.

122. E.g., Stat. *Prerogativa regis* (ca. 1324), S.R. I, 226–27.

123. E.g., Pawlett v. Att'y Gen. (Exch. 1668), Hard. 465, 469, 145 E.R. 550, 552.

124. 5 Edw. II, c. 28 (1311); 12 Co. Rep. 130, 77 E.R. 1404–05; see also Helen Lacey, *The Royal Pardon: Access to Mercy in Fourteenth-Century England* (2009), 73–81.

125. Newton v. Shafto (1632), 2 Keb. 111, 84 E.R. 70; see also Wilkes v. Broadbent (1744), 1 Wils. K.B. 63, 64, 95 E.R. 494, 495 (invalidating a lord's claim to sink pits in his tenant's lands and remove coals because it "savours much of arbitrary power"); Mayor of Winchester v. Wilks (1705), 3 Salk. 349, 91 E.R. 866 (refusing a restriction on trading within the city to freemen of the merchants' guild, but admitting that a similar custom would be good for London "because their customs are confirmed by many Acts of Parliament"). See also Cudden v. Eastwick (1704), 6 Mod. 123, 124, 87 E.R. 881; Pierce v. Bartrum (1775), 1 Cowp. 269, 98 E.R. 1080.

126. 13 Edw. I, c. 1 (1285).

127. Anon. (Chan. 1599), Cary 9, 21 E.R. 5. Other cases to the same effect: Mildmay's Case (1605), 6 Co. Rep. 40a, 41b, 77 E.R. 311, 315; Hoel's Case (1622), Win. 54, 57, 124 E.R. 46, 49.

128. Pells v. Brown (1620), 2 Rolle 216, 221, 81 E.R. 760, 763. See also Duke of Norfolk's Case (Chan. 1681) sub nom. Marshall v. Holloway, 2 Swans. 454,

460, 36 E.R. 690, 692: "[S]uch perpetuities fight against God by affecting a stability which human providence can never attend to."

129. See A. W. B. Simpson, *A History of the Land Law* 2d ed. (1986), 225–29.

130. See Joseph Biancalana, *The Fee Tail and the Common Recovery in Medieval England, 1176–1502* (2001).

131. (1608–1609), 8 Co. Rep. 107a, 113b, 77 E.R. 638, 646.

132. The author's fuller analysis of the case can be found in "Bonham's Case, Judicial Review and the Law of Nature," *J. Legal Analysis* 1 (2009), 324–54; the article also contains a more complete bibliography of the enormous body of relevant secondary literature.

133. See D. E. C. Yale, "*Iudex in propria causa:* An Historical Excursus," *Cambridge L.J.* 33 (1974), 80–96.

134. 14–15 Hen. VIII, c. 5 (1523) (with exception for graduates of Oxford and Cambridge); 1 Ph. & Mary, St. 2, c. 9 (1553) (without the exception).

135. 8 Co. Rep. at 118a, 77 E.R. at 652.

136. See 8 Co. Rep. at 119a, 77 E.R. at 654: "[I]f it be so in a deed, *a fortiori* it shall be so in an Act of Parliament."

137. *Institutes of Natural Law,* Bk. I, c. 2, no. 6.

138. E.g., Rex v. Earl of Banbury (1694), Skin. 517, 526–27, 90 E.R. 231, 236 (asserting that judges often "construe and expound Acts of Parliament, and adjudge them to be void"); Charles Viner, *General Abridgement of Law and Equity* 19, tit. Statutes (E.6), no. 31 (1793) (asserting that judges "have taken by equity of the text contrary to the text, to make them agree with reason and equity"); T. Wood, *Institute of the Laws of England, Intro.* 10: "Acts of Parliament that are against common justice and reason or impossible to be performed shall be judged void." See also Day v. Savadge (1614), Hob. 85, 80 E.R. 235; Earl of Oxford's Case (Chan. 1615), 1 Chan. Rep. 1, 11–12, 21 E.R. 485, 487–88; Rex v. Prin (1663), Keb. 594, 83 E.R. 1131; Proctor v. Philips (Exch. 1663), Hard. 327, 145 E.R. 481; Att'y Gen. v. Mico (Exch. 1658), Hard. 137, 140, 145 E.R. 419, 421; City of London v. Wood (1702), 12 Mod. 669, 687–88, 88 E.R.1592, 1601–1602; Thornby v. Fleetwood (1718), 10 Mod. 406, 412, 88 E.R. 784, 787. For commentary, see esp. Rudolf Vollmer, *Die Idee der materiellen Gesetzeskontrolle in der englischen Rechtsprechung* (1969).

139. Compare 1 *Bl. Comm.* *120 with ibid., *156. On this point, Blackstone has been described as "[e]loquent, suave, [and] undismayed in the presence of palpable contradictions in his pages." See Edward Corwin, *The "Higher Law" Background of American Constitutional Law* (2008), 80. For a useful Continental perspective on the subject, see Maurizio Fioravanti, "Constitutionalism," in: *History of the Philosophy of Law in the Civil Law World, 1600–1900,* D. Canale, P. Grossi, and H. Hofmann eds. (2009), 263–300, esp. 270–72.

140. Compare Thomas v. Sorrell (Exch. Ch.), Vaugh. 330, 337, 124 E.R. 1098, 1102 (listing a series of possible acts beyond the power of king or Parliament), with Dixon v. Harrison (1670), Vaugh. 36, 39, 124 E.R. 958,

959: "These defects, if they happen in the law, can only be remedied by Parliament." For comment, see Williams, "Sir John Vaughan," above chapter 3, note 125, at 140–41.

141. Rex v. Inhabitants of Haughton (1718), 1 Str. 83, 85, 93 E.R. 399, 400.

142. W. J. Zwalve, "The Equity of the Law: Law and Equity since Justinian," in: *Law and Equity. Approaches in Roman Law and Common Law*, E. Koops and W. J. Zwalve eds. (2014), 17–37, at 25–27.

143. These proceedings are reported in Moo. K.B. 824, 72 E.R. 929.

144. Moo. K.B., at 825, 72 E.R. at 930.

145. Hugh Davis (d. 1694), *De jure uniformitatis ecclesiasticae* (1669); the work is more fully described in my "Notable English Ecclesiastical Lawyers," *Ecclesiastical L.J.* 15 (2013), 344–48.

146. Fuller treatments are found in my *Marriage Litigation in Medieval England* (1974), 172–78; see also Charlotte Christensen-Nugues, "Mariage consenti et mariage contraint: L'abjuration sub pena nubendi à l'officialité de Cerisy, 1314–1346," 40 *Médiévales* (2001), 101–11.

147. Gloss to Statutes of Exeter II, in: *Councils and Synods with Other Documents Relating to the English Church II*, F. M. Powicke and C. R. Cheney eds. (1964), II, 999, note 4.

148. Ex officio c. Ditchfield (1635), Cheshire Record Office, Chester, Act book EDC/1/52, s.d. 21 January.

149. Test. of Anstye (Rochester 1467), Kent History and Library Centre, Maidstone, Act book DRb Pa 3, f. 548v.

150. See H. Swinburne, *Briefe Treatise*, Pt. II § 3, nos. 8, 13.

151. See above note 113.

152. The case is printed in "Notebook of William Colman," no. 34, in: *Three Civilian Notebooks, 1580–1640*, R. H. Helmholz ed., S.S. 127 (2010), 126–27.

153. Further information about the subject is found in Christopher Kemp, *Floating Gold: A Natural (and Unnatural) History of Ambergris* (2012).

154. Case of *Modus Decimandi* (1608), 13 Co. Rep. 12, 77 E.R. 1424.

155. This was also the *communis opinio* among the Continental jurists; see P. Rebuffus, *Tractatus de decimis*, Quaest. I, no. 2.

156. 13 Co. Rep. at 16, 77 E.R. at 1428.

157. See, e.g., the conclusions of S. E. Thorne, "*Statuti* in the Post-Glossators," *Speculum* 11 (1936), 452–61, at 459.

158. A suggestive and useful article on the subject is Caroline Dunn, "Ending English Exceptionalism: Bryce Lyon's Legacy for Constitutional and Legal Historians," in: *Comparative Perspectives on History and Historians*, D. Nicholas, B. Bachrach, and J. M. Murray eds. (2012), 149–68.

5. Legal Education in the United States

1. See Lawrence Friedman, *History of American Law*, 3d ed. (2005), 16–23.

2. Perry Miller, *The Life of the Mind in America: From the Revolution to the Civil War* (1965), 156–85.

3. Erwin Surrency, "Law Reports in the United States," *A.J.L.H.* 25 (1981), 48–66.

4. Two colonies, Maryland and Pennsylvania, had printed law reports prior to Independence. Eight states—Connecticut, Delaware, New Jersey, New York, North Carolina, South Carolina, Vermont, and Virginia—had instituted printed reports prior to 1800. Federal cases, including the decisions of the U.S. Supreme Court, were printed from 1789 to 1790.

5. E.g., Edward Corwin, "The 'Higher Law' Background of American Constitutional Law," *Harvard L. Rev.* 42 (1928–1929), 149–85, 365–409; Charles G. Haines, *The Revival of Natural Law Concepts* (1930); Morton White, *The Philosophy of the American Revolution* (1978), 142–84; Michael Zuchert, *The Natural Rights Republic* (1996), 56–89; Lester Cohen, "The American Revolution and Natural Law Theory," *J. Hist. of Ideas* 39 (1978), 491–502. But cf. Daniel Rodgers, *Contested Truths* (1987), 45–57, and John P. Reid, "The Irrelevance of the Declaration," in: *Law in the American Revolution and the Revolution in the Law,* H. Hartog ed. (1981), 46–89 (denying any lasting or substantive importance to these natural law principles).

6. See generally Dieter Grimm, "Europäisches Naturrecht und Amerikanische Revolution," *Ius commune* 3 (1970), 120–51.

7. "The Declaration of Independence (Appendix One A)," in: Alfred Kelly, Winfred Harbison, and Herman Belz, *The American Constitution: Its Origins and Development,* 7th ed. (1991) (assertion that colonists were called upon by "the Laws of Nature and of Nature's God" to separate from Great Britain).

8. See, e.g., *The Federalist,* No. 43, Jacob E. Cooke ed. (1961), 297 (reference to "the transcendent law of nature" that declares the aim of all government is to rest on the self-preservation of its society).

9. Virginia Bill of Rights §§ 1, 3: in *Federal and State Constitutions,* F. N. Thorpe ed. (1909), VII, 3813.

10. The arguments pro and con are admirably laid out, together with historical examples, in H. Grotius, *De jure belli ac pacis,* Lib. I, c. 4. Or see their less nuanced expression by James Otis, "Rights of the British Colonies Asserted and Proved (1764)," in: *Pamphlets of the American Revolution, 1750–1776,* Bernard Bailyn ed. (1965), 419–82.

11. Locke, Second Treatise §§ 11–13, in: *Two Treatises of Government,* Peter Laslett ed. (1960), 314–17. See generally Deborah Baumgold, *Contract Theory in Historical Context: Essays on Grotius, Hobbes, and Locke* (2010), 27–49.

12. *Papers of John Adams,* Robert Taylor ed. (1977), II, 288–93.

13. Morris Cohen, "Thomas Jefferson Recommends a Course of Law Study," *Univ. Pennsylvania L. Rev.* 119 (1971), 823–44.

14. See *Catalogue of the Library of Thomas Jefferson,* E. M. Sowerby ed. (1983), II, 67–88.

15. See his proposed "Bill for Establishing Religious Freedom," in *Writings of Thomas Jefferson,* Merrill Peterson ed. (1984), 347 (assertion of a natural right to religious freedom).

16. See Benjamin F. Wright Jr., *American Interpretations of Natural Law* (1931, repr. 1962), 62–148.

17. *The Legal Papers of John Adams*, L. Kinvin Wroth and Hiller Zobel eds. (1965), I, 3 (the importance of his study of *lex naturae* as a young man).

18. John Quincy Adams, *The Social Compact: Exemplified in the Constitution of the Commonwealth of Massachusetts* (1842), 25 (discussion of marriage and marital contracts as founded upon the law of nature).

19. See *The Writings of Samuel Adams*, H. A. Cushing ed. (1904), I, 46–47: "The Rights of Nature are happily interwoven in the British Constitution."

20. *The Speeches of Fisher Ames in Congress, 1789–1796*, P. W. Ames ed. (1871), 45 (argument for full repayment of debts based upon "that moral sense, to that law written upon the heart").

21. *Enquiry into the Rights of the British Colonies* (1769), 10 (arguing that the laws enacted by Parliament were to be obeyed because they were founded upon "principles of the law of nature, true, certain, and universal").

22. *Essay on the Constitutional Power of Great-Britain over the Colonies in America* (1774), 43–45 (consideration of natural law and the rights of colonies, with reference to Grotius and Pufendorf). See also Jane Calvert, *Quaker Constitutionalism and the Political Thought of John Dickinson* (2009), 213–15.

23. See "The Farmer Refuted," in: *Selected Writings and Speeches of Alexander Hamilton*, Morton Frisch ed. (1985), 21 (natural right to liberty).

24. *Correspondence and Public Papers of John Jay*, Henry Johnston ed. (1902), II, 396, 406 (that rights to Western lands and navigation of the Mississippi River were "deducible from the laws of nature").

25. *Substance of Two Speeches, Delivered in the Senate of the United States on the Subject of the Missouri Bill* (1819) (importance of the protection of "the rights of conscience and other natural rights").

26. *Letter to the Right Reverend Father in God, John, Lord Bishop of Landaff* (1768) 8 (assertion of rights of private judgment as "sacred by the laws of God and of nature").

27. See, e.g., "Address to the States" (1783), in: *Papers of James Madison*, W. T. Hutchinson and W. M. E. Rachal eds. (1969) VI, 493–94 (that the rights contended for in the American Revolution were "the rights of human nature").

28. See Ogden v. Saunders (1827), in: *Papers of John Marshall*, Charles Hobson ed. (2000), X, 367 (reference to "writers on natural and national law, whose opinions have been viewed with profound respect by the wisest men of the present, and of past ages").

29. Virginia Declaration of Rights, c. 1 (1776), in: *Constitutions*, F. N. Thorpe ed., above note 9, VII, 3813; see also *Natural Rights and Natural Law: The Legacy of George Mason*, Robert P. Davidow ed. (1986), 247 (assertion that "by nature" men possess "certain inherent rights").

30. See *Observations on the American Revolution Published According to a Resolution of Congress* (attributed to Morris) (1779), 50 (that the rights of American

colonists were derived both from the law of nature and the English constitution).

31. *Of the Political and Civil Rights of the British Colonies* (1764), in: *Pamphlets,* Bailyn ed., above note 10, 454 (assertion of power over the colonists by act of Parliament void if they were "against any of [God's] natural laws").

32. *Charge of Judge Paterson to the Jury in the Case of Vanhorne's Lessee against Dorrance* (1795), 15–17 (discussion of natural rights, relating to religion and compensation for property taken by the government).

33. *Political Truth, or Animadversions on the Past and Present State of Public Affairs* (1796), 5 (unfavorable view of the bulk of mankind's ability to profit from the rights "which the God of nature destined for them").

34. "Plea for Establishing Public Schools in Pennsylvania," in: *Essays, Literary, Moral and Philosophical,* 2d ed. (1806) (plea that "the law of nature and nations" be taught at university to be established in Pennsylvania).

35. See "Course of Study for Law Students," in: Paul Hamlin, *Legal Education in Colonial New York* (1939), 197–200 (placing the law of nature and nations among subjects of study that were necessary for lawyers). The ascription to the son rather than the father of the same name is disputed. See Milton Klein, "Rise of the New York Bar," *William & Mary Law Q.* 15 (1958), 337n.

36. See St. George Tucker, "Appendix to Volume 1" § 1, in: *Blackstone's Commentaries with Notes of Reference to the Constitution and Laws of the Federal Government of the United States and of the Commonwealth of Virginia* (1803), I, 11 (arguing that "the laws of nature and of moral obligation" continue in force under all circumstances).

37. *The Plea of the Colonies: On the Charges against Them by Lord M[ansfiel]d and Others* (1775), 26 (discussion of whether the case of the colonists was "founded on the natural rights of mankind").

38. *Works of James Wilson,* Robert McCloskey ed. (1967) I, 126–47 (a chapter devoted to the exploration of the law of nature).

39. Yales v. Salle (1792), in: *Decisions of Cases in Virginia by the High Court of Chancery* (1852), 163, at 168 (quoting from the Roman Law Digest on the subject).

40. See, e.g., the *Institutio legalis,* a club formed by New Jersey law students in 1783, described with a mention of natural law dilemmas, in Philip Hamburger, *Law and Judicial Duty* (2008), 632–41.

41. See D. W. Robson, *Educating Republicans* (1985), 82–87, 148–52, 162–71, 206–209; Douglas Sloan, *The Scottish Enlightenment and the American College Ideal* (1971), 92–93.

42. See *Signers of the Constitution,* Robert Ferris ed. (1976), 136.

43. See, e.g., Hamlin, *Legal Education,* above note 35, 171–96; Herbert Johnson, *Imported Eighteenth-Century Law Treatises in American Libraries 1700–1799* (1978); W. Hamilton Bryson, *Census of Law Books in Colonial Virginia* (1978), 27–30; Daniel Coquillette, "Justinian in Braintree: John Adams, Civilian

Learning, and Legal Elitism, 1758–1775," in: *Law in Colonial Massachusetts 1630–1800* (1984), 359–418, esp. 367–69.

44. Friedman, *History of American Law,* above note 1, at 235–37; Hugh Macgill and R. Kent Newmyer, "Legal Education and Legal Thought, 1790–1920," in: *Cambridge History of Law in America,* M. Grossberg and C. Tomlins eds. (2008), II, 36–67, at 36–48.

45. See, e.g., "Apprenticeship Agreement," in: Hamlin, *Legal Education,* above note 35, at 165–66. See also Charles McKurdy, "The Lawyer as Apprentice: Legal Education in Eighteenth Century Massachusetts," *J. Legal Education* 28 (1976), 124–36; Albert Coates, "Beginnings of the Legal Profession in North Carolina," *North Carolina L. Rev.* 24 (1946), 307–26.

46. The evidence for one state is explored in: Gerard Gawalt, "Massachusetts Legal Education in Transition, 1766–1840," *American J. Legal Hist.* 17 (1973), 27–50.

47. They are listed, with brief biographical descriptions, in: E. A. Jones, *American Members of the Inns of Court* (1924).

48. "Experiences as a Law Student, 1828," in: *History of Legal Education in the United States: Commentaries and Primary Sources,* Steve Sheppard ed. (1999), I, 128.

49. R. Kent Newmyer, *Supreme Court Justice Joseph Story: Statesman of the Old Republic* (1985), 40–41.

50. Compare, for example, Duncan Kennedy, "The Structure of Blackstone's Commentaries," *Buffalo L. Rev.* 28 (1979), 209–382, with Albert Alschuler, "Rediscovering Blackstone," *Univ. Pennsylvania. L. Rev.* 145 (1996), 1–55.

51. Dennis Nolan, "Sir William Blackstone and the New American Republic: A Study of Intellectual Impact," *New York Univ. L. Rev.* 51 (1976), 731–68 (minimizing his impact on American substantive law, but confirming it on the process of legal education). See also Macgill and Newmyer, "Legal Education," above note 44, at 39–40.

52. Michael Hoeflich, *Subscription Publishing and the Sale of Law Books in Antebellum America* (2007), 8–11; Robert Ferguson, *Law and Letters in American Culture* (1986), 11, 15.

53. See Kunal Parker, "Historicising Blackstone's *Commentaries on the Laws of England:* Difference and Sameness in Historical Time," in: *Law Books in Action,* A. Fernandez and M. D. Dubber eds. (2012), 22–42, and Philip Girard, " 'Of Institutes and Treatises': Blackstone's Commentaries, Kent's *Commentaries* and Murdoch's *Epitome of the Laws of Nova-Scotia,"* ibid., 43–62.

54. Quoted in James Ogden, "Lincoln's Early Impressions of the Law in Indiana," *Notre Dame L. Rev.* 7 (1932), 325–329, at 328. See also Mark Steiner, *An Honest Calling: The Law Practice of Abraham Lincoln* (2006), 31–37.

55. James Kent, "Experiences, 1828," above note 48, at I, 120.

56. See Fannie M. Farmer, "Legal Education in North Carolina, 1820–1860," *North Carolina Hist. Rev.* 28 (1951), 271–97, at 293.

57. See Morris S. Arnold, "Blackstone, William," in: *Yale Biographical Dictionary of American Law,* Roger K. Newman ed. (2009), 54–55; similar is O. F. Robinson, T. D. Fergus, and W. M. Gordon, *European Legal History,* 3d ed. (2000), 153, describing Blackstone's references to natural law as "timid."

58. 1 *Bl. Comm.* Intro. § 2, *41. See also David Lieberman, *The Province of Legislation Determined: Legal Theory in Eighteenth-Century Britain* (1989), 36–40.

59. 1 *Bl. Comm.* Intro. § 1, *33 (stating the student's need to have "impressed on his mind the sound maxims of the law of nature, the best and most authentic foundation of human laws").

60. 1 *Bl. Comm.* Intro. § 2, *40.

61. Ibid., *42.

62. Ibid., *47.

63. E.g., ibid., *52 (St. George Tucker ed.), n. 9 (discussing the fundamental principles of the law of the United States in which the supreme power (or *Jura summi imperii*) resides in the people).

64. Ibid., § 14, *211.

65. 2 *Bl. Comm.* **390, 411.

66. Ibid., § 2, *18.

67. 3 Cai. Rep. 175 (N.Y. 1805).

68. 4 *Bl. Comm.* § 2, *29

69. Ibid., *30.

70. Ibid., **31–32.

71. So described in Alschuler, "Rediscovering Blackstone," above note 50, at 4.

72. See Anton-Hermann Chroust, *Rise of the Legal Profession in America* (1965), II, 173–223.

73. Lists have been compiled, but none claims to be complete; see, e.g., George Dargo, *Law in the New Republic* (1983), 52 (listing nineteen law schools established before 1835).

74. Its history is told in Marian C. McKenna, *Tapping Reeve and the Litchfield Law School* (1986).

75. Ibid., at 145.

76. Ibid., at 112.

77. A. Z. Reed, *Training for the Public Profession of the Law* (1921), 112–14.

78. Arthur Sutherland, *The Law at Harvard: A History of Ideas and Men, 1817–1967* (1967), 59.

79. E.g., "William and Mary: America's First Law School," *William & Mary L. Rev.* 2 (1960), 424–36.

80. E.g., "Lecture of Daniel Mayes at Transylvania University (1834)," in: *The Gladsome Light of Jurisprudence,* Michael Hoeflich ed. (1988), 145–64, at 147–48 (stating the value to lawyers of understanding law's "principles, founded in reason and the fixed nature of things"); "Introductory Lecture of Henry St. George Tucker (1841)," in: *Essays on Legal Education in 19th Century Virginia,* W. Hamilton Bryson ed. (1998), 129–49, at 131 (description of the law of nature and its relation to positive law). See generally Steve

Sheppard, "Casebooks, Commentaries, and Curmudgeons: An Introductory History of Law in the Lecture Hall," *Iowa L. Rev.* 82 (1997), 547–644.

81. See Robert Stevens, *Law School: Legal Education in America from the 1850s to the 1980s* (1983), 35–72; Bruce Kimball, *The Inception of Modern Professional Education, C. C. Langdell, 1826–1906* (2009).

82. *Treatise on the Common Law in Relation to Watercourses,* 2d ed. (1833), 10 (asserting that watercourses derive their name and principal characteristics from the law of nature).

83. *General View of the Origin and Nature of the Constitution and Government of the United States* (1837) (insistence that the rights of English inhabitants of North America were held "by the immutable laws of nature").

84. *Dissertation on the Freedom of Navigation and Marine Commerce* (1802): "the law of Nature comprehends all the Laws promulgated to man by Right Reason."

85. See Charles C. Binney, *The Life of Horace Binney, with Selections from His Letters* (1903), 82 (favoring the regulation of commerce by the law of nature rather than governmental regulation).

86. *An Introductory Lecture on the Study of the Law: Delivered at Transylvania University on Monday, November 4, 1822* (1822) ("The Great Author of Nature" as the source of rules regulating conduct between peoples and nations).

87. *Institutes of American Law* (1851), 6 (distinguishing scope of municipal law from natural law).

88. *Law Miscellanies* (1814), 122–24 (law of nature as the source of claims to land).

89. *Disquisition on Government and a Discourse on the Constitution and Government of the United States* (1851), 1 (necessity of understanding the law of nature in order "to have a clear and just conception of the nature and object of government").

90. *Reclamation of Fugitives from Service* (1847), 83, 94 (slavery incompatible with natural rights).

91. *An Essay on the Law of Contracts* (1822), 61 (basic property rights asserted to be in accord with "a principle of the common law, founded on the law of nature").

92. *Principles of Government: A Treatise on Free Institutions* (1833), 158–70 (chapter devoted to the law of nature).

93. *Treatise on the Law of Libel and the Liberty of the Press* (1830), 59 (definition of libel to encompass offenses against the law of nature).

94. *General Abridgement and Digest of American Law* (1823–29), VI, 626–28 (providing legal maxims connected with the law of nature).

95. *A View of South-Carolina* (1802), 147 (defense of slavery as compatible with the "unerring laws" of Nature).

96. *The Law of Nations Investigated in a Popular Manner* (1809), 7: "[u]nless the law of nature sanctions the artificial law of men or states, the latter is of no force nor effect."

97. *Lecture on the Law of Representations in Marine Insurance* (1844), 1–2 (argument that the law of marine insurance was "not merely a branch of municipal law" but "synonymous with the moral law, or as some modern writers have chosen to term it, the law of nature").

98. *The New York Justice* (1815), 171 (wives not to be prosecuted for crimes committed under coercion of their husbands, except for those crimes that contravened the law of nature).

99. *Historical Sketches of the Principles and Maxims of American Jurisprudence* (1819), 7 (describing the law of nature as "common to all rational beings and the revealed law of God").

100. *Considerations upon the Nature and Tendency of Free Institutions* (1848), 459 (consideration of the extent to which American institutions were compatible with the laws of nature).

101. *Remarks on the Law of Imprisonment for Debt* (1823), 13–14 (status of imprisonment for debt evaluated under the law of nature). Herttell also believed that the common law restrictions on the ability of married women to hold property violated the law of nature; see Norma Basch, *In the Eyes of the Law: Women, Marriage, and Property in Nineteenth-Century New York* (1982), 116–20.

102. *The Elements of Law* (1848), 386–87 (compulsion no excuse for committing a crime forbidden under the law of nature).

103. *The Alabama Justice of the Peace* (1822), 184 (attributing the rule protecting nonparties to litigation, *res inter alios acta*, to principles of natural justice).

104. *Syllabus of a Course of Lectures* (1821), 14 (defining and outlining the law of nature).

105. *An Address Delivered before the Law Academy of Philadelphia at the Opening of the Session 1826–79* (1826) (American defense of their rights "as established and protected by the laws of nature and nations").

106. *A Compendium of the Common Law in Force in Kentucky* (1822), 488 (homicide in self-defense not to be punished because authorized by the law of nature).

107. *The Law of Freedom and Bondage in the United States* (1958), 1–3 (definition and endorsement of the law of nature).

108. *View of the Rights and Wrongs, Power and Policy of the United States of America* (1808), 78 (actions of France on the high seas asserted to be crimes against the law of nature).

109. *Digest of the Laws of South Carolina* (1822), 548 (asserting trespass to be a crime against the law of nature).

110. *Commentaries on American Law*, 1st ed. (1826–1830, repr. 1971), I, 3 (describing the law of nations as at least in part based upon "the principles of natural law [and] equally binding in every age and upon all mankind").

111. See *Writings of Hugh Swinton Legaré, Late Attorney General and Acting Secretary of State of the United States* (1845–1846) I, 276 (observance by sover-

eigns of the law of nations and nature, there being no positive law to bind them).

112. *Amendments to the Constitution Submitted to the Consideration of the American People* (1865), 8 (law of nature and nature's rules above the rules of men). See, however, Charles Merriam, *History of American Political Theories* 305–10 (1903) (giving credit to Lieber for starting movement among political scientists to discredit natural law, although also stating that in Lieber's writing "the concept of natural law was still defended").

113. *Treatise on the Law of Principal and Agent and of Sales by Auction* (1818), 310–11 (endorsement of "just and equitable" principle of law of nature that compels performance of promise but recognition of its imperfect reception in the common law).

114. See *Complete Works of Edward Livingston on Criminal Jurisprudence* (1973), 65 (the law of nature described as "innate in the mind of man" and to be used to test the legality of human conduct).

115. *Legal Rights, Liabilities and Duties of Women* (1845), 114: "The natural law, then, is one of those classes of laws which apply to women in the same manner as men."

116. *The Genuine Information Delivered to the Legislature of the State of Maryland Relative to the Proceedings of the General Convention* (1839), 14–16 (mentioning the law of nature and some of its consequences).

117. *Address to the Students of Law in Transylvania University* (1835), 6 (stressing the importance of the study of "natural foundations of justice").

118. *The Pennsylvania Justice of the Peace* (1839), 5 (discussing and classifying crimes against nature).

119. *Institutes of Common and Statute Law,* 3d ed. (1882–1895), I, 21–22 (outline of the law of nature in dealing with the several categories of law).

120. *Commentaries on American Law* (1836), 333 (marriages incestuous under the law of nature to be treated as void).

121. *Memoirs of the Life of John Quincy Adams* (1853), 372–73 (discussion of troubled relationship between law of nature and slavery).

122. See *Proceedings and Debates of the Virginia State Convention of 1829–1830* (1830, repr. 1971), 161–62, 319 (natural law as the source guaranteeing the sanctity of property rights).

123. *A View of the Constitution of the United States of America* (1825), 252 (stating that the law of nature is "implanted in us by nature itself . . . and though not always observed, never is forgotten").

124. *Law of Baron and Femme,* 2d ed. (1846), 283 (duty of parents to support their children founded on the law of nature).

125. See Margaret Horsnell, *Spencer Roane: Judicial Advocate of Jeffersonian Principles* (1986), 83 (describing Roane's application of the law of nature to unsolved problems in the law of slavery).

126. See his Introduction to *Reports of Cases Adjudged in the Superior Court [of Connecticut]* (1898), I, pp. ix–x (describing the common law of the state of Connecticut in the same terms used to describe the law of nature).

127. *Sampson's Discourse, and Correspondence with Various Learned Jurists upon the History of the Law* (1826), 9 (connection between American law and the law of nature).
128. *Treatise on the Measure of the Law of Damages,* 2d ed. (1852), 11 (endorsing view that damages for injury to property were founded upon the law of nature).
129. See Alfred Konefsky, "Shaw, Lemuel," in: *Yale Biographical Dictionary of American Law,* Roger Newman ed. (2009), 492 (slavery said to be illegal in Massachusetts as "contrary to natural right and the plain principles of justice"). See also Shaw's *Address Delivered before the Bar of Barkshire on the Occasion of His First Taking His Seat as Chief Justice* (1830), 13–14 (praising his predecessor for following "the plain dictates of natural justice").
130. *Address Delivered before the Alumni Association of Nassau Hall, September 26, 1832* (promoting education based upon "the constitution of our nature— adapted to all our relations").
131. *An Essay on the Trial by Jury* (1852), 135: "And this rule is, that the language of statutes and constitutions shall be construed, as nearly as possible, consistently with natural law."
132. See 2 Joseph Story, *Commentaries on the Constitution of the United States,* Bk. III, c. 34 § 1381, 3d ed. (1858), 274 (constitutional prohibition of impairment of obligation of contracts based upon "general principles of natural, or [as it is sometimes called] universal law").
133. *History of Land Titles in Massachusetts* (1801), 282 (rights to air, water, and sea "were given to man by the Law of Nature").
134. *A System of the Laws of the State of Connecticut,* Introduction § 2 (1795), I, 7 (describing the law of nature as consisting of "general laws resulting from the original principles and fitness of things" and established by God).
135. See Samuel Tyler, *Memoir of Roger Brooke Taney, LL.B. Chief Justice of the Supreme Court* (1872), 366–67 (acknowledging the contradiction between the law of nature and slavery, but defending it under the law of nations).
136. *A Review of the Criminal Law of the Commonwealth of Kentucky* (1804), 3: "felonious homicide is the highest crime against the law of nature."
137. See his "Introductory Lecture to Law Students," in: *Essays on Legal Education in 19th Century Virginia,* W. Hamilton Bryson ed. (1998), 43–56, at 46 (praising the efforts of lawyers "to imitate the divine model").
138. *The Theory of the Common Law* (1852), 125 (distinguishing the part of Roman law that survived as that part stating the law of nature).
139. *Introduction to American Law: Designed as a First Book for Students* (1869), 338–39 (rights in unowned property derived from first occupancy founded upon the law of nature).
140. *Manual of Criminal Law,* 2d ed. (1889), 8 (equating crimes classed as *mala in se* with those prohibited by the law of nature).
141. The *Papers of Daniel Webster: Legal Papers,* Andrew King ed. (1989) III:3, 879 (rights acquired by invention "stand on plainer principles of natural law").

142. *The Connecticut Town-Officer* (1814), 114 (the duty of parents to support their children described as dictated by the law of nature).

143. *A Treatise on American Law Designed for the Use of the People* (1843), 49 (pursuit of happiness as the great principle of the law of nature).

144. From Edward Barradall (1704), 43, as described in A. G. Roeber, *Faithful Magistrates and Republican Lawyers* (1981), 106–07.

145. See Stuart Banner, "When Christianity Was Part of the Common Law," *L.H.R.* 27 (1998), 27–62; Perry Miller, *Life of the Mind,* above note 2, at 192–206; Sarah Barringer Gordon, "Law and Religion, 1790–1920," in: *Cambridge History of Law in America,* above note 44, 417–48.

146. *The First Book of the Law* §§ 85–95 (1868), 137–42. See also David Flaherty, "Law and Morals in Early America," in: *Law in American History,* D. Fleming and B. Bailyn eds. (1971), 203–53.

6. The Law of Nature in American Courts

1. For this distinction, see, e.g., S. Pufendorf, *Elementorum jurisprudentiae,* Lib. I, def. XIII §§ 1–2, 14–15; see also its recognition and statement in: *The Federalist,* No. 78 (Alexander Hamilton) (Jacob B. Cook ed., 1961), and its modern form in: T. Khaitan, "'Constitution' as a Statutory Term," *L.Q.R.* 129 (2013), 589–609; Jürgen Heideking, "The Law of Nature and Natural Rights. Die Positivierung von Naturrecht im Amerika des ausgehenden 18. Jahrhunderts," in: *Naturrecht, Spätaufklärung, Revolution,* O. Dann and D. Klippel eds. (1995), 48–60.

2. E.g., Blanchard v. Maysville, Washington, Paris and Lexington Turnpike Co., 31 Ky. (1 Dana) 86, 91 (1833); Whicher v. Board of Commissioners of Cedar County, 1 Greene 217, 218 (Iowa 1848).

3. Art. 1 § 1 (1776), in *Federal and State Constitutions,* F. N. Thorpe ed. (1909), VII, 3813.

4. Pt. I (Bill of Rights), Art. 2 (1784), in *Constitutions,* Thorpe ed., IV, 2453–54. Similar language stressing that all men are "by nature free" appeared also in the constitutions of Pennsylvania, Vermont, Massachusetts, Connecticut, and New Jersey. See Robert Cover, *Justice Accused: Antislavery and the Judicial Process* (1975), 43.

5. Constitution of Maryland (1776), Art. 39, in *Constitutions,* Thorpe ed., III, 1690.

6. Form of Government, Pt. I, c. 11 (1780), in *Constitutions,* Thorpe ed., III, 1891.

7. See David Ritchie, *Natural Rights* (1924), 263–71; J. B. Dyer, *Natural Law and the Antislavery Constitutional Tradition* (2012), 17–21. Compare, for example, the Constitution of Kansas—1857, Art VII § 1, in: *Constitutions,* Thorpe ed., II, 1210: "The right of property is before and higher than any constitutional sanction, and the right of the owner of a slave . . . is the same and as inviolable as the right of the owner of any property whatever."

8. See Kent, *Commentaries,* Pt. IV, lect. 24 (p. 6).
9. Compare, for instance, Michael Zuckert, *The Natural Rights Republic* (1996), 108–17, with John Phillip Reid, *Constitutional History of the American Revolution: The Authority of Rights* (1986), 87–102.
10. For the phrase's origins and meaning, see Jerome Hall, "Nulla poena sine lege," *Yale Law J.* 47 (1937), 165–93.
11. For modern settings, see Geoffrey Walker, *The Rule of Law: Foundation of Constitutional Democracy* (1988), 322–24.
12. See C. J. G. Sampford, *Retrospectivity and the Rule of Law* (2006), for discussion of the treatment of retrospective legislative acts.
13. 3 U.S. (3 Dall.) 386.
14. See Chapter 4.
15. 3 U.S. (3 Dall.), at 388.
16. Ibid., at 394.
17. Compare, for example, J. H. Ely, *Democracy and Distrust: A Theory of Judicial Review* (1980), 210–11, with David Currie, *The Constitution in the Supreme Court. The First Hundred Years 1789–1888* (1985), 46–49.
18. Bartolus, *Commentaria* ad Dig. 1.1.9, no. 39.
19. The starting points were set out in Cod. 1.14(17).9 and X 1.2.13. See also F. C. von Savigny, *Treatise on the Conflict of Laws,* William Duthrie trans. (1880), 433–516, where relevant treatments by Bartolus, Molinaeus, Voet, and Huber are printed.
20. Bartolus, *Commentaria* ad Dig. 1.1.9, no. 41: "negotia praeterita decisa seu finita."
21. See Rosamaria Alibrandi, "British Ideas, American Parliamentarism: Republican and Liberal Echoes in the Philadelphia Constitutional Convention of 1787," *Parliaments, Estates & Representation* 33 (2013), 20–33, at 22.
22. Calder v. Bull, 3 U.S. (3 Dall.) at 399.
23. Ibid., at 398.
24. Ibid., at 399.
25. Ibid.
26. Currie, *The Constitution,* above note 17, at 47–48.
27. The discussion in Robert Clinton, *God and Man in the Law* (1997), 38–40 seems to me to be entirely correct on this point.
28. E.g., Green v. Biddle, 21 U.S. (8 Wheat.) 1, 82–3 (1823) (interpreting the rights of occupants of property owned by another according to "that maxim of equity and of natural law, *nemo debet locupletari aliena jactura*)"; The Antelope, 23 U.S. (10 Wheat.) 66, 120 (1825): "That it [the slave trade] is contrary to the law of nature will scarcely be denied"; Martin v. Waddell's Lessee, 41 U.S. (16 Pet.) 367, 420 (1842) (legislative power to grant rights in flowing water was restricted "consistently with the principles of the law of nature") (Thompson, J. dissenting).
29. See, e.g., Lapsley v. Brashears & Barr, 14 Ky. (4 Litt.) 47, 54, 94 (1823); Lindsay v. Commissioners, 2 S.C.L. (2 Bay) 38, 57 (1796). See also the valu-

able evidence found in C. G. Haines, *The Revival of Natural Law Concepts* (1930), 75–103, and Sylvia Snowiss, *Judicial Review and the Law of the Constitution* (1990).

30. E.g., People v. Gallagher, 4 Mich. 244 (1856) (enforcing a restriction on the sale of liquor despite an argument, at 253, that it was an "unjust exercise of legislative power."). See also Commonwealth v. Hitchings, 71 Mass. 482, 486 (1855); McCormick v. Alexander, 2 Ohio 65, 77–78 (1825); Norris v. Clymer, 2 Pa. 277, 284–85 (1845); Lincoln v. Smith, 27 Vt. 328, 339–40 (1855).

31. The phrase is taken from Reid, *Constitutional History*, above note 9, 88.

32. Lapsley v. Brashears & Barr, 14 Ky. (4 Litt.) 47, at 90, 94 (1823); Town of Goshen v. Town of Stonington, 4 Conn. 209, at 225–27 (1822). See also the evidence uncovered by Suzanna Sherry, "Natural Law in the States," Univ. of *Cincinnati L. Rev.* 61 (1992), 171–222.

33. Billings v. Hall, 7 Cal. 1, 11 (1857) (refusing to enforce the Act for the Protection of Actual Settlers and stressing that "the law of nature stands as an eternal rule to all men, binding upon legislatures as well as others"). See also In the Matter of J. L. Dorsey, 7 Port. 293, 377–78 (Ala. 1838) (rejecting Justice Iredell's approach to the question).

34. See Susan Reynolds, *Before Eminent Domain: Toward a History of Expropriation of Land for the Common Good* (2010); Robert Feenstra, "Expropriation et *dominium eminens* chez Grotius," in: *Histoire du droit savant (13e–18e siècle)* (2005), No. IV.

35. The leading case was Gardner v. Village of Newburgh, 2 Johns. Ch. 162 (N.Y. Ch. Ann. 1816). Accord: Ex parte Martin, 13 Ark. 198, 209 (1853); Hooker v. New Haven & Northampton Co. 14 Conn. 146, 158 (1841); Parham v. Justices of Decatur County, 9 Ga. 341, 350 (1851); Concord R.R. v. Greely and Magee, 17 N.H. 47 (1845); In re Public Highway, 22 N.J.L. 293, 303 (1849); Bradshaw v. Rogers, 20 Johns. 103, 106 (N.Y. 1822); Blanchard v. Maysville, Washington, Paris and Lexington Turnpike Co., 31 Ky. (1 Dana) 86, 91 (1833); Mims v. Macon & Western Railroad Co., 3 Ga. 333, 339 (1847); Kramer v. Cleveland & Pittsburgh Railroad Co., 5 Ohio St. 140, 150 (1855). See also Harry Schreiber, "The Road to Munn: Eminent Domain and the concept of Public Purpose in the State Courts," in: *Law in American History*, D. Fleming and B. Bailyn eds. (1971), 327–402, esp. 360–62; Edward Corwin, "The Basic Doctrine of American Constitutional Law," *Michigan L. Rev.* 12 (1914), 247–75.

36. John Locke, *Two Treatises of Government* (1988), II, c. 11 § 135 (that the Legislator is supreme, yet "it is not, nor can it possibly be, absolutely arbitrary over the lives and fortunes of the people").

37. Concord R.R. v. Greely and Magee, 17 N.H. 48, 56 (1845); see also J. Mazzone, "The Bill of Rights in the Early State Courts," *Minnesota L. Rev.* 92 (2007), 1–82.

38. See Daniel Farber & Suzanna Sherry, *History of the American Constitution*, 2d ed. (2005), 373, 383.

39. Henfield's Case, 11 F. Cas. 1099, 1107 (C.C.D. Pa. 1793) (No. 6,360) (from jury charge by Wilson, J.)
40. Worcester v. Georgia, 31 U.S. 515, 579 (1832) (concurrence by McLean, J.).
41. Billings v. Hall, 7 Cal. 1, 11 (1857).
42. Arnold v. Mundy, 6 N.J.L. 1, 11 (1821).
43. Bell v. State, 31 Tenn. (1 Swan) 42, 44 (1851) (citing Blackstone). Other examples: Chappell v. Causey & Stallings, 11 Ga. 25, 31 (1852); Stanley v. Earl, 15 Ky. (5 Litt.) 281, 284 (1824); Adams v. People, 1 N.Y. 173, 175 (1848).
44. See Robert Lowry Clinton, "The Supreme Court before John Marshall," *J. Supreme Court Hist.* 27 (2002), 222–39, at 235–36; Peter Hoffer, *The Law's Conscience: Equitable Constitutionalism in America* (1990), 85–106.
45. *Encyclopédie,* v. *droit naturel,* in D. Diderot, *Oeuvres complètes* (1973) XV, 229–36; see generally Elaine Martin-Haag, "Droit naturel et histoire dans la philosophie de Diderot," in: *Recherches sur Diderot et sur l'Encyclopédie* (1999), 37–47.
46. Bank of Utica v. Wager, 2 Cow. 712, 765 (N.Y. 1824).
47. E.g., Borden v. State, 11 Ark. 519, 528–29 (1851).
48. McCormick v. Alexander, 2 Ohio 66, 76 (1825).
49. Schoonmaker v. Roosa & DeWitt, 17 Johns. 301, 304 (N.Y. 1820); University of Vermont v. Buell, 2 Vt. 48 (1829).
50. Livingston v. Jefferson, 15 F. Cas. 660, 662–63 (C.C.D. Va. 1811) (No. 8,411); see also U.S. v. Holmes, 26 F. Cas. 360 (C.C.E.D. Pa. 1842) (No. 15,383); Roberts v. Roberts, 1 Ohio Dec. Reprint 368, 369 (1850), and see generally Morton Horwitz, *The Transformation of American Law, 1870–1960* (1992), 158–59.
51. Harris v. Hardeman, 55 U.S. (1 How.) 334, 340–41 (1852). See also D'Arcy v. Ketchum, 52 U.S. 165, 174 (1850); Hollingsworth v. Duane, 12 F. Cas. 367, 369 (C.C.D. Pa. 1801) (No. 6,617); Astor v. Winter, 8 Mart. (o.s.) 171, 178 (La. 1820).
52. Mathewson v. Sprague, 16 F. Cas. 1103, 1105 (C.C.D.R.I. 1853) (No. 9,278); Bartlet v. Knight, 1 Mass. 401, 406 (1805); Borden v. Fitch, 15 Johns. 121, 134 (N.Y. Sup. Ct. 1818).
53. 55 U.S. at 341.
54. E.g., Borden v. State, 11 Ark. 519 (1851).
55. Dorsey v. Dorsey, 7 Watts 349, 350 (Pa. 1838); Tobin v. Walkinshaw, 23 F. Cas. 1331, 1336 (N.D. Cal. 1855) (No. 14,068).
56. E.g., D'Arcy v. Ketchum 52 U.S. 165, 170 (1850); Este & Longworth v. Strong, 2 Ohio 401 (1826). See also the ante-bellum cases collected in Haines, *Revival of Natural Law,* above note 29, at 104–39.
57. In the Matter of J. L. Dorsey, 7 Port. 293, 320–21, 347–48, 360–61 (Ala. 1838).
58. Ibid., at 375–77 (finding sufficient authority in the reservation of rights to the people in the Alabama constitution).
59. Foster v. Directors of the Essex Bank, 16 Mass. 245 (1819).

60. 16 Mass. at 252.

61. Fletcher v. Peck, 10 U.S. (6 Cranch) 87 (1810); Dartmouth College v. Woodward, 17 U.S. (4 Wheat.) 518 (1819), Sturges v. Crowninshield, 17 U.S. (4 Wheat.) 122 (1819).

62. 16 Mass. at 271.

63. 16 Mass. at 273.

64. 16 Mass. at 271.

65. Other examples: Livingston v. Moore, 15 F. Cas. 677 (C.C.E.D. Pa. 1830) (No. 8,416); Baltimore & Ohio R. Co. v. Van Ness, 2 F. Cas. 574, 576 (C.C.D.C. 1835) (No. 830).

66. See, e.g., U.S. v. Holmes, 26 F. Cas. 360, 368 (C.C.E.D. Pa. 1842) (No. 15,383); Levering v. Levering, 14 Md. 30 (1859).

67. For its more theoretical aspects, see Stephen Buckle, *Natural Law and the Theory of Property: Grotius to Hume* (1991).

68. This is the central theme of William Novak, *The People's Welfare: Law and Regulation in Nineteenth-Century America* (1996); see esp. 26–35. For the common law background, see Joan Kent, "Attitudes of Members of the House of Commons to the Regulation of 'Personal Conduct' in late Elizabethan and Early Stuart England," *B.I.H.R.* 46 (1973), 41–71.

69. See, e.g., Johnson v. M'Intosh, 21 U.S. (8 Wheat.) 543 (1823).

70. Pierson v. Post, 3 Cai. R. 175 (N.Y. Sup. Ct. 1805).

71. Goff v. Kilts, 15 Wend. 550, 552 (N.Y. Sup. Ct. 1836); Gillet v. Mason, 7 Johns. 16 (N.Y. Sup. Ct. 1810); Idol v. Jones, 13 N.C. 162, 163 (1829). See also Kent, *Commentaries*, Pt. V, lect. 52 (2) (pp. 281–83).

72. See 3 *Bl. Comm.* *390–93; Holden v. Smallbrooke (1668), Vaugh. 187, 124 E.R. 1030.

73. 6 N.J.L. 1 (1821). The holding of the case as to legislative power was later limited by Gough v. Bell, 22 N.J.L. 441 (1850).

74. 6 N.J.L. at 79 (Rossell, J.).

75. 6 N.J.L. at 76–77 (Kirkpatrick, C.J.). See Dig. 1.8.5.

76. 6 N.J.L. at 59.

77. See, e.g., Martin v. Waddell, 41 U.S. 367, 412–13 (1842); Mitchell v. Warner, 5 Conn. 497 (1825); Haywood v. Mayor and Aldermen of Savannah, 12 Ga. 404 (1853); Morgan v. Livingston, 6 Mart. (o.s.) 19 (La. 1819); Moulton v. Libbey, 37 Me. 472 (1854); Morgan & Harrison v. Reading, 11 Miss. (3 S. & M.) 366, 397 (1844); Livingston v. Van Ingen, 9 Johns. 507, 518–19 (N.Y. Ct. of Errors 1812); Roberts & Co. v. Cunningham, 8 Tenn. 67, 69–70 (1827). Contra: Commissioners of the Canal Fund v. Kempshall, 26 Wend. 404 (N.Y. Ct. of Errors 1841).

78. See Kent, *Commentaries*, Pt. VI, lect. 51, I (2) (pp. 329–37).

79. See, e.g., Dale Goble and Eric Freyfogle, *Wildlife Law*, 2d ed. (2010), 245–89. The possibility of state regulation, as opposed to ownership, was recognized from the start; see, e.g., Commonwealth v. Alger, 61 Mass. (7 Cush.) 53.

80. Patterson's Devisees v. Bradford, 3 Ky. (1 Hard.) 101, 111 (1807): "deducible from the principles of natural law"; Hanes v. Peck's Lessee, 8 Tenn.

Notes to Pages 157–159

(1 Mart. & Yer.) 228, 231 (1827): that the rule is "founded upon and accordant with the law of nature"; Lessee of Ludlow's Heirs v. Barr, 3 Ohio 388, 390–91 (1828): "Occupancy is the first right under the laws of nature" and a court "resorts to the law of nature for title."

81. This seems to have been the view of America's most influential work on the subject, John Chipman Gray, *Restraints on the Alienation of Property* (1894) § 21.

82. *De iure belli ac pacis,* C. VI, I, 1.

83. Kent, *Commentaries,* Pt. VI, lect. 52, I(2) (p. 406).

84. Buckner v. Real Estate Bank, 5 Ark. 536, 540 (1844) (case dealing with the customs of merchants).

85. E.g., De Peyster v. Michael, 6 N.Y. 467, 493–94 (1852); see also Dawes v. Head, 20 Mass. (3 Pick.) 128, 132 (1825) (by counsel).

86. U.S. Constitution, Art. III § 1.

87. Sutton v. Warren, 51 Mass. 451, 452 (1845): "There is an exception, however, to this principle where the marriage is considered as incestuous by the law of Christianity, and as against natural law." The most common reference point for this position was the opinion of Chancellor Kent, in Wightman v. Wightman, 4 Johns. Ch. 343 (N.Y. 1820). See also Maberry & Pollard v. Shisler, 1 Del. (1 Harr.) 349, 354 (1834); Stevenson v. Gray, 56 Ky. (17 B. Mon.) 193 (1856); Thornton v. Western Reserve Farmers' Ins. Co., 1 Grant 472 (Pa. 1858) (counsel). For a clear statement in the context of its modern relevance, see Patrick Borchers, "The Essential Irrelevance of the Full Faith and Credit Clause to the Same-Sex Marriage Debate," *Creighton L. Rev.* 38 (2004) 353–63.

88. See Annot. 71 A.L.R. 2d 676 § 5.

89. See Rogers v. Cruger, 7 Johns. 557, 634 (N.Y. 1808): "[E]very sympathy of nature, every dictate of policy, and every injunction of religion rise up and declare in favor of the rights of inheritance." See also Blackburn v. Hawkins, 6 Ark. 50, 58 (1845), (interpreting a legacy to take effect at twenty-one to take effect earlier, "since by the law of nature [the father] was obliged to provide not only for the future but the present maintenance of his child, and shall not be presumed to have left him destitute"); Jackson v. Jackson, 2 Pa. 212, 215 (1845) ("obligation of a parent to provide for the sustenance and education of his children" used to help determine whether a trust had been created by will).

90. Except, of course, in Louisiana, where the civil law governed this area of law.

91. Johnson & Henderson v. Dilliard, 1 S.C.L. (1 Bay) 232 (1792). See Adam Hirsch, "Inheritance: United States Law," in: *Oxford International Encyclopedia of Legal Hist.* 3 (2009), 235–40.

92. See Stanley Katz, "Republicanism and the Law of Inheritance in the American Revolutionary Era," *Michigan L. Rev.* 76 (1977), 1–29; Susanna Blumenthal, "The Deviance of the Will: Policing the Bounds of Testamentary Freedom in Nineteenth-Century America," *Harvard L. Rev.* 119 (2006),

959–1034; Richard Morris, "Primogeniture and Entailed Estates in America," *Columbia L. Rev.* 27 (1927), 24–51. Much of the controversy about this question has centered around the question of whether the movement followed or preceded the Revolution; see, e.g., Holly Brewer, "Entailing Aristocracy in Colonial Virginia: 'Ancient Feudal Restraints' and Revolutionary Reform," *William & Mary Q.* 3d ser. 54 (1997), 307–46; Toby Ditz, "Ownership and Obligation: Inheritance and Patriarchal Households in Connecticut, 1750–1820," *William & Mary Q.* 3d ser. 47 (1990), 235–65. Claire Priest has brought a different and more economic perspective to the subject, but it seems not wholly inconsistent with traditional views of the subject; see her "Creating an American Property Law: Alienability and Its Limits in American History," *Harvard L. Rev.* 120 (2006), 385–459.

93. E.g., Van Duyne v. Vreeland, 12 N.J. Eq. 142, 144 (1858).

94. E.g., Heath v. White, 5 Conn. 228, 232 (1824) (allowing illegitimate child to inherit from mother upon her intestacy).

95. Hawes v. Cooksey & James, 13 Ohio 242, 246 (1844): "[I]t was not the design of the bankrupt law to overturn all society by discharging men from the performance of those moral and natural duties which constitute the foundation of the whole social fabric."

96. The Etna, 8 F. Cas. 803, 806 (D. Me. 1838) (No. 4,542). See also Thompson v. Buckhannon, 25 Ky. (2 J. J. Marsh.) 416, 419 (1829); Wilkes v. Rogers, 6 Johns. 566, 579 (1810).

97. Donald Kramer, *Legal Rights of Children,* 2d ed. rev. (2005), I § 4:2 (with relevant cases and statutory references).

98. Ira Ellman et al., *Family Law: Cases, Text, Problems,* 5th ed. (2010), 503: "The precise rationale for imposing the duty to support children on their parents is rarely discussed or articulated."

99. E.g., Scott Altman, "A Theory of Child Support," *International J. of Law* 17 (2003), 173–210, at 175 (suggesting that the obligation arises from causing the child "to suffer, by failing to demonstrate love to the child").

100. Foster v. Alston, 7 Miss. (6 Howard) 406 (1842) (allowing mother to keep custody of children against the claims of a guardian appointed by the father).

101. Mifflin v. Commonwealth, 5 Watts & Serg. 461, 463 (Pa. 1843) (allowing conspiracy prosecution for removing a daughter from her father, thus asserting a right that "is deeply seated, not only in the law of nature, but in the public welfare"); Commonwealth v. Downes, 41 Mass. (24 Pick.) 227, 231 (1836) (law of nature cited in allowing a father to "reclaim" son who had enlisted in the Navy without his consent); Town of Woodstock v. Hooker, 6 Conn. 35, 38 (1825) (status of illegitimate children settled with mother described as "agreeable to the law of nature and reason," quoting Canaan v. Salisbury 1 Root 155, at 156 (Conn. 1790)).

102. State ex rel. Paine v. Paine, 23 Tenn. (4 Hum.) 523, 533 (1843). See also Chappell v. Causey & Stallings, 11 Ga. 25, 32 (1852): "We never love equity more, than when it . . . interposes to protect the rights of a feme

covert"; Osborn v. Allen, 26 N.J.L. 388, 391 (1857): "The duties of parents to their children, by the law of nature, rest equally on both." But cf. Lawson v. Scott, 9 Tenn. (1 Yer.) 92, 95 (1825) (showing greater hesitation).

103. E.g., Gishwiler v. Dodez, 4 Ohio St. 615, 617 (1855) (holding that both parents had a natural right to their child but that "neither of the parties has any rights that can be made to conflict with the welfare of the child"). A similar case is State v. Smith, 6 Me. 462 (1830); see also Lewis Hochheimer, *Treatise on the Law Relating to the Custody of Infants* 2d ed. (1891) §§ 15–17.

104. Van Valkinburgh v. Watson & Watson, 13 Johns. 480 (N.Y. 1816).

105. Finch v. Finch, 22 Conn. 411, 415 (1853); Hunt v. Thompson, 4 Ill. (3 Scam.) 179 (1841); Van Duyne v. Vreeland, 12 N.J. Eq. 142 (1858); Edwards v. Davis, 16 Johns. 281 (N.Y. 1819). Contra: Stanton v. Willson & Smith, 3 Day 37 (Conn. 1808); Forsyth v. Ganson, 5 Wend. 558 (N.Y. 1830).

106. Angel v. McLellan, 16 Mass. 28 (1819).

107. The leading case was Commonwealth v. Aves, 35 Mass (18 Pick.) 193; see also In re Matter of Archy, 9 Cal. 147, 162 (1858); Jackson v. Bulloch, 12 Conn. 38 (1837); Jarrot v. Jarrot, 7 Ill. (2 Gilm.) 1 (1845); Mahoney v. Ashton, 4 H. & McH. 295, 304 (Md. 1799); Marguerite v. Chouteau, 3 Mo. 540 (1834); Lemmon v. People, 26 Barb. 270 (N.Y. Sup. Ct. 1857). See also Alan Watson, *Slave Law in the Americas* (1989), 122–24.

108. Cover, *Justice Accused,* above note 4; Justin Dyer, *Natural Law and the Antislavery Constitutional Tradition* (2012); William M. Wiecek, "Somerset: Lord Mansfield and the Legitimacy of Slavery in the Anglo-American World," *Univ. of Chicago L. Rev.* 42 (1974), 86–146.

109. Cover, *Justice Accused,* above note 4, at 105.

110. Rankin v. Lydia, 9 Ky. (2 A.K. Marsh.) 467 (1820). Something close to the opposite result was reached under English law, declared by Lord Stowell in "The Slave Grace," 2 Hag. Adm. 94, 166 E.R. 179 (1827); it was known as "the reattachment doctrine." The operative distinction was drawn by the American courts between merely "sojourning" and establishing one's domicile in the free state; see Note, *Columbia L. Rev.* 71 (1971), 74–99, at 87–92.

111. Rankin, prior note, at 472. Cases are collected in Jacob Wheeler, *A Practical Treatise on the Law of Slavery* (1837, repr. 1968), 335–88. See also William Wiecek, *Sources of Antislavery Constitutionalism in America, 1760–1848* (1977), 202–27.

112. See Cover, *Justice Accused,* above note 4, at 111. Some of the difficulties and complexities of that position are explored in Wiecek, "Somerset: Lord Mansfield," above note 108, at 128–40.

113. See Note, 71 *Columbia L. Rev.* 71 (1971), 74–99, at 92–98.

114. *Justice Accused,* above note 4, at 154–58; Wiecek, *Sources of Antislavery Constitutionalism,* above note 111, at 259–61. See also David Schrader, "Natural Law in the Constitutional Thought of Frederick Douglass," in: *Frederick Douglass: A Critical Reader,* Bill Lawson and Frank Kirkland eds. (1990), 85–99.

115. Spooner, *The Unconstitutionality of Slavery* (1860), 7, 15. See Helen Knowles, "Seeing the Light: Lysander Spooner's Increasingly Popular Constitutionalism," *Law & Hist. Rev.* 31 (2013), 231–58.

116. *Justice Accused,* above note 4, at 159–91. See, e.g., Jones v. Vanzandt, 13 F. Cas. 1040, 1045 (C.C.D. Ohio 1843) (No. 7,501); In re Ralph, Morris 1 (Iowa 1839) (giving a narrow reading to the term "fugitive"); Gray v. Combs, 30 Ky. (7 J. J. Marsh.) 478, 481–82, 484 (1832) (frequent reference to law of nature in dealing with slave's criminal acts). See also Christopher Eisgruber, "Justice Story, Slavery, and the Natural Law Foundations of American Constitutionalism," *Univ. of Chicago L. Rev.* 55 (1988), 273–327.

117. An example of the former is Rice v. Parkman, 16 Mass. 326, 330 (1820); of the latter George v. State, 37 Miss. 316, 320 (1859). See David B. Davis, *Inhuman Bondage: The Rise and Fall of Slavery in the New World* (2006), 175–92; William Wiethoff, *A Peculiar Humanism:* the *Judicial Advocacy of Slavery in High Courts of the Old South, 1820–1850* (1996), 35–74.

118. Dave v. State, 22 Ala. 23, 34 (1853). See also State v. Reed, 9 N.C. (2 Hawks) 454 (1823).

119. State v. Jones, 1 Miss. (1 Walker) 83 (1821); Fields v. State, 9 Tenn. (1 Yer.) 156 (1829); Nix v. State, 13 Tex. 575 (1855). See also Jacob Wheeler, *Practical Treatise,* above note 111, at 200–04. But cf. Commonwealth v. Turner, 26 Va. (5 Rand.) 678 (1827); Mark Tushnet, *American Law of Slavery, 1810–1860* (1981), 54–70; Thomas Morris, *Southern Slavery and the Law, 1619–1860* (1996), 161–81.

120. Jackson v. Phillips, 96 Mass. 539, 564 (1867).

121. Biscoe v. Biscoe, 6 G. & J. 232, 233 (Md. 1834). On some of the problems involving slavery raised by the Rule, see Morris, *Southern Slavery,* above note 119, at 418–23.

122. See, e.g., the interesting question on whether manumission could be made contingent on election by the slave himself, a question determined differently in Virginia and North Carolina. Compare Osborne v. Taylor's Administrator, 53 Va. (12 Gratt.) 117, 128 (1855) (rejecting "this impracticable and repugnant alternative") with Redding v. Long & Findley, 57 N.C. (4 Jones Eq.) 216, 218–19 (1858) (permitting it). See generally Paul Finkelman, "Slavery in the United States. Persons or Property?" in: *The Legal Understanding of Slavery,* Jean Allain ed. (2012), 105–34; Judith Schafer, *Slavery, the Civil Law, and the Supreme Court of Louisiana* (1994), 1–27.

123. Morrison v. Barksdale, 16 S.C.L. (Harp.) 101, 102 (1824); very similar language also appears in Jim v. State, 3 Mo. 147, 158–59 (1832).

124. 115 N.Y. 506 (1889).

125. 115 N.Y. at 511; see Chapter 2.

126. See Reinhard Zimmermann, "'Unworthiness' in the Roman Law of Succession," in: *Judge and Jurist: Essays in Memory of Lord Rodger of Earlsferry,* A. Burrows, D. Johnston, and R. Zimmermann eds. (2013), 325–44.

127. 115 N.Y. at 511.

128. 115 N.Y. at 517.

129. E.g., James Barr Ames, "Can a Murderer Acquire Title by His Crime and Keep It?" in: *Lectures on Legal History and Miscellaneous Legal Essays* (1913), 310–22; William McGovern, "Homicide and Succession to Property," *Michigan L. Rev.* 68 (1969), 65–110.
130. E.g., Kelley v. State, 105 N.H. 240, 242, 196, 198 A.2d 68 (1963).
131. Uniform Probate Code § 2–803.
132. Sinnickson v. Johnson & Johnson, 17 N.J.L. 129, 153 (1839). The case was decided before the U.S. Constitution had been incorporated into state law in this situation. See also Fanning v. Gregoire & Bogg, 57 U.S. 524 (1850).
133. Cases where government authorities destroyed private property to prevent harm to society, as in a conflagration, were an exception. Some purported to rest on the law of nature itself; see, e.g., Surocco v. Geary, 3 Cal. 69, 73 (1853): "The individual rights of property give way to the higher laws of impending necessity." See also American Print Works v. Laurence, 23 N.J.L. 590, 615 (1851).
134. E.g., Briscoe v. Bronaugh, 1 Tex. 326, 337 (1846); Richards, Truesdale & Co. v. Hunt, 6 Vt. 251, 253 (1834).
135. *Law and Judicial Duty* (2008), 612–15.
136. Haywood v. Mayor and Aldermen of Savannah, 12 Ga. 404, 411–12 (1853).
137. Id.
138. Buckner v. Real Estate Bank, 5 Ark. 536, 540 (1844) (that bills of exchange are assignable founded upon "the general principle of natural law"); Mayor of Philadelphia v. Commissioners of Spring Garden, 7 Pa. 348, 363 (1847) (grant of exclusive right to draw water given minimalist reading).
139. Cook v. Corn, 1 Tenn. (1 Overt.) 340, 342 (1808): "Self-preservation is the first law of nature."
140. E.g., Duncan v. Commonwealth, 4 Serg. & Rawle 449 (Pa. 1818).
141. See above notes 34–37.
142. Walton v. Willis, 1 U.S. (1 Dall.) 351, 353 (1788): "[N]atural justice and the constant rules of all courts require that every person who is interested in the proceedings should be summoned and heard."
143. Mayor v. Commissioners of Spring Garden, 7 Pa. 348, 363–64 (1847).
144. See William Fisher III, "The Development of Modern American Legal Theory and the Judicial Interpretation of the Bill of Rights," in: *A Culture of Rights,* M. J. Lacey and Knud Haakonssen eds. (1991), 266–365.
145. Sturges v. Crowninshield, 17 U.S. (4 Wheat.) 122, 155 (1819).
146. See, e.g., Warden v. Greer, 6 Watts 424, 426 (Pa. 1837). See also Benjamin Wright Jr., *American Interpretations of Natural Law* (1931, repr. 1962), 216 (noting a general tendency "to think of natural law in terms of the laws of the physical world").
147. Moore v. Moore, 22 Tex. 237, 239 (1858).
148. Beebe v. Beebe, 10 Iowa 133, 135 (1859).
149. E.g., T. Sanchez, *De matrimonii sacramento,* Lib. II, disp. 2–4.
150. Marshall v. Clark, 8 Va. (4 Call) 268, 273 (1791).

151. Beard v. Smith, 22 Ky. 430, 492 (1828). See also Stanley v. Earl, 15 Ky. (5 Litt.) 281, 284 (1824).
152. E.g., Burke v. Hale, 9 Ark. 328, 334–35 (1849) (Walker, J.).
153. See, e.g., Pirate v. Dalby 1 U.S. (1 Dell.) 167, 169 (1786), Dawes v. Head, 20 Mass. (3 Pick.) 128, 132 (1825); Rogers v. Cruger, 7 Johns. 557, 633 (1808), Richards & Truesdale v. Hunt, 6 Vt. 251, 253 (1834). Contra: Moore's Trustees v. Howe's Heirs, 20 Ky. (4 T.B. Mon.) 199 (1826).
154. Willard v. People, 5 Ill. (4 Scam.) 461, 462 (1843).
155. People ex rel. Attorney-General v. Folsom, 5 Cal. 373, 379 (1855) (citing "the principles of natural law" to that effect); Goodell v. Jackson, 20 Johns. 693, 707 (N.Y. 1823): "part of the law of our nature and deeply rooted in the social affections."
156. Livingston v. Herman, 9 Mart. (o.s.) 656, 691 (La. 1821).
157. Synder v. Warford & Thomas, 11 Mo. 513, 516 (1848). See also Carey v. Daniels, 49 Mass. (8 Met.), 466, 473 (counsel).

Conclusion

1. *Novus Ordo Seclorum: The Intellectual Origins of the Constitution* (1985), 58.
2. 3 *Bl. Comm.* *330.
3. Stout v. Jackson, 23 Va. (2 Rand.) 132, 150 (1823).
4. Henry Gally (1696–1769), *Some Considerations upon Clandestine Marriages* (1750), 6.
5. *Summa theologiae*, 1a2ae, qu. 94, art. 4.

Bibliography

Treatises and Other Works on Law and Procedure Written before 1850

Note: Citations to the published treatises and legal literature are given in abbreviated form in the footnotes; for full references to the authors and editions cited, readers should have recourse to this bibliography. The many early works used in Chapters 3 and 5 to show the widespread acceptance of natural law's existence and value have, with few exceptions, not been included here.

Accarisius, Joannes (fl. 1645), *Decisiones Rotae Florentinae* (Florence 1713).

Afflictis, Matthaeus de (d.a. 1528), *Decisiones sacri consilii Neapolitani* (Venice 1604).

Albericus de Rosate (d. 1354), *Dictionarium iuris quam civilis quam canonici* (Venice 1573, repr. 1971).

Albizzi, Franciscus (d. 1684), *De inconstantia in judiciis tractatus* (Rome 1698).

——, *Sacrae Rotae Romanae decisiones* (Rome 1698).

Almici, Giovanni Battista (d. 1793), *Institutiones iuris naturae et gentium secundum catholica principia* (Brescia 1768).

Altogradi, Josephus (fl. seventeenth century), *Controversiae forenses* (Geneva 1701).

Amendola, Flavius (d. ca. 1616), *Additiones aureae et annotationes ad tres partes decisionum regii consilii Neapolitani* (Venice 1616).

Ancharano, Petrus de (d. 1416), *Commentaria in libros decretalium* (Bologna 1580).

Andreae, Joannes (d. 1348), *In quinque decretalium libros novella commentaria* (Venice 1581, repr. 1963).

Angelus Carlettus, de Clavasio (d. 1495). See *Summa angelica.*

Arumaeus, Dominicus (d. 1637), *Decisionum et sententiarum facultate et dicasterio provinciali Jenensi pronunciatarum liber primus* (Jena 1612).

Aufrerius, Stephanus. See *Capella Tholosana.*

Avila, Stephanus de (d. 1601), *De censuris ecclesiasticis tractatus* (Lyons 1608).

Ayliffe, John (d. 1732), *Parergon juris canonici Anglicani* (London 1726).

Ayton, John (d. 1350), *Constitutiones legatinae domini Othonis et domini Othoboni cum annotationibus Johannis de Athona* (Oxford 1679).

Azo (d. ca. 1230), *Summa codicis* (Basel 1563).

Balbus, J. Lanfrancus (d.p. 1518), *Observationes nonnullarum in jure decisionum . . . centurias quinque* (Paris 1541).

Baldus de Ubaldis (d. 1400), *Commentaria omnia* (Venice 1599, repr. 2004).

———, *In decretalium volumen commentaria* (Venice 1595, repr. 1971).

Barbosa, Augustinus (d. 1649), *Summa apostolicarum decisionum extra ius commune vagantium* (Lyon 1680).

Barbosa, Simon Vaz (d. 1681), *Principia et loci communes seu regulae tam decisionum quam argumentorum* (Utrecht 1651).

Barrington, Daines (d. 1800), *Observations upon the Statutes* (London 1766).

Bartolus de Saxoferrato (d. 1357), *Opera omnia* (Venice 1570–1571).

Barzius, Caesar, *Decisiones almae rotae Bononiensis* (Venice 1610).

Bellapertica, Petrus de (d. ca. 1308), *Lectura institutionum* (Lyon 1536, repr. 1972).

Bellemere, Egidius (d. 1407), *Decisiones Romanae* (Lyon 1538).

Bellone, Marc'Antonio (fl. 1580), *Decisiones rotae Genuae de mercatura et ad eam pertinentibus* (Venice 1606).

Berlich, Mattheus (d. 1631), *Decisiones aureae* (Leipzig 1673).

Bertachinus, Johannes (d. ca. 1506), *Repertorium iuris utriusque* (Venice 1590).

Blackstone, William (d. 1780), *Commentaries on the Laws of England* (Oxford 1765–1769).

Blancus, Marcus Antonius (d. 1548), *Practica criminalis* (Venice 1555).

Boerius, Nicholaus (d. 1539), *Decisiones aureae . . . Burdegalenses* (Lyon 1544).

Bohic, Henricus (d. ca. 1350), *In quinque decretalium libros commentaria* (Venice 1576).

Bondino, Vincenzo (d. 1704), *De iure controverso colluctationum legalium . . . opus* (Venice 1665).

Bracton: De legibus et consuetudinibus Angliae, George Woodbine ed. and S. E. Thorne trans. (Cambridge, Mass. 1968–1977).

Brunnemannus, Johannes (d. 1672), *Decisionum Centuriae V* (Frankfurt 1704).

Brydall, John (d. ca. 1705), *Enchiridion legume: Speculum juris anglicani* (London 1673).

Burlamaqui, Jean Jacques (d. 1748), *Principles of Natural and Public Law,* Thomas Nugent trans. (Indianapolis Ind. 2006).

Butrio, Antonius de (d. 1408), *Commentaria in libros decretalium* (Venice 1578, repr. 1967).

Caballus, Petrus (d. 1616), *Resolutionum criminalium centuriae duae* (Venice 1694).

Cabedo, Georgius de (fl. 1600), *Practicarum observationum sive decisionum supremi Senatus regni Lusitaniae pars secunda* (Antwerp 1610).

Caccialupus, Giovanni Baptista (d. 1496), *De debitore suspecto et fugitivo tractatus* (Lyon 1621).

————, *Tractatus de modo studendi in utroque iure* (Venice 1569).

Cacheranus, Octavianus (d. 1580), *Decisiones sacri senatus Pedemontani* (Frankfurt 1599).

Camarela, Franciscus, *De legatis et singulis rebus per fideicommissum relictis* (Venice 1681).

Capella Tholosana, Decisiones (Frankfurt 1614).

Capycius, Antonius (d. ca. 1585), *Decisiones sacri regii consilii Neapolitani* (Venice 1556).

Carletti, Angelo (d. 1495). See *Summa angelica*.

Cartari, Fliminio (d. 1593), *Decisiones Rotae causarum executivarum Reipublicae Genuensis* (Mainz 1604).

Cavalcanus, Borgninus (d. 1607), *Decisionum fori Fivizanensis aliorumque tribunalium in Italia* (Venice 1602).

Censius, Ludovicus (d. 1637), *Decisiones sacrae Romanae Rota* (Turin 1638).

Chartarius, Flaminio (d. 1593), *Decisiones Rotae causarum executivarum reipublicae Genuensis* (Mainz 1604).

Christinaeus, Paulus (d. 1631), *Practicarum quaestionum rerumque in supremis Belgarum curiis actarum et observatarum decisiones* (Antwerp 1671).

Claperius, Franciscus de (fl. 1536), *Decisiones in summa curia Provinciae* (Lyon 1602).

Clarus, Julius (d. 1575), *Liber sententiarum receptarum V: Practica criminalis* (Venice 1595).

Clavasio. See *Summa Angelica*.

Clerke, Francis (fl. 1596), *Praxis in curiis ecclesiasticis* (London 1684).

Coccini, Giovanni Baptista (d. ca. 1641), *Decisiones sacrae Romanae Rota* (Lyon 1623).

Codex Fabrianus definitionum forensium et rerum in sacro Sabaudiae senatu tractatarum [Antoine Favre (d. 1624)] (Cologne 1620).

Coke, Edward (d. 1634), *Commentary on Littleton* [Pt. I of prior entry] (1628).

————, *First (Second etc.) Part of the Institutes of the Lawes of England* (London 1628–1644).

Corpus iuris canonici cum glossis (Venice 1615).

Corpus iuris civilis cum glossis (Venice 1606).

Corserius, Joannes. See *Capella Tholosana*.

Costantini, Francesco Maria (d. 1713), *Decisiones diversorum Sacrae Romanae Rota auditorum* (Rome 1702).

Costanus, Antonius Gubertus (fl. 1550), *De sponsalibus matrimoniis et dotibus commentarius* (Marburg 1597).

Covarruvias y Leyva, Didacus (d. 1577), *Quaestionum practicarum earumque resolutionum liber* (Frankfurt 1573).

Cowell, John (d. 1611), *The Interpreter or Booke containing the Signification of Words* (Cambridge 1607).

Cumberland, Richard (d. 1718), *A Treatise of the Laws of Nature*, John Maxwell trans. (London 1727, repr. 2005).

Damhouder, Jodocus (d. 1581), *Praxis rerum criminalium* (Antwerp 1601, repr. 1978).

Díaz de Luco, Joannes Bernardus (d. 1556), *Aureae decisiones criminales* (Venice 1544).

——, *Practica criminalis canonica* (Mainz 1610).

Dodderidge, John (d. 1628), *The English Lawyer* (London 1631).

Dunozetus, Guilelmus (d. 1657), *Decisiones sacrae Romanae Rotae* (Rome 1673).

Durante, Giovanni Diletto (sixteenth century), *De arte testandi et cautelis ultimarum voluntatum* (Venice 1564).

Durantis, William (d. 1296), *Speculum iudiciale* (Basel 1574, repr. 1975).

Everhardus, Nicholaus (d. 1532), *Consilia sive responsa* (Antwerp 1643).

Farinacius, Prosper (d. 1618), *Sacrae Rotae Romanae decisionum recentiorum* (Lyon 1603).

——, *Variarum quaestionum et communium opinionum criminalium liber* (Venice 1589–1593).

Favre, Antoine. See *Codex Fabrianus.*

Fenzonius, Joannes Baptista (fl. 1630), *Annotationes sive ius municipale Romanae urbis* (Rome 1636).

Ferrariis, Johannes Petrus de (fl. 1400), *Practica aurea* (Venice 1610).

Finch, Henry (d. 1625), *Law, or a discourse thereof* (London 1613).

Finetti, Joannes Franciscus (d. 1842), *De principiis juris naturae et gentium adversus Hobbesium, Puffendorfium, Thomasium, Wulfium et alios* (Venice 1764).

Fontanella, Joannes Petrus (d. 1680), *Sacri regii senatus Catholoniae decisiones* (Barcelona 1645).

Franchis, Vincentius de (d. 1601), *Decisiones sacri regii consilii Neapolitani* (Milan 1609).

Fulbecke, William (d. 1603), *Direction or Preparative to the Study of Lawe* (London 1613).

——, *Parallele or Conference of the Civil, Canon, and the Common Law of England* (London 1602).

Gaill, Andreas (d. 1587), *Practicarum observationum imperialis camerae . . . libri V* (Turin 1595).

Gamma, Antonio de (d. 1595), *Decisiones supremi senatus regni Lusitaniae* (Barcelona 1597).

Gattus, Bartholomeus, *Consilia* (Parma 1688).

Geoffrey of Trani (d. 1245), *Summa super titulis decretalium* (Lyon 1519, repr. 1992).

Gibalini, Josephus (d. 1671), *De usuris, commerciis, deque aequitate et usu fori Lugdunensis . . . tractatio perutilis* (Lyon 1656).

Giurba, Mario (d. 1649), *Consilia seu decisiones criminales* (Venice 1626).

Gizzarello, Nicola Antonius (d. ca. 1622), *Aureae decisiones sacri regii concilii Neapolitani* (Naples 1656).

Godolphin, John (d. 1678), *The Orphan's Legacy or a Testamentary Abridgment* (London 1674).

Grammaticus, Thomas (d. 1556), *Decisiones sacri regii concilii Neapolitani* (Frankfurt 1600).

Grassus, Michaelis (fl. 1580), *Tractatus de successione tam ex testamento quam ab intestato* (Venice 1606).

Gratianus, Stephanus (fl. 1615), *Decisiones Rotae provinciae Marchiae* (Rome 1619).

Grivel de Perrigny, Jean (d. 1624), *Decisiones celeberrimi sequanorum senatus Doleni* (Antwerp 1618).

Grotius, Hugo (d. 1645), *De iure belli ac pacis* (Lyon 1919).

———, *De jure praedae commentarius* (1604, repr. Oxford 1950).

Gutiérrez, Juan (d. 1618), *Practicarum quaestionum civilium . . . libri* (Frankfurt 1607).

Ghewiet, George de (d. 1745), *Jurisprudence du parlement de Flandre,* Serge Dauchy and Veronique Demars-Sion eds. (2008).

Guido Papa. See Papa.

Haberkorn, Heinrich Peter von (d. 1711), *Variarum iuris tam publici quam privati materiarum decisiones* (Leipzig 1672).

Heineccius, Johann Gottlieb (d. 1741), *Elementa juris civilis secundum ordinem Pandectarum* (Strasbourg 1732).

———, *Methodical System of Universal Law, with Supplements and a Discourse by George Turnbull,* T. Ahnert and P. Schröder eds. (2008).

Henricus de Segusio. See Hostiensis.

Hostiensis (d. 1271), *In decretalium libros lectura* (Venice 1581, repr. 1965).

———, *Summa aurea* (Venice 1574, repr. 1963).

Huber, Ulrich (d. 1694), *De Ratione juris docendi et discendi diatribe* (Nijmegan 2010).

Imola, Joannes ab (d. 1436), *In libros decretalium commentaria* (Venice 1575).

Kent, James (d. 1847), *Commentaries on American Law* (New York 1826).

Lancelottus, Joannes Paulus (d. 1590), *Institutiones iuris canonici* (Venice 1703).

Laurentiis, Hieronymus a (fl. 1600), *Decisiones Rotae sacri palatii apostolici Avenionis* (Frankfurt 1600).

Leeuwen, Simon van (d. 1682), *Censura forensis* (Lyon 1662).

Leoncillus, Antonius (fl. seventeenth century), *Decisiones causarum quas in almo Ferrariensis rotae praetorio iudicavit* (Ferrara 1642).

Lezana, Johannes Baptista de (fl. 1630), *Consulta varia* (Venice 1651).

Locatus, Umbertus (d. 1587), *Opus quod iudiciale inquisitorum dicitur* (Rome 1570).

Locke, John (d. 1704), *Two Treatises of Government,* Student edition, Peter Laslett ed. (Cambridge 1988).

Luca, Carolus Antonius de (fl. seventeenth century), *Ad Decisiones Rotae Marchiae D. Stephani Gratiani Romani Scholia* (Naples 1692).

Luca, Giovanni Battista de (d. 1683), *Theatrum veritatis et iustitiae* (Naples 1758).

Ludovicus, Joseph (sixteenth century), *Decisiones seu diffinitiones causarum Perusinarum et provinciae Umbriae* (Venice 1572).

Lyndwood, William (d. 1446), *Provinciale (seu Constitutiones Angliae)* (Oxford 1679, repr. 1968).

Magonius, Hieronymus (d. 1596), *Decisiones causarum tam Rotae Florentianae quam Rotae Lucencis* (Venice 1597).

Mangilius, Joannes Antonius (d. 1642), *De imputationibus et detractionibus in legitima, trebellianica et aliis quartis contingentibus . . . tractatus* (Venice 1618).

Mantica, Franciscus (d. 1614), *Decisiones Rotae Romanae* (Rome 1599).

――――, *Tractatus de conjecturis ultimarum voluntatum* (Cologne 1735).

Mantova Benavides, Marco (d. 1582), *Praxis iudiciariae centuria* (Venice 1545).

Maranta, Robertus (d. ca. 1530), *Tractatus de ordine iudiciorum . . . intitulatus Speculum aureum* (Venice 1549).

Marcus, Franciscus (d. 1522), *Decisiones aureae in sacro Delphinatus senatu discussae ac promulgatae* (Venice 1561).

Marta, Giacomo Antonio (d. 1629), *Tractatus de clausulis . . . cum suis resolutionibus et decisionibus* (Venice 1612).

Marzimedici, Christopherus (d. 1654), *Decisiones rotae et fori ordinarii Senensis* (Florence 1665).

Mascardus, Josephus (d. 1588), *Conclusiones probationum omnium quae in utroque foro quotidie versantur* (Frankfurt 1593).

Matthaeu y Sanz, Laurentius (d. 1680), *Tractatus de re criminali sive controversiarum usu frequentium in causis criminalibus* (Lyon 1702).

Meichsner, Johann, *Decisiones sive res in camera imperiali iudicatae* (Frankfurt 1603).

Mendes de Castro, Manuel (fl. 1604), *Practica Lusitana* (Lisbon 1767).

Menochius, Jacobus (d. 1607), *De praesumptionibus, coniecturis, signis, et indiciis commentariorum* (Venice 1587).

Merlino Pignatelli, Francesco (d. 1650), *Controversiarum forensium iuris communis et regni Neapolitani . . . Centuria* (Venice 1657).

Mevius, David (d. 1670), *Decisiones super causis praecipuis ad summum tribunal regium Vismariense delatis* (Frankfurt 1712).

Milanese, Francesco (d. 1595), *Aureae decisiones magnae regiae curiae regni Siciliae* (Venice 1602).

Monaldus, Franciscus (fl. sixteenth century), *Consilia sive responsa ac decisiones* (Venice 1597).

Muta, Mario (d. 1636), *Decisiones novissimae magnae regiae curiae . . . Siciliae* (Palermo 1620).

Mynsinger, Joachim (d. 1587), *Apotelesma sive corpus perfectum scoliorum ad quatuor libros Institutionum iuris civilis* (Venice 1699).

――――, *Observationes practicae imperialis camerae . . . insignes decisiones* (Wittenberg 1624).

Neostadius, Cornelius van (d. 1606), *Utriusque, Hollandiae, Zelandiae, Frisiaeque curiae decisiones* (The Hague 1667).

Nicholaus de Tudeschis. See Panormitanus.

Noodt, Gerard (d. 1725), *Three Books on Interest-Bearing Loans and Interest* (Capetown 2009).

Odofredus (Bononiensis) (d. 1265), *Lectura super codice* (Bologna 1552, repr. 1968).

Ointomos. See Schneidewein.

Oldradus da Ponte (d. 1335), *Consilia, seu responsa, et quaestiones aureae* (Venice 1570).

Olivarus-Razzalius, Seraphinus (d. 1609), *Aureae decisiones* (Venice 1625).

Oppenritter, Joannes (fl. eighteenth century), *Decisionum imperatoriarum syntagma* (Vienna 1735).

Page, John, *Jus fratrum: the Law of Brethren* (London 1657/1658).

Panormitanus (Nicolaus de Tudeschis) (d. 1445 or 1453), *Commentaria super decretalium libros* (Venice 1615).

———, *Consilia, iuris responsa et quaestiones* (Venice 1617).

Papa, Guido (d. 1487), *In augustissimo senatu Gratianopolitano decisiones* (Geneva 1667).

Papon, Jean (d. 1590), *Recueil d'arrests notables des cours souveraines de France* (Lyon 1557).

Paucapalea (fl. 1140s), *Die Summa des Paucapalea über das Decretum Gratiani*, J. F. von Schulte ed. (Giessen 1890, repr. 1965).

Peguera, Ludovicus a (d. 1610), *Decisiones aureae civiles et criminales ex variis sacri Cathaloniae senatus conclusionibus* (Turin 1613).

Pellegrino, Carlo (fl. 1660), *Praxis vicariorum et omnium in utroque foro jusdicentium . . . ac Sacrae Rotae decisiones* (Venice 1643).

Perez, Antonius (d. 1673), *Praelectionis in duodecim libros Codicis* (Naples 1755).

Phaebus, Melchior (d. 1632), *Decisiones senatus regni Lusitaniae* (Lisbon 1619–1625).

Postius, Ludovicus (fl. 1644), *Decisiones rotae Bononiae* (Parma 1694).

Praetis, Simon de (d. 1602), *De ultimarum voluntatum interpretatione tractatus* (Frankfurt 1583).

Prierio, Sylvestro Mazzolini de (d. 1527). See *Summa Sylvestrina*.

Pufendorf, Samuel von (d. 1694), *Elementorum jurisprudentiae universalis libri duo* (1672, repr. Oxford 1931).

Rebuffus, Petrus (d. 1557), *Tractatus de decimis* (Antwerp 1615).

Reinharthus, Tobias Jacobus (d. 1743), *Selectae observationes ad Pauli Christianei decisiones* (Erfurt 1743).

Riccio, Giovanni Luigi (d. 1643), *Praxis aurea et quotidiana rerum fori ecclesiastici complectens* (Cologne 1621).

Ridley, Thomas (d. 1629), *A View of the Civile and Ecclesiastical Law* (Oxford 1662).

Roccus, Franciscus (d. 1706), *Responsorum legalium cum decisionibus centuria* (Naples 1655).

Rosate. See Albericus de Rosate.

Rota Romana, *Rotae Romanae auditorum decisiones novae, antiquae et antiquiores*
(Venice 1570).

Rovitus, Scipio (d. 1636), *Consilia cum decisionibus supremorum regni Neapolitani
tribunalium* (Naples 1699).

Rutherforth, Thomas (d. 1771), *Institutes of Natural Law,* 2d Amer. ed. (Baltimore 1832).

St. German, Christopher (d. 1540), *Doctor and Student,* T. F. T. Plucknett
and J. L. Barton eds., S.S. 91 (London 1974).

Samuelli, Francisco Maria, (d. 1660), *Praxis nova observanda in ecclesiasticis
supulturis* (Turin 1678).

Sanchez, Thomas (d. 1610), *De sancto matrimonii sacramento tomi tres* (Lyons
1739).

Sande, Joannes van den (d. 1638), *Decisiones Frisicae sive rerum in suprema
Frisiorum curia iudicatarum* (Amsterdam 1698).

Sanfelice, Giovanni Francesco (d. 1648), *Decisionum supremorum tribunalium
Neapolitani* (Naples 1733).

Scaccia, Sigismundo (fl. seventeenth century), *De iudiciis causarum civilium,
criminalium et haereticalium* (Venice 1663).

Schneidewein, Joannes (d. 1568–1569), *In quatuor libros Institutionum imperialium commentarii* (Venice 1701).

Scialoya, Angiolo (fl. 1645), *Tractatus de foro competenti* (Naples 1663).

Seraphinus. See Olivarus-Razzalius.

Sesse, Josephus de (d. 1629), *Decisionum sacri senatus regii regni Aragonum*
(Frankfurt 1619).

Sheppard, William (d. 1675), *Faithful Counsellor or the Marrow of the Law in
English* (London 1675).

Soefve, Lucien, *Nouveau recueil de plusieurs questions notables . . . du Parlement de
Paris* (Paris 1682).

Sola, Antonio (d. 1593), *Commentaria ad universa serenissimorum Sabaudiae
ducum decreta* (Turin 1625).

Soto, Domingo de (d. 1560), *De iustitia et iure libri decem* (Madrid 1967–1968).

Speckhan, Eberhardus (d. 1627), *Quaestionum et Decisionum iuris Caesaraei,
Pontificii, statutarii et consuetudinarii centuria* (Wittenberg 1620).

Speculator. See Durantis, William.

Sperelli, Alexandro (d. 1672), *Decisiones fori ecclesiastici* (Venice 1651).

Stracca, Benvenuto (d. 1578), *De mercatura . . . decisiones et tractatus varii*
(Amsterdam 1669).

Suárez, Francisco (d. 1617), *Tractatus de legibus et deo legislatore* (Coimbra 1612),
in: *Selections from Three Works of Francisco Suárez,* Vol. I (1944).

Suarez de Paz, Gonzalo (d. 1590), *Praxis ecclesiasticus et secularis* (n.p. 1609).

Summa Angelica (Lyon 1520).

Summa Silvestrina (Venice 1601).

Surdus, Joannes Petrus (Sordi) (d. 1588), *Decisiones Mantuanae universae*
(Frankfurt 1664).

————, *Tractatus de alimentis* (Venice 1602).

Swinburne, Henry (d. 1624), *Brief Treatise of Testaments and Last Willes* (London 1590–1591).

————, *Treatise of Spousals or Matrimonial Contracts* (London 1686).

Tancred (of Bologna) (d. 1236), *Ordo iudiciarius*, in: *Libri de iudiciorum ordine*, F. C. Bergmann ed. (Göttingen 1842, repr. 1965).

Tartagni, Alexander [de Imola] (d. 1477), *Consiliorum seu responsorum . . . libri* (Lyon 1549).

Tesauro, Gaspar Antonio (d. 1628), *Novae decisiones sacri senatus Pedemontani* (Turin 1626).

————, *Quaestionum et decisionum forensium seu practicarum liber singularis* (Frankfurt 1608).

Thomingius, Jacobus (d. 1576), *Decisiones quaestionum illustrium* (Leipzig 1579).

Tortus, Flavius (d. 1617), *Annotationes seu lucubrationes ad statuta inclytae civitatis Papie* (Pavia 1617).

Tractatus universi iuris (Venice 1549).

Trentacinque, Alexander (d. 1599), *Consiliorum sive Responsorum . . . Pars Prima (- Secunda)* (Venice 1610).

Tudeschis, Nicholaus de. See Panormitanus.

Tuschus, Dominicus (d. 1620), *Practicarum conclusionum iuris in omni foro frequentiorum* (Rome 1605–1670).

Ubaldis, Baldus de. See Baldus.

Urceoli [Ursilli], Caesar (d. 1568), *[Additiones* to] *Decisiones inclytae Rotae Florentinae* (Alborg 1694).

Valascus [Vaz], Alvarus (d. 1593), *Decisionum, consultationum ac rerum iudicatarum in regno Lusitaniae libri duo* (Coimbra 1686).

Vantius, Sebastianus (d. 1570), *Tractatus de nullitatibus processuum ac sententiarum* (Venice 1567).

Ventriglia, Joannes Baptista (d. 1662), *Praxis rerum notabilium praesertim fori eccleiastici* (Venice 1694).

Venturini, Marzio (fl. seventeenth century), *Decisiones Rotae Florentinae* (Florence 1709).

Vestrius, Octavianus (d. 1573), *In Romanae aulae actionem et iudiciorum mores introductio* (Venice 1547).

Vinnius, Arnoldus (d. 1657), *In quatuor libros Institutionum imperialium commentarius* (Nürnberg 1676).

Voet, Johannes (d. 1713), *Commentarius ad Pandectas* (The Hague 1716).

Wehner, Paulus Matthias (d. 1612), *Dubiorum seu quaestionum aliquot in iure controversarum decisiones* (Frankfurt 1601).

Wheeler, Jacob (fl. 1825), *Practical Treatise on the Law of Slavery* (1837).

Wood, Thomas (d. 1722), *Institute of the Laws of England,* 3d ed. (London 1772, repr. 2005).

Wynants, Goswinus de (d. 1732), *Supremae curiae Brabantinae decisiones recentiores* (Brussels 1744).

Zasius, Ulrich (d. 1535), *Commentaria seu lecturas in titulos Pandectarum*, in: *Opera omnia* (Lyon 1550).

Zuccaro, Octavianus (fl. seventeenth century), *Decisiones civiles et criminales almae rotae Lucensis* (Venice 1632).

Zuffus, Joannes (fl. 1650), *Tractatus criminalis processus libri tres* (Rome 1665).

Index

Absolution, 35, 67–68. *See also* pardons
absolutism, natural law and, 75, 114
abuse: of persons, 59, 122–123; of
    power, 75, 101, 107, 145–169; of right,
    75, 168. *See also* injury, avoidance of
Acherley, Roger, 91
Adam and Eve, 48, 102, 206n93
Adams, John, 129, 130
Adams, John Quincy, 130
Adams, Samuel, 130
admiralty, courts of, 121–124. *See also*
    maritime law
adoption. *See* children: adoption of
adultery, crime of, 44, 54
adverse possession, 36, 113, 144, 171.
    See also limitations, statutes of
Alabama, state of, 152–153
alienation, freedom of, 117–118, 157–158,
    214n67
ambergris, 123–124
Ames, Fisher, 130
analogy, reasoning by, 20, 38, 64, 80
Angell, Joseph, 139
animals: characteristics of, 115, 135,
    155–156; mistreatment of, 63;
    natural law and, 2–3, 18, 26–27, 54,
    59, 64; punishment of, 63; wild, 18,
    54, 135, 155–156. *See also individual
    animals*
Antwerp, city of, 64
appeals, law of, 51–53, 60, 71–72, 101
apprenticeship. *See* clerkships, legal
Aquinas, Thomas, 4–7, 32, 69, 125, 173,
    178
argument *a contrario sensu*, 52
Aristotle, 1, 6, 34, 64

arson, crime of, 136
Ashe, Thomas, 91
Ashley, Francis, 91
assaults, 2–3, 32, 42–43, 59–60, 87, 136,
    164. *See also* self-defense
atheism, 6, 141
aunts and uncles, 57
Avignon, 61

Bacon, Francis, 90–91, 202n22,
    203n52
Bacon, Matthew, 91, 166
Baker, J. H., 86, 201nn10–16
Baldwin, Henry, 139
Ballow, Henry, 130
banking, regulation of, 65, 153–154,
    238n138
bankruptcy, 50, 110, 159
Barbeyrac, Jean, 129
Barrington, Daines, 91, 113
Bartolus of Saxoferrato, 19, 23, 82, 145,
    186n27
bats, 188n53
Bentham, Jeremy, 92
Bible: general references, 21, 26, 64,
    125, 133; knowledge of, 21, 26, 107,
    133; natural law and, 3, 7, 17, 19, 26,
    61, 107, 133, 150; New Testament
    references, 2–4, 7, 17, 22–24, 51, 56;
    Old Testament references,17, 19, 48,
    61–62, 72, 102, 106, 150; Roman law
    and, 22, 24. *See also* divine law; Ten
    Commandments
Bishop, Joel Prentiss, 141
Blackstone, William, 89, 105, 120,
    132–137, 140, 166, 175, 218n139

Spanish law, 7, 63, 77, 176, 193n57
Spelman, Henry, 92, 202n28, 217n115
Spooner, Lysander, 139, 163–164
starvation, as reason for theft, 136
state of nature, 60, 129, 165, 171–172, 209n131
statutes: ecclesiastical, 30, 107, 121–122; interpretation of, 19, 52, 60, 69–71, 73–75, 111, 115, 120, 165–168; "mind" of, 73, 80, 116, 120, 166; natural law and, 11, 24, 40, 46–47, 51, 62, 112, 116, 175; odious, 51, 68–70, 108–109, 111–112, 143; retrospective, 144–146, 153–154, 171; strict construction of, 38, 68–69, 73, 112, 118. *See also specific subjects*
statutes, English, 87, 98, 104, 111, 113–115, 124, 126, 202n4, 204n65, 211n23, 217n114
Staunford, William, 92
St. German, Christopher, 86, 90, 92, 125, 137
storks, 188n54
Story, Joseph, 132, 139
Style, William, 92
succession. *See* inheritance; intestacy
summons. *See* citation, requirement of
Swift, Zephaniah, 139

takings, of property. *See* eminent domain
Taney, Roger, 139
Ten Commandments, 4–5, 22–23, 27
Tennessee, state of, 150
testaments, last wills and, 20, 73, 144, 166, 212n36
textbook examples, 4, 48, 55, 70, 102
texts, juridical: centrality of, 7, 14–18, 22–25; glossing of, 15, 18, 22–23, 34, 37, 135; interpretation of, 38, 44–45, 51–54, 68, 75, 80, 112, 116
theft, crime of, 59–61, 119–120, 136
Tierney, Brian, 75
tithes, law of, 125–126, 233–234n80
title, to property, 36–37, 145, 155, 157–158, 171
Toledo, church of, 68, 77
torture, use in courts, 101, 177, 202n22, 211n26
trade, restraint of, 63, 67, 74, 111–112, 169. *See also* commerce
translations, works on natural law, 90, 95, 129, 140, 176

Transylvania, university of, 138
treason, crime of, 56, 61, 76, 100, 209n132
treatises, legal: American, 139–140; Continental, 10, 25, 41–42, 174, 176; English, 89–92, 124, 132; natural law in, 19, 43, 90, 95, 129, 142. *See also individual authors*
trespass, action of, 109, 226n109
trusts, law of, 106, 165, 167, 234n89
Tucker, St. George, 130, 134–135, 139, 224n80
turtles, 188n54
Tuschus, Dominicus, 51
tyranny, resistance to, 75, 128–130. *See also* self-defense

Ulpian, 18, 26, 51, 54, 63
Uniform Probate Code, 167
universities, 2, 14–15, 21, 39, 82, 102, 131, 137–138, 174. *See also* legal education
unjust enrichment, 38, 68, 110, 189nn75–79
usury: canon law and, 64–65, 111; natural law and, 23, 65, 67, 111, 150; Roman law and, 24, 195n95, 196n111; treatment in courts, 24, 64–66, 99, 111, 150
usus modernus Pandectarum, 16, 38
utopians, constitutional, 163–164

Vattel, Emmerich de, 95
Vaughan, John, 92, 120, 218–219n140
vices, human, 64, 81. *See also* morality; *specific crimes*
villeinage, English law of, 84, 86, 109
Virginia, state of, 108, 128, 135, 138, 143, 178, 237n122
Voet, Johannes, 97, 131
Vogenauer, Stefan, 69
void acts, concept of, 87, 95, 119–120, 146, 152, 165, 168, 203n53, 206n91, 207n101

wardship, English, 98–99, 159. *See also* guardianship
wars: American Civil, 5, 138–139, 149, 155, 162, 167, 170; American Independence, 128–129, 141; on crime, 177; slavery and, 32, 108; soldiers in, 57, 177